PANEL DATA ECONOMETRICS

T0291392

In the last 20 years, econometric theory on panel data has developed rapidly, particularly for analyzing common behaviors among individuals over time. Meanwhile, the statistical methods employed by applied researchers have not kept up-to-date. This book attempts to fill in this gap by teaching researchers how to use the latest panel estimation methods correctly.

Almost all applied economics articles use panel data or panel regressions. However, many empirical results from typical panel data analyses are not correctly executed. This book aims to help applied researchers to run panel regressions correctly and avoid common mistakes. The book explains how to model cross-sectional dependence, how to estimate a few key common variables, and how to identify them. It also provides guidance on how to separate out the long-run relationship and common dynamic and idiosyncratic dynamic relationships from a set of panel data.

Aimed at applied researchers who want to learn about panel data econometrics by running statistical software, this book provides clear guidance and is supported by a full range of online teaching and learning materials. It includes practice sections on MATLAB, STATA, and GAUSS throughout, along with short and simple econometric theories on basic panel regressions for those who are unfamiliar with econometric theory on traditional panel regressions.

Donggyu Sul is currently the John Kain Professor of Economics at the University of Texas at Dallas, USA. He specializes in panel data econometrics, international finance, and empirical economic growth, and his articles have been published in numerous major research journals.

PANEL DATA ECONOMETRICS

Common Factor Analysis for Empirical Researchers

Donggyu Sul

Routledge
Taylor & Francis Group

LONDON AND NEW YORK

First published 2019
by Routledge
2 Park Square, Milton Park, Abingdon, Oxon OX14 4RN

and by Routledge
52 Vanderbilt Avenue, New York, NY 10017

Routledge is an imprint of the Taylor & Francis Group, an informa business

British Library Cataloguing-in-Publication Data
A catalogue record for this book is available from the British Library

Library of Congress Cataloging-in-Publication Data
Names: Sul, Donggyu, 1965– author.
Title: Panel data econometrics : common factor analysis for empirical
  researchers / Donggyu Sul.
Description: 1 Edition. | New York : Routledge, 2019. | Includes
  bibliographical references and index.
Identifiers: LCCN 2018050049 (print) | LCCN 2019000836 (ebook) |
  ISBN 9780429423765 (Ebook) | ISBN 9781138389663 (hardback :
  alk. paper) | ISBN 9781138389670 (pbk. : alk. paper) |
  ISBN 9780429423765 (ebk)
Subjects: LCSH: Panel analysis. | Econometric models.
Classification: LCC H61.26 (ebook) | LCC H61.26 .S85 2019 (print) |
  DDC 330.01/5195—dc23
LC record available at https://lccn.loc.gov/2018050049

ISBN: 978-1-138-38966-3 (hbk)
ISBN: 978-1-138-38967-0 (pbk)
ISBN: 978-0-429-42376-5 (ebk)

Typeset in Times New Roman
by Apex CoVantage, LLC

Visit the eResources at: www.routledge.com/9781138389670

MIX
Paper from
responsible sources
FSC
www.fsc.org   FSC® C013056

Printed and bound in Great Britain by
TJ International Ltd, Padstow, Cornwall

CONTENTS

FIGURES

TABLES

PREFACE

Almost all recent empirical papers have used panel data. Many applied researchers have believed that a panel regression provides more accurate estimates
simply because the panel regression uses more data points than either cross-
sectional or time series regression. Under this principle, the following panel
regression, which is called 'panel two-way fixed effect regression,' has been
very popularly used.

$$y_{it} = a_i + \theta_t + \beta x_{it} + e_{it},$$

where 'i' stands for each cross-sectional unit, 't' is a time index, a_i is an individual fixed effect, and θ_t is called either a time dummy or year fixed effect.
Running the panel fixed effect regression sounds 'harmless' and seems to
provide a better estimate. Of course, the use of the 'robust' option in STATA
to construct the 'correct' variance seems to be good enough. Such a belief
leads to the following wild conclusion: Learning more econometric methods
or theories is more likely 'harmful.'

It would be wonderful if this belief were true. Unfortunately, what most
researchers have believed about the panel fixed effect regression is either
completely wrong or useless, except for a few cases. The purpose of this monograph is to explain the underlying reasons why the panel fixed effect regression
may capture elusive results. A journey for this quest starts with understanding
the fact that panel data provides important information, which is hidden or
cannot be identified by using only cross-sectional or time series data. Let's
take property crime rates across states as an example. Some parts of the crime
rates may be explained by state-specific variables. We may further decompose
these individual specific crime rates into two parts: Time invariant term and
time-varying component. The rest of the crime may be purely due to some

common variables. It is important to note that it is impossible to identify or estimate accurately all three components – time invariant individual specific terms, time-varying idiosyncratic terms, and common components – by using only cross-sectional or time series data. Nonetheless, depending on which variable becomes of interest, the panel fixed effect regression becomes useless or meaningful. Suppose that the national property crime rate is of interest. If the common components among the property crime rates across states can be summarized by a single common factor – which is the case (see Chapter 3) – then the panel fixed effect regression is not helpful at all to explain the behavior of the national property crime over time. The underlying reason is simple. The time dummy or year fixed effect, θ_t, captures the national average of the property crimes, and the panel two-way fixed effect regression eliminates them completely by controlling for year fixed effect in the regression.

The dependence among cross-sectional units has been treated as a nuisance rather than key information. Recent development in panel econometrics, however, has provided more tools to understand the economic meanings of the cross-sectional dependence. New econometric methods have been developed to identify and estimate a few common factors, which cause the dependence among cross-sectional units. More interestingly, these common variables usually explain the major dynamic behaviors of the panel data of interest. Meanwhile, traditional determinant variables in economic theories are not able to explain, or little explain, the dynamic behaviors of the panel data. Along with recent econometric development, applied researchers have gained an increased understanding of the importance of cross-sectional dependence. Rather than ignoring or eliminating cross-sectional dependence from the panel data of interest, applied researchers have started to estimate the common variables, which cause the dependence among cross-sectional units and, more importantly, give economic meaning and logical explanation of why these common variables become of interest. This monograph aims to help empirical researchers who want to learn the recent econometric development of cross-sectional dependence. Except for the first two introductory chapters, each chapter includes an appendix of practical exercises with three major statistical software: MATLAB, STATA and GAUSS. By running example codes, readers can digest econometric theory more effectively. For those who do not have basic knowledge about panel data regressions, I provide a condensed summary of a panel regression under cross-sectional independence at the end of this book.

Finally, I express my appreciation to Wukki Kim, who corrected typos and mistakes in the earlier draft of the manuscript, and thanks to Jianning Kong for teaching me how to program STATA codes.

1

BASIC STRUCTURE
OF PANEL DATA

This chapter is the most basic and important chapter in this book. I encourage readers to digest this first chapter carefully. This chapter provides the basic structure of a panel data, which can be decomposed into time invariant individual specific variables, time-varying common variables, and time-varying individual specific variables. We will study how to identify each component statistically. By doing so, we will learn the economic meaning of each component.

Let y_{it} be a data of interest for the i–th individual (or firm, region, group, country) at time t.[1] The i–th unit is called the cross-sectional unit. The total number of the cross-sectional unit is denoted as n. That is, $i = 1, ..., n$. The range of the time index is denoted as $t = 1, ..., T$. The variable y must have the same attributes across i over t. For example, a panel of household income includes only income data for each household during a certain time period.

In the end, we will consider the following general structure of a panel data.

$$y_{it} = a_i + b_{it}t + \lambda'_{it}\theta_t + y^o_{it}, \tag{1.1}$$

where a_i is a time invariant term, b_{it} is a time-varying individual growth rate, λ_{it} is a vector of time-varying factor loading coefficients, θ_t is a vector of common factors, and y^o_{it} is a leftover term or purely idiosyncratic term. However, we start from a basic and simple model by assuming that $b_{it} = 0$ for all i and t, and $\lambda_{it} = 1$ for all i and t. These assumptions lead to

$$y_{it} = a_i + \theta_t + y^o_{it}. \tag{1.2}$$

Later we will relax these strong assumptions one by one.

1.1 Meaning of fixed effect

In this section, we study the economic meaning of the time invariant terms – a_i (individual mean) and b_i (slope coefficient on the trend term). First, we consider the economic meaning of a_i with non-trended data.

1.1.1 Fixed effects with non-trended data

We rewrite (1.2) as

$$y_{it} = a_i + y_{it}^*, \tag{1.3}$$

where a_i is a time invariant unobserved variable, and y_{it}^* is a time-varying variable with a mean of zero and finite variance. In this section, the parameter of interest is a_i, which is often called "fixed effect" among applied ecometricians.[2] Nonetheless, this unobserved time invariant variable can be identified and estimated if the number of time series observations is large. Since y_{it}^* has a zero mean, the sample time series mean of y_{it} can be written as

$$\frac{1}{T}\sum_{t=1}^{T} y_{it} = a_i + \frac{1}{T}\sum_{t=1}^{T} y_{it}^* := \bar{y}_{iT}. \tag{1.4}$$

As $T \to \infty$, the probability limit of $\bar{y}_{iT}$ becomes[3]

$$\text{plim}_{T\to\infty}\bar{y}_{iT} = a_i + \text{plim}_{T\to\infty}\frac{1}{T}\sum_{t=1}^{T} y_{it}^* = a_i. \tag{1.5}$$

In other words, the fixed effect, a_i, is identified as the long-run average of y_{it}.

Suppose that y_{it} is the growth rate of an individual's annual income. Then (1.3) implies that the annual income growth rate for the i-th individual at time t can be decomposed into the long-run average, a_i, and the temporal variation of y_{it}^*. Note that the equation in (1.3) is not a determinant model for y_{it}, but just a simple decompositional equation. In other words, a_i is not a long-run determinant of y_{it}, but just a time invariant mean. To find out the determinant of a_i, one may want to consider an individual's education level, personality, intellectual level, gender, health, and other individual specific variables.

It is worth noting that the result in (1.5) holds only with a very large T. In a finite sample, the sample time series mean, of course, becomes an estimator of a_i. There are various ways to estimate the unobserved but time invariant heterogeneity. In real situations, the number of the time series observations is given. Hence it is worth analyzing how accurately the time series sample mean approximates the unobserved parameter a_i. Under regularity conditions, the limiting distribution of the sample time series mean is given by

$$\sqrt{T}(\bar{y}_{iT} - a_i) \to^d N(0, \sigma_i^2) \tag{1.6}$$

so that the sample time series mean can be rewritten as

$$y_{iT} = a_i + \Delta_T, \tag{1.7}$$

where Δ_T is a small random number, but as $T \rightarrow \infty$, $\Delta_T \rightarrow 0$ in probability. Hence the sample mean becomes a more accurate estimate as more T is available.

1.1.2   Fixed effects with trended panel data

Consider the following exponentially growing panel data series.

$$Y_{it} = \exp(a_i)\exp(b_i t)\exp(y_{it}^*). \tag{1.8}$$

Taking logarithm in Y_{it} yields

$$y_{it} = \ln Y_{it} = a_i + b_i t + y_{it}^*. \tag{1.9}$$

The parameters of interest here are a_i and b_i: The expected initial value of y_{i0} becomes a_i, and the expected growth rate becomes b_i. The economic meaning of a_i in (1.9) is, hence, changed. Also, there is no long-run average with y_{it} because y_{it} grows infinity. However, the notion of the long-run average can be obtained by taking the first difference in y_{it}. The first difference in y_{it} becomes

$$\Delta y_{it} = b_i + \Delta y_{it}^* \tag{1.10}$$

so that the equation in (1.10) falls into the statistical model in (1.3), except for the notational changes.

Taking the sample mean of Δy_{it} yields

$$\frac{1}{T-1}\sum_{t=2}^{T} \Delta y_{it} = \frac{1}{T-1}(y_{i2} - y_{i1} + y_{i3} - y_{i2} + \cdots + y_{iT} - y_{iT-1}) = \frac{y_{iT} - y_{i1}}{T-1}, \tag{1.11}$$

which is called 'long-run difference.' In economic growth literature, this long-run difference method has been popularly used to estimate the long-run value of Δy_{it}. See Chapter 6 for a more detailed discussion.

The trend model in (1.9) has been used to explain the trending behaviors of time series data, particularly macro time series. However, this trend model implies the divergence of the cross-sectional dispersion in the long run. Suppose that y_{it} is the annual earning for the i-th individual or country at time t. Then the expected sample cross-sectional variance at time t can be written as

$$\mathbb{E}\frac{1}{n}\sum_{i=1}^{n}\left(y_{it} - \frac{1}{n}\sum_{i=1}^{n}y_{it}\right)^2 = \sigma_a^2 + \sigma_b^2 t^2 + 2\sigma_{ab}t + \sigma_t^2, \tag{1.12}$$

where σ_a^2, σ_b^2, and σ_t^2 are the variance of a_i, b_i and y_{it}^* at time t, respectively, and σ_{ab} is the covariance between a_i and b_i. Here we assume that $\mathbb{E}(a_i y_{it}^*) = \mathbb{E}(b_i y_{it}^*) = 0$. When the variance of the time varying term is fluctuating over time, then the cross-sectional dispersion (or variance) increases over time, even when there is negative correlation between a_i and b_i. The negative correlation between a_i and b_i implies that those with initially lower earnings will make faster earning growth than those with initially higher earnings. If the earning growth – which is roughly equivalent to b_i – reflects on labor productivity, the negative correlation between a_i and b_i implies also that the earning growth rates of higher productivity workers are lower than those of lower productivity workers. Even in this case, the income inequality becomes inevitable as long as the slope coefficient, b_i, is time invariant. We will study the long-run convergence in Chapter 7.

We can introduce a more general and realistic trend function. However, in this case, the trend function can be viewed as one of common factors, which we will study next.

1.2   Meaning of common components

In this section, we will study the economic meaning of the common components, particularly common factors. The most general model for the common components can be written as

$$y_{it}^* = \underbrace{\lambda_{it}' \theta_t}_{\text{common components}} + \underbrace{y_{it}^o}_{\text{idiosyncratic component}} \tag{1.13}$$

where θ_t is a vector common unobserved factor across the cross-sectional units, λ_{it} is a vector of time varying factor loadings, and y_{it}^o is a pure idiosyncratic term, which is cross-sectionally independent. Later, we will introduce 'weak' cross-sectional dependence form in y_{it}^o, but here we assume that there is no dependence among y_{it}^o. It is important to note that the model in (1.13) is just a hypothetical one since the time-varying factor loadings cannot be identified statistically without imposing further restrictions. For example, one can impose a restriction that λ_{it} follows AR(1), y_{it}^o follows AR(1) also, but θ_t follows a random walk. Under these restrictions, one can estimate λ_{it} by using the Kalman filter method. However, it is very hard to justify whether such restrictions are valid.

For the intuitive explanation, we start to use the following simplest form.

$$y_{it} = a_i + \theta_t + y_{it}^o \tag{1.14}$$

There are three economic meanings of the common factor: Aggregation or macro factor, the source of the cross-sectional correlation, and the central location parameter for each t.

1.2.1   Aggregation or macro factor

The common factor θ_t can be identified as the population average of y_{it}. That is,

$$\text{plim}_{n\to\infty} \frac{1}{n} \sum_{i=1}^{n} y_{it} = a + \theta_t + \text{plim}_{n\to\infty} \frac{1}{n} \sum_{i=1}^{n} y_{it}^o = a + \theta_t, \tag{1.15}$$

where $a = \text{plim}_{n\to\infty} \frac{1}{n}\sum_{i=1}^{n} a_i$, which can be treated as a constant. Note that the second equality holds because y_{it}^o has a zero mean across i and over t. Suppose that y_{it} is a log annual wage of the i-th individual at time t. Then the sum of all household wages becomes gross national income. Hence the common factor, θ_t, is equivalent to the log per capita national income. Suppose that y_{it} is the per capita income for the i-th country at time t. Then the common factor is equivalent to the per capita world GDP. In this sense, the common factor can be interpreted as the aggregation variable or macro factor.

Then what is the role of the common factor on each cross-sectional unit? It depends on the size of variation of each term. Consider the time series variation of y_{it}. That is,

$$\mathbb{E}\frac{1}{T}\sum_{t=1}^{T}\left(y_{it} - \frac{1}{T}\sum_{t=1}^{T}y_{it}\right)^2 = \sigma_\theta^2 + \sigma_i^2, \tag{1.16}$$

where σ_θ^2 is the variance of θ_t and σ_i^2 is the variance of y_{it}^o. Usually in a micro panel data, σ_θ^2 is relatively tiny compared with σ_i^2. In other words, usually the macro factor has little influence on an individual's decision. Meanwhile, in aggregated panel data (such as a panel of states, cities or firms), the relative size of σ_θ^2 is not ignorable. We will provide an empirical evidence later in Chapter 4.

Now, we need to discuss the economic meaning of the equation in (1.15). Suppose that y_{it} is an individual opinion on a particular social issue, such as gender and racial discrimination. The equation in (1.15) provides an interesting interpretation: The entire national or population average for each year is stochastic or random – θ_t is a random variable. The probability limit of the sample cross-sectional mean becomes random due to the existence of the common factor. In other words, the current national opinion or norm changes over time. In fact, we cannot predict the future outcome unless the common factor, θ_t, has a clear trending behavior. Since the size of θ_t relative to y_{it}^o is very tiny, each individual may not notice a change in θ_t every year. However, by looking back at historical changes, one can see how the national opinion has evolved.

Eliminating θ_t from y_{it} is rather simple as long as the common factor follows the simplest form, like in (1.14). The sample cross-sectional average approximates θ_t accurately when n is large. In a panel regression, the inclusion of year dummies eliminates the common factor effectively if the common factor structure is given in (1.14). If the common factor is removed, then the remaining panel consists of only individual specific components. What does it mean? If one wants to explain national or aggregated behavior of a certain variable, one should not eliminate the common factor (or equivalently should not include year dummies in the panel regression). We will study this case in Chapter 6.

1.2.2 Source of cross-sectional dependence

The common factor, θ_t, is literally common across cross-sectional units. The expected sample covariance between the i–th and j–th units is given by

$$\mathbb{E}\frac{1}{T}\sum_{t=1}^{T}\left(y_{it} - \frac{1}{T}\sum_{t=1}^{T}y_{it}\right)\left(y_{jt} - \frac{1}{T}\sum_{t=1}^{T}y_{jt}\right) = \sigma_\theta^2 \neq 0. \tag{1.17}$$

The equation in (1.17) implies that y_{it} is cross-sectionally correlated with y_{jt} by sharing the same variable θ_t. In other words, if y_{it} is not sharing the same variable with y_{jt}, they must be independent of each other.

The common variable can influence each cross-section unit differently. For example, an increase in the market interest rate leads to a decrease in consumption by those in debt, but an increase in consumption by others. Consider a single factor case given by

$$y_{it} = a_i + \lambda_i \theta_t + y_{it}^o, \tag{1.18}$$

where λ_i measures the economic distance between the common factor θ_t and y_{it}. The expected sample covariance between the i–th and j–th units in (1.18) is given by

$$\mathbb{E}\frac{1}{T}\sum_{t=1}^{T}\left(y_{it} - \frac{1}{T}\sum_{t=1}^{T}y_{it}\right)\left(y_{jt} - \frac{1}{T}\sum_{t=1}^{T}y_{jt}\right) = \lambda_i \lambda_j \sigma_\theta^2,$$

where we treat λ_i as if it were a constant. Definitely, the heterogeneous factor loading model is more flexible compared with the homogenous factor loading model in (1.17).

When there is more than a single common variable, the common components can be written as

$$y_{it} = a_i + \sum_{j=1}^{r} \lambda_{i,j} \theta_{j,t} + y_{it}^o = a_i + \lambda_i' \theta_t + y_{it}^o, \tag{1.19}$$

where $\lambda_i = [\lambda_{i1}, \ldots, \lambda_{i,r}]'$ and $\theta_t = [\theta_{1t}, \ldots, \theta_{rt}]$. The number of common factors is unknown, so it must be estimated. The number of common factors is usually assumed to be small, say one to three. In fact, it is hard to find an empirical panel data of which the common factors are more than four. We will study in Chapter 3 how to identify or estimate the number of common factors in detail.

The common factor model assumes that the influence of the common variable on each individual is time invariant. However, the time invariant assumption is not realistic. Usually, a relationship between two people (you and your academic advisor, or you and your coauthor) is time varying so that the sample covariance between the two becomes varying over time as well. Such a time-varying pattern can be modeled by time-varying factor loadings. That is, y_{it} can be written as

$$y_{it} = a_i + \lambda_{it}' \theta_t + y_{it}^o.$$

We will study this model in Chapter 7 in detail.

1.2.3 Central location parameter

The last interpretation of the common factor is the 'center of the distribution' of y_{it} for each t. Mean and median are good examples for the central location of random variables. When a distribution is symmetric, the mean is an efficient estimator for the central location or center. Meanwhile, when a distribution is not symmetric, the median is usually used to measure the central location. For example, a median of real estate prices is usually of interest.

The robust estimation of the central location parameter has been an important issue in nonparametric statistics. There are many theoretical papers regarding how to estimate the central location robustly (against potential outliers). In practice, economists also want to measure central tendencies of economic data. For example, the estimation of the headline or core inflation among many disaggregate components becomes of interest to Bureau of Economic Analysis (BEA), Bureau of Labor Statistics (BLS), and Federal Reserve Banks (FRBs). Another example is the estimation of the nominal effective exchange rates becoming of interest to central banks and BIS.

Suppose that y_{it} has multiple factors. Then the common components include main informations about the center of the distribution for each t; meanwhile, the idiosyncratic components provide only nuisance informations. That is,

$$y_{it} = a_i + \underbrace{\lambda_i' \theta_t}_{\text{key info}} + \underbrace{y_{it}^\rho}_{\text{nuisance info}} \ .$$

Hence how to isolate or eliminate the nuisance information becomes the most important issue in the core inflation literature.

Several estimation methods for the central location are available. Among them, the most popular estimation method in statistics is the so-called depth weighted estimator. The depth weighted estimator is less efficient compared to the sample mean if there is no outlier. However, under the presence of many outliers, the depth weighted or the depth trimmed estimator has been known to be the most efficient estimator. Especially when researchers are interested in subtracting the representative common variable from a panel data, the depth weighted estimator can be a good alternative. We will not study further about the depth weighted estimator in the current version of this book.

1.3 Meaning of idiosyncratic components

The 'leftover' or idiosyncratic term provides valuable information about how each individual behaves. There are three idiosyncratic components: the fixed effect or long-run mean, the factor loadings, and the pure idiosyncratic time varying components. The first two – particularly fixed effects – are not time varying. The directions of the correlations among idiosyncratic terms are unknown, and theoretically, this area has not ever been explored. The part most theoretically explored is the last time-varying component.

The Latin phrase 'ceteris paribus' is one of the most popularly used economic terms. Under ceteris paribus, usually economists seek the causal effect of an exogenous variable x on an endogenous variable y. To be specific, consider the following question: A mayor wants to know the effectiveness of hiring an additional policeman to cover the violent crime in her city. The answer to this question is not simple at all. First, consider the number of sworn police officers across cities. We will show it later, but this number is highly cross-sectionally dependent. In other words, when other cities hire more sworn police officers, the city of interest also hires more officers. Also, the violent crime is – sounds very strange but – also cross-sectionally dependent. It is not negatively correlated, but highly positively correlated. That is, if the number of violent crimes in a neighbor city increases, then more likely the number of violent crimes in your city is also increasing at the same time. Such positive correlation is due to the common factor. Hence after controlling for the effects of all these common factors, one should estimate the effect of the idiosyncratic increase in the number of the sworn police officers on the idiosyncratic violent crime. When the factor loadings are all identical, it is rather easy to control for the common factors.

A typical panel regression with a single regressor of x_{it} can be written as

$$y_{it} = \alpha_i + \tau_t + \beta x_{it} + u_{it}. \tag{1.20}$$

Assume that both y_{it} and x_{it} have a single factor. That is, $y_{it} = a_{y,i} + \theta_{y,t} + y_{it}^o$, and $x_{it} = a_{x,i} + \theta_{x,t} + x_{it}^o$. Then running (1.20) is asymptotically equivalent – when T and n are very large – to running the following regression.

$$y_{it}^o = \beta x_{it}^o + u_{it}$$

The underlying reason is simple. To eliminate the fixed effect, α_i and the year dummy τ_t, we can transform y_{it} as

$$y_{it} - \frac{1}{n}\sum_{i=1}^n y_{it} - \frac{1}{T}\sum_{t=1}^T \left(y_{it} - \frac{1}{n}\sum_{i=1}^n y_{it} \right)$$

$$= y_{it}^o - \frac{1}{n}\sum_{i=1}^n y_{it}^o - \frac{1}{T}\sum_{t=1}^T \left(y_{it}^o - \frac{1}{n}\sum_{i=1}^n y_{it}^o \right).$$

Similarly, the regressor x_{it} can be transformed in this way. When n and T are large, then the transformed data approximates the idiosyncratic term very well. Later, we will study the economic meaning of the typical panel regression given in (1.20), and we will study how to identify and estimate the dynamic relationship among idiosyncratic components and among common components as well.

Notes

1   We use a capital letter for a level data usually. A small letter for a logged level data. Note that all data used in the regression analysis must be taken logarithm first (except for growth variables). For example, national GDP data usually grows exponentially. Hence if you do not take log, then the GDP data must be modeled by a nonlinear function. If you have many 'zero' but level observations (for example, household nominal incomes), then I strongly recommend dropping this variable. For example, suppose that $Y_{1t} = [100, 0, 800, 400]$. In this case, the second observation becomes an outlier, which causes a number of statistical problems. If you include this zero, then the sample average and variance become biased. Also, other statistics related to the sample mean and variances are all biased.

2   When a_i is treated as if it were a given constant, it is called 'fixed effect' in a panel regression setting. When a_i is treated as if it were a random variable, it is called 'random effect.' Since in most panel regressions a_i is included as 'fixed effect,' this time invariant unobserved variable is called 'fixed effect.'

3   Suppose that $\operatorname{plim}_{T \to \infty} x_T = a$. This implies (i) $\lim_{T \to \infty} \mathbb{E}(x_T) = a$ and (ii) $\lim_{T \to \infty} \mathbb{E}(x_T - a)^2 = 0$. In other words, $\operatorname{plim}_{T \to \infty} x_T = a$ implies that the chance that x_T becomes a is getting larger as T increases.

2

STATISTICAL MODELS FOR CROSS-SECTIONAL DEPENDENCE

Not like the time series dependence, the cross-sectional dependence is hard to model econometrically because the ordering of the cross-sectional units is usually unknown. Let $\{x\}$ be a variable of interest. When x is a time series data, the ordering of x is unique, along with time: Past, current, and future. Assume x has a zero mean. Then the covariance between x_t and x_{t-1} is expressed as $\mathbb{E}x_t x_{t-1}$. To identify this value with actual data, one needs the assumption of stationarity. That is, $\mathbb{E}x_t x_{t-1} = \mathbb{E}x_s x_{s-1}$ for all t and s. In this case, this value can be estimated consistently by the sample mean of $T^{-1}\sum_{t=1}^{T}x_t x_{t-1}$. Can we apply the same logic to the cross-sectional data? The first requirement is the exact ordering of the sequence. When x is cross-sectional data, it is impossible to pin down the unique ordering of x. For example, let x be household incomes at a certain time. Then x can be ordered by various ways: Location (zip code), value itself (from smallest to highest), age of household, family size and educational level, etc. Depending on the ordering, cross-sectional dependence changes. In other words, unless the ordering of sequence is known, the covariance between a pair of cross-sectional observations, $\mathbb{E}x_i x_j$, cannot be identified. Only when the time series information is available can the dependence be identified. That is, the sample mean of $T^{-1}\sum_{t=1}^{T}x_{it}x_{jt}$ becomes a consistent estimator for the covariance of $\{x_i\}$ and $\{x_j\}$.

When the time series information is not available (or pure cross-sectional data), the notion of cross-sectional dependence is purely hypothetical. Here we will study how researchers have attempted to model cross-sectional dependence.

2.1   Spatial dependence

The most popular way to order cross-sectional units is the use of their geographic locations. The simplest spatial autocorrelation model is given by

$$x_i = e_i + \rho \sum_{\substack{j \neq 0, j=-J}}^{j=J} e_{i+j}, \tag{2.1}$$

where i is the location index, e_i is usually assumed to be iid (identical and independently distributed), and J is the neighborhood range. Here we assume that individuals are located on a straight line. Assume that e_i has a zero mean. If $J = 1$, then x_i is correlated with next two neighbors.

$$\mathbb{E}x_i x_{i+1} = \sigma_e^2 \times 2\rho, \quad \mathbb{E}x_i x_{i+2} = \sigma_e^2 \times \rho^2, \quad \mathbb{E}x_i x_{i+k} = 0 \text{ if } k \geq 3$$

When $J = 2$, then x_i is correlated with the next four neighbors.

$$\mathbb{E}x_i x_{i+1} = \sigma_e^2 \times [2\rho + 2\rho^2], \quad \mathbb{E}x_i x_{i+2} = \sigma_e^2 \times [2\rho + \rho^2]$$
$$\mathbb{E}x_i x_{i+3} = \sigma_e^2 \times 2\rho, \quad \mathbb{E}x_i x_{i+4} = \sigma_e^2 \times \rho^2, \quad \mathbb{E}x_i x_{i+k} = 0 \text{ if } k \geq 5$$

The covariance between x_i and x_{i+1} is dependent both on J and ρ. More general spatial autocorrelation model can be written as

$$x_i = e_i + \rho \sum_{\substack{j \neq 0, j=-J}}^{j=J} \omega_{i,j} e_{i+j}, \tag{2.2}$$

where $\omega_{i,j}$ is the i–th and j–th weight function. Usually, the weights are assumed to be known. This model might be useful when there is no time series information at all. Except for some obvious cases, such as the location of a wireless communication center, however, the actual cross-sectional dependence may not follow the spatial autocorrelation model. In social science and economics, hence, the spatial autocorrelation has been used as a filtering rule. That is, after eliminating the spatial dependence (by using the spatial structure), if there exists cross-sectional dependence still, then this result becomes supportive evidence for the social interaction. In fact, spatial dependence is treated as an example of weak dependence in panel econometrics because the cross-sectional correlation goes away very quickly as the physical distance between i and j gets larger.

The spatial model has been popularly used, particularly in geographic information science or urban economics. In fact, the spatial model is useful to explain the correlation among housing prices in some regions and epidemic and natural events including earthquake or flooding. However, it is not certain whether or not we can apply this model to explain the cross-sectional dependence of any economic or social variable. Figure 2.1 shows a county map with roads and cities in one area of northwestern Texas. There are a total of

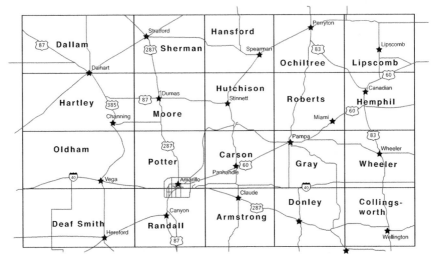

FIGURE 2.1   County map in north Texas

TABLE 2.1   Correlation coefficients with respect to Hutchinson County

Dallam	Sherman	Hansford	Ochiltree	Lipscomb
0.179	0.271	0.115	0.410	0.420
Hartley	Moore	Hutchinson	Roberts	Hemphill
0.091	0.217	1.000	0.198	0.422
Oldham	Potter	Carson	Gray	Wheeler
0.124	0.525	0.290	0.758	0.446
Deaf Smith	Randall	Armstrong	Donley	Collingsworth
0.040	0.506	0.278	−0.048	−0.057

20 counties in Figure 2.1. I download a panel data of per capita personal income from 1960 to 2015 from BEA, and calculate the correlation matrix with the growth rates of the per capita personal income in this region.

Table 2.1 shows the correlation coefficients of other counties with respect to Hutchinson, which is located in the center of the map. The nearest adjunct counties are in dark gray. The correlation coefficients vary from 0.115 (Hansford) to 0.758 (Gray). The median correlation becomes around 0.28. The next neighboring countries are in light gray. The median correlation is around 0.18, which is lower than that of the nearest regions. So overall, the spatial dependence seems to work. However, if we consider the correlations with the right counties of Hutchinson, then it does not make sense. For example, the correlations with Lipscomb and Hemphill are 0.420 and 0.422, respectively. These correlations

TABLE 2.2 Correlation coefficients with respect to Potter County

Dallam −0.105	Sherman 0.062	Hansford 0.143	Ochiltree 0.342	Lipscomb 0.333
Hartley 0.012	Moore 0.276	Hutchinson 0.525	Roberts 0.008	Hemphill 0.089
Oldham 0.037	Potter 1.000	Carson 0.074	Gray 0.501	Wheeler 0.329
Deaf Smith 0.041	Randall 0.454	Armstrong −0.038	Donley 0.000	Collingsworth −0.140

are much higher than the correlation with Roberts (0.198) or with Sherman (0.271).

Table 2.2 shows the correlation coefficients with respect to Potter County, which includes the largest city, Amarillo. In fact, Randall shares Amarillo with Potter. Nonetheless, the median correlations among the nearest counties (in dark gray) and among nearer counties (in light gray) are around 0.05 and 0.06, respectively. However, the median correlation with the farthest counties (in white) is 0.21. Hence spatial dependence is not helpful at all in this case.

In sum, spatial dependence is a useful tool for some specific variables (for example, housing prices). However, as shown, the spatial dependence model is not general enough to explain the dependent structure among social and economic variables. We study another simple approach next.

2.2   Gravity model

Newton's gravity law is given by

$$F = G\frac{m_1 m_2}{r^2},$$ (2.3)

where F is force, G is gravity constant, m_1 and m_2 are the mass of two objects, and r is the distance between two objects. Tinbergen (1962) used this formula to explain the trade flow between any pair of countries. Tinbergen's formula is given by

$$F_{ij} = G\frac{m_i^{\beta_1} m_j^{\beta_2}}{d_{ij}^{\beta_3}},$$ (2.4)

where F_{ij} is the trade flow between the i–th and j–th countries, m_i is the economic mass, d_{ij} is the distance, and G is a constant. Taking logarithm yields,

$$\ln F_{ij} = \ln G + \beta_1 \ln m_i + \beta_2 \ln m_j + \beta_3 \ln d_{ij}.$$ (2.5)

This simple gravity model has been empirically investigated. Also, the gravity model is used to explain the interaction between two places in urban economics. For example, traffic volume and immigration between any pair of cities have been explained by this gravity model. Historically, the gravity model is the first economic model to take the cross-sectional dependence seriously. Contrasted with the Heckscher-Ohlin model, the gravity model can be statistically interpreted as a factor model. To see this, consider a panel version of the gravity model given by

$$f_{ij,t} = \ln G + \beta_1 \ln m_{it} + \beta_2 \ln m_{jt} + \beta_3 \ln d_{ij} + \varepsilon_{ij,t}, \tag{2.6}$$

where $\varepsilon_{ij,t}$ is the regression error, and $f_{it,t} = \ln F_{ij,t}$. Hence $\ln m_{it}$ and $\ln m_{jt}$ become common factors to $f_{ij,t}$. Interestingly, the relative physical distance becomes just an individual fixed effect.

Note that the panel gravity model can be written as a three-way fixed effect regression given by

$$f_{ij,t} = a_{ij} + \theta_{it} + \theta_{jt} + \varepsilon_{ij,t}. \tag{2.7}$$

If the panel gravity model in (2.6) is correctly specified, then both $\ln m_{it}$ and $\ln m_{jt}$ do not need to be specified as a certain variable. By using the following simple transformations, the unknown factors of θ_{it} and θ_{jt} can be approximated. To approximate θ_{it} and θ_{jt}, we consider the following transformation.

$$\frac{1}{T}\sum_{t=1}^{T} f_{ij,t} = a_{ij} + \frac{1}{T}\sum_{t=1}^{T} \theta_{it} + \frac{1}{T}\sum_{t=1}^{T} \theta_{jt} + \frac{1}{T}\sum_{t=1}^{T} \varepsilon_{ij,t} \tag{2.8}$$

Denote '~' as the deviation from its time series mean. For example, $\tilde{f}_{it,t} = f_{it,t} - T^{-1}\sum_{t=1}^{T} f_{ij,t}$. Subtracting (2.8) from (2.9) yields

$$\tilde{f}_{ij,t} = \tilde{\theta}_{it} + \tilde{\theta}_{jt} + \tilde{\varepsilon}_{ij,t}. \tag{2.9}$$

Taking the cross-sectional average of $\tilde{f}_{ij,t}$ over i yields

$$\frac{1}{n}\sum_{i=1}^{n} \tilde{f}_{ij,t} = \frac{1}{n}\sum_{i=1}^{n} \tilde{\theta}_{it} + \tilde{\theta}_{jt} + \frac{1}{n}\sum_{i=1}^{n} \tilde{\varepsilon}_{ij,t}. \tag{2.10}$$

Subtracting (2.10) from (2.9) results in

$$f_{ij,t}^{+} = \tilde{f}_{ij,t} - \frac{1}{n}\sum_{i=1}^{n} \tilde{f}_{ij,t} = \tilde{\theta}_{it} - \frac{1}{n}\sum_{i=1}^{n} \tilde{\theta}_{it} + \tilde{\varepsilon}_{ij,t} - \frac{1}{n}\sum_{i=1}^{n} \tilde{\varepsilon}_{ij,t}. \tag{2.11}$$

Taking the cross-sectional average of $f_{ij,t}^+$ over j becomes

$$\frac{1}{m}\sum_{j=1}^{m} f_{ij,t}^+ = \theta_{it}^+ + \frac{1}{m}\sum_{j=1}^{m}\tilde{\varepsilon}_{ij,t} - \frac{1}{m}\sum_{j=1}^{m}\frac{1}{n}\sum_{i=1}^{n}\tilde{\varepsilon}_{ij,t} \qquad (2.12)$$

$$\simeq \theta_{it}^+ \text{ if } m \text{ is large.}$$

Or, we can write as

$$\theta_{it}^+ \simeq \frac{1}{m}\sum_{j=1}^{m}\left(f_{ij,t} - \frac{1}{T}\sum_{t=1}^{T} f_{ij,t} - \frac{1}{n}\sum_{i=1}^{n} f_{ij,t} + \frac{1}{T}\sum_{t=1}^{T}\frac{1}{n}\sum_{i=1}^{n} f_{ij,t}\right), \qquad (2.13)$$

Similarly, we can identify or approximate θ_{jt} as

$$\theta_{jt}^+ \simeq \frac{1}{n}\sum_{i=1}^{n}\left(f_{ij,t} - \frac{1}{T}\sum_{t=1}^{T} f_{ij,t} - \frac{1}{m}\sum_{j=1}^{m} f_{ij,t} + \frac{1}{T}\sum_{t=1}^{T}\frac{1}{m}\sum_{j=1}^{m} f_{ij,t}\right). \qquad (2.14)$$

However, it is not easy to test precisely whether $\ln m_{it}$ is truly a determinant of θ_{it}^+ since the two equations in (2.13) and (2.14) are justified only under the assumption that the equation in (2.9) was true. As Anderson and Wincoop (2003) showed, if the number of determinants may be more than two, then the approximation in (2.13) fails.

Hence the number of common factors with $\ln F_{ij,t}$ becomes of interest. Nonetheless, the gravity model does not provide any solution to this issue.

2.3   Common factor approach

When there are too many regressors compared with the sample size, a few principal components (PC hereafter) with regressors can be used traditionally. That is, the common factor or PC approach has been used to reduce the dimensionality.

Even though this method was useful, there was an issue of how many PC factors should be extracted from the data and whether the estimated common factors are consistent. Around the 1980s, financial econometricians developed a consistent estimation method of the unknown common factors. In the 2000s, econometricians made a link between the common factor and cross-sectional dependence, and developed methods to select the factor number and to estimate the common factors. We will study these methods in the next chapter. Here we study the reasons why the common factor approach is more general than the other two and the limitations of the common factor approach.

The common factor model assumes that a few common variables are the source of cross-sectional dependence. A single factor model is given by

$$y_{it} = a_i + y_{it}^* = a_i + \alpha_i\theta_t + y_{it}^o, \qquad (2.15)$$

where θ_t is the common variable to y_{it}, a_i is the economic distance between θ_t and y_{it}, and y_{it}^o are the leftover terms, or purely idiosyncratic terms. Note that y_{it}^* has a zero mean. The cross-sectional covariance between the i-th and j-th units can be identified by the sample covariance between y_{it}^* and y_{jt}^*. That is,

$$\mathbb{E}\frac{1}{T}\sum_{t=1}^{T} y_{it}^* y_{jt}^* = a_i a_j \mathbb{E}\theta_t^2 = a_i a_j \sigma_\theta^2, \tag{2.16}$$

where $\sigma_\theta^2 = \mathbb{E}\theta_t^2$ for all t.

This simple common factor model can be interpreted in various ways. First, the common factor, θ_t, can be interpreted as a common shock to the system, and the factor loading, a_i, is the degree of the i-th individual reaction to the common shock. The total impact from the common shock on y_{it}^* is $a_i\theta_t$, which is the common component. The remaining term becomes y_{it}^o, which is independent from the common component. Second, the common factor can be interpreted as the macro or aggregation factor. For example, let y_{it} be the unemployment rate of the i-th state. After controlling out the long-run mean $\left(y_{it}^* = y_{it} - a_i\right)$, the state-level unemployment can be influenced by the nationwide unemployment, θ_t – which is the simple cross-sectional average of the unemployments across states. Third, the common factor can be just a common determinant of y_{it}^*. For example, let y_{it}^* be the price movement of the i-th firm in a particular industry. Suppose that there is a price leader (for example, y_{1t}^*), and the rest of the firms are followers $(y_{2t}^*, \ldots, y_{nt}^*)$. Then θ_t becomes y_{1t}^*. That is,

$$y_{1t}^* = y_{1t}^o, \quad y_{it}^* = a_i y_{1t}^* + y_{it}^o \text{ for } i = 2, \ldots, n. \tag{2.17}$$

We will study further how to identify the unknown common factors in detail.

Figure 2.2 shows the common factor structure graphically. We assume that the variance of the idiosyncratic component is identical across i; then the dependence structure relies totally on the value of the factor loading. The factor loading of point A is unity. The factor loading for B is between 1 and 0.9. The factor loading for C is between 0.9 and 0.8, and so on. In the single-factor structure, the contours cannot cross out each other. This implies that the cross-sectional dependences among points in upper contours must be higher than those in lower contours. For example, the cross-sectional correlation between points C and D must be higher than that between E and F. Also, the dependence between points A and C or D is higher than that between points A and E or F.

A two-factor model can be written as

$$y_{it} = a_i + a_{1i}\theta_{1t} + a_{2i}\theta_{2t} + y_{it}^o, \tag{2.18}$$

where the common factors are possibly correlated with each other. $\mathbb{E}\theta_{1t}\theta_{2t} \neq 0$. Since cross-sectional dependence does not depend on the values of two-factor

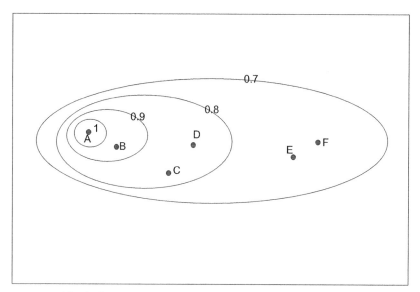

FIGURE 2.2   Single-factor structure

loadings, a two-factor model provides more a complicated dependent structure. The economic interpretations are exactly the same though. The common factors are interpreted as either common shocks, macro factors, or leaders. A more important fact is how much the common factors can explain the variation of y_{it}.

Figure 2.3 shows a two-factor case graphically. A, B, C, and D have one factor. Hence the second factor loadings, α_{2i}, are all zero for A, B, C, and D. Meanwhile, E and F have two factors. Point F is near the center of the second factor. Contrasted with Figure 2.2, the dependence between points C and D is lower than the dependence between points E and F. Note that the dashed contour – second-factor loadings – can cross over the solid contour – first-factor loadings.

Even though the dependence among common factors can be permitted, it is impossible to identify them separately. Usually, the following two identifying conditions are imposed: Orthogonality between common factors and unitary variance of each common factor. To see this, we rewrite the common component with independent factors. Assume $\theta_{2t} = \alpha\theta_{1t} + \theta_{2t}^{*}$ where $\mathbb{E}\theta_{2t}^{*}\theta_{1s} = 0$ for any t and s. Then we have

$$\alpha_{1i}\theta_{1t} + \alpha_{2i}\theta_{2t} = (\alpha_{1i} + \alpha_{2i}\alpha)\sigma_{\theta_1}\left(\sigma_{\theta_1}^{-1}\theta_{1t}\right) + \alpha_{2i}\sigma_{\theta_2^*}\left(\sigma_{\theta_2^*}^{-1}\theta_{2t}^*\right) = \lambda_{1i}F_{1t} + \lambda_{2i}F_{2t},$$

$$(2.19)$$

where $\sigma_{\theta_1}^2$ and $\sigma_{\theta_2^*}^2$ are the true variances of θ_{1t} and θ_{2t}^*, respectively. Note that we impose the restriction of the unitary variance for F_{1t} and F_{2t}. Also note that F_{1t} is orthogonal to F_{2t}. That is, $T^{-1}\sum_{t=1}^{T} F_{1t}F_{2t} = 0$. The common factor, F_t, is called

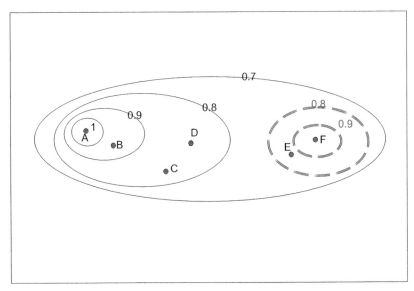

FIGURE 2.3 Two-factor structure

the 'statistical' factor. Only in this case, the number of common factors becomes the number of non-zero eigenvalues of the covariance matrix of y_{it}. Then the associated eigenvectors become the factor loadings. Hence the statistical factors and factor loadings are not equivalent to the true factors and loadings.

2.4 Other variations

In this section, we study various factor models, and consider how each model is different from the standard factor model.

2.4.1 Dynamic factor model

The common factor model we have studied in the previous section is sometimes called the 'static' factor model to contrast with a dynamic factor model, which we will study now. A single dynamic factor model can be written as

$$y_{it} = \lambda_{1i} F_{1t} + \lambda_{2i} F_{1t-1} + y_{it}^o, \text{ with } F_{1t} = \rho F_{1t-1} + v_{1t}.$$

Of course, the number of static factors becomes two, but the source of the dependence comes from the single common factor F_{1t}. Statistically, this dynamic factor model can always be rewritten with two independent factors. In the aforementioned example, we can rewrite the common component as

$$\lambda_{1i} F_{1t} + \lambda_{2i} F_{1t-1} = \left[(\lambda_{1i}\rho + \lambda_{2i})\sigma_{F_1} \right]\sigma_{F_1}^{-1} F_{1t-1} + (\lambda_{1i}\sigma_v)\sigma_v^{-1} v_{1t} = \delta_{1i} F_{1t}^* + \delta_{2i} F_{2t}^*,$$

where $F_{1t}^* = \sigma_{F_1}^{-1} F_{1t-1}$, and $F_{2t}^* = \sigma_v^{-1} v_{1t}$. Hence it is not easy at all to identify the latent static factor in this case.

2.4.2   Hierarchical factor model

The hierarchical factor approach has sometimes been used in practice, particularly in psychology. In economics, the hierachical factor model is usually used for describing local or regional factors. For example, consider property crime rates across counties in the United States. There are 48 contiguous states, which can be divided further into a total of 3,007 counties. One may consider national and state factors to explain common behaviors of property crime rates across counties. In this case, a total of 49 common factors may be used for the crime rates across 3,007 counties. That is, the hierarchical factor structure becomes like this:

$$
\theta_t \rightarrow
\begin{cases}
\eta_{1t} \rightarrow
\begin{cases}
\xi_{1,1t} \\
\vdots \\
\xi_{1,c_1 t}
\end{cases} \\
\quad \vdots \\
\eta_{48,t} \rightarrow
\begin{cases}
\xi_{48,1t} \\
\vdots \\
\xi_{48,c_{48} t}
\end{cases}
\end{cases}
, \qquad (2.20)
$$

where $\eta_t = (\eta_{1t}, \dots, \eta_{48,t})'$ is a vector of state factors, and $\xi_{i,j,t}$ is the crime rate in the j-county in the i-th state at time t. Once we aggregate crime rates for all counties for each state, then we can identify the state level crime rates. That is,

$$
\eta_{1t} = \frac{1}{c_1} \sum_{j=1}^{c_1} \xi_{1,jt}, \quad \cdots, \quad \eta_{48t} = \frac{1}{c_{48}} \sum_{j=1}^{c_{48}} \xi_{48,jt}.
$$

Note that η_{it} is not an estimate but the population average for the i-th state. Once the state-level aggregration is done, η_{it} is no longer a common factor, but an idiosyncratic component. Hence the hierarchical factor model can be thought of as several layers of the static factor models.

3

FACTOR NUMBER IDENTIFICATION

In this chapter, we study how to select the optimal the number of common factors. In econometric studies on the factor number estimation, theoretical econometricians allow weak cross-sectional dependence among the idiosyncratic component, y_{it}^o, and allow weak dependence between the common factors and the idiosyncratic components. For example, the spatial dependence among y_{it}^o is usually allowed.

There are broadly two methods available in the literature. The first method is using penalty functions. The methods proposed by Bai and Ng (2002), Hallin and Liska (2007), and Ahn and Horenstein (2013) are classified in this category. The second method is using the statistical inference proposed by Onatski (2009, 2010). Hallin and Liska's (2007) method is based on Bai and Ng (2002). See Choi and Jeong (2018) for recent survey and finite sample comparisons among various criteria. All methods utilize the PC estimates of the common factors.

I will provide a step-by-step procedure for the determination of the optimal factor number, and right after that, I will demonstrate how the step-by-step procedure works in practice. The underlying econometric theory will be provided later.

3.1   A step-by-step procedure for determining the factor number

There are a number of criteria and estimation methods for selecting the factor number. Among them, the following criterion has been popularly used. It is called Bai and Ng's IC_2 (information criterion 2). See Section 3.2 for more discussions about alternative criteria functions and their empirical performance.

$$IC_2(k) = \ln V\left(k, \hat{F}^k\right) + k\left(\frac{n+T}{nT}\right) \ln C_{nT}, \qquad (3.1)$$

where $V\left(k, \hat{F}^k\right) = \frac{1}{nT}\sum_{i=1}^{n}\sum_{t=1}^{T}\left(\tilde{y}_{it} - \hat{\lambda}_{i}^{k'}\hat{F}_{t}^k\right)^2$, $\hat{\lambda}_{i}^{k}$ and $\hat{F}_{t}^{k}$ are the PC estimates of the factor loadings and common factors up to k, and $C_{nT} = \min[n, T]$. The optimal factor number can be obtained by minimizing this IC$_2$ function in (3.1). As k increases, V decreases uniformly. The second term in (3.1) is a penalty function, which is an increasing function of k. The PC estimates of the k common factors are simply the eigenvectors associated with the first largest k eigenvalues. Once the eigenvectors are estimated, the factor loadings are estimated by running $\tilde{y}_{it}$ on $\hat{F}_{t}^{k}$ for each i.

If the idiosyncratic components are independent and identically distributed, then IC$_2$ selects the true factor number very accurately. Hence it would be ideal to transform the panel data of interest that the idiosyncratic parts become iid. The following step-by-step procedure is important to get a reasonable esti-mate of the factor number and common factors. The first two steps make the idiosyncratic components more likely near iid. Also note that it is critically important that the number of the cross-sectional and time series units must be moderately large (let's say more than 20 each). Otherwise, the performance of the IC$_2$ is not reliable at all.

Step 1 Check the serial correlation, ρ. If the serial correlation is high (let's say $\rho > 0.8$), then take the first difference. See Section 3.3 for a more detailed explanation of why the first difference or alternative prewhitening method is needed.

Step 2 Standardize all data for each individual's standard deviation. That is, modify y_{it} as follows:

$$y_{it}^{+} = y_{it}/\hat{\sigma}_{i}, \quad \text{with } \hat{\sigma}_{i}^2 = (T-1)^{-1}\sum_{t=1}^{T}\left(y_{it} - T^{-1}\sum_{t=1}^{T}y_{it}\right)^2. \qquad (3.2)$$

See Section 3.3 also for the underlying reasons why the standardization is required.

Step 3 Set the maximum k, $k_{\max}$. Usually, $k_{\max}$ is greater than four but less than ten. Get IC$_2$ (k) for each k and then minimize the criterion.

Step 4 Repeat Step 2 and Step 3 with various subsamples. Make sure that the selected factor numbers are stable over time.

Step 1 is required for highly persistent data. If the serial correlation is high – if the first order autocorrelation coefficient is greater than 0.5 – it is always safe to take the first difference. See the next section for more discussion. The IC$_2$ always chooses $k_{\max}$ as the optimal factor number. Do not mix the panel data with the first difference and non-difference data. If some time series are highly persistent but the rest of them are not, then all series should be first differenced. However, if some series have trend terms, but the other series do not, then taking the first difference for all series leads to an inaccurate result. In this case, one should separate the trended series and make a separate panel. Step 2 is also very important. Without standardization, the IC$_2$ always picks $k_{\max}$. Step 4 is also important. Check your data with the same amount of rolling samples. Increase your rolling windows and check whether you can get a stable factor number estimate.

Next, I provide how the step-by-step procedure works with actual data. FBI reports crime statistics for each state from 1960, except for New York. The crime rates of New York state start from 1965. The FBI crime data set is called the 'Uniform Crime Reports' (UCR). Crimes are classified into two types broadly: Violent and property crimes. Violent crime includes murder, robbery, rape, and assault. Property crime consists of burglary, larceny theft, and motor vehicle theft. Each panel data consists of a crime rate (reported offenses per 100,000 population) across 50 states (including Hawaii and Alaska) from 1965 to 2014: $n = 50$ and $T = 50$. I take the logarithm in the crime rate and transform the log crime rate into three variations. A total of four different types of the panel data are examined.

y_{it} :   No difference, y_{it}^{+} :   No difference but standardized
Δy_{it} :   Differenced, Δy_{it}^{+} : Differenced and standardized

Table 3.1 reports the selected factor number by IC_2. The maximum k is eight. Evidently, the selected factor numbers with y_{it} are more or less around the maximum k. The selected numbers with y_{it}^{+} are usually smaller than those with y_{it}, but they are still closed to the maximum k. With the first differenced series – Δy_{it}, the selected factor numbers suddenly dropped to around unity, but the selected factor numbers for four crime rates out of nine are still above unity. With the first differenced and the standardized series – Δy_{it}^{+}, the selected factor numbers become one for all cases.

Figure 3.1 displays the selected factor numbers with rolling samples of the property crime rate. The rolling window is 30 years. Evidently, the general

TABLE 3.1 Selected factor number with various crime rates

		y_{it}	y_{it}^{+}	Δy_{it}	Δy_{it}^{+}
Differenced		No	No	Yes	Yes
Standardization		No	Yes	No	Yes
Violent		8	8	1	1
	Murder	5	2	3	1
	Robbery	7	7	3	1
	Rape	7	6	1	1
	Assault	6	8	1	1
Property		7	7	1	1
	Burglary	8	8	2	1
	Larceny Theft	6	7	1	1
	Motor Vehicle Theft	8	8	1	1

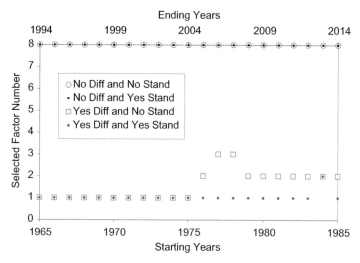

FIGURE 3.1   Robust check for property crime rate (30 years rolling window)

patterns are very similar: A series should be first differenced (because of high serial correlation) and standardized by its standard deviation. However, the pre-whitening and standardization do not always yield a good result. See Section 3.3 for more detailed discussion.

3.2   Information criteria and alternative methods

Let $\tilde{y}_{it}$ be the deviation from its time series mean, $\hat{\Sigma}_T$ be the sample $(T \times T)$ covariance matrix, and $\hat{\Sigma}_n$ be the sample $(n \times n)$ covariance matrix. If $n < T$, the kth largest eigenvectors from $\hat{\Sigma}_n$ become the PC estimates for the factor loadings, then the common factors are estimated from the regression of $\tilde{y}_{it}$ on the k estimated eigenvectors for each t. If $T < n$, the kth largest eigenvectors from $\hat{\Sigma}_T$ become the PC estimates for the common factors. The PC estimates for the factor loadings are obtained from the regression of $\tilde{y}_{it}$ on the eigenvectors for each i. Define ϱ_i as the ith largest eigenvalue of the $(nT)^{-1}\hat{y}^{o\prime}\hat{y}^o$ matrix, where $\hat{y}^o$ is the $T \times n$ matrix of the residual of $\hat{y}_{it}^o$. The maximum number of the eigenvalues becomes h, where $h = \min[n, T]$.

Bai and Ng's (2002) criteria minimize the following statistics.

$$\text{IC}_{BN} = \underset{0 \le k \le k_{\max}}{\arg\min} \left[\ln \left(\sum\nolimits_{i=k+1}^{h} \varrho_i \right) + k \times p(n, T) \right], \tag{3.3}$$

where $p(n, T)$ is a penalty or threshold function, and $k_{\max}$ is the maximum factor number usually assigned by a practitioner. In detail, the penalty functions considered by Bai and Ng (2002) are as follow:

$$IC_1(k) = \ln\left(\sum_{i=k+1}^{h} \varrho_i\right) + k\left(\frac{n+T}{nT}\right)\ln\frac{nT}{2(n+T)},$$

$$IC_2(k) = \ln\left(\sum_{i=k+1}^{h} \varrho_i\right) + k\left(\frac{n+T}{nT}\right)\ln h, \qquad (3.4)$$

$$IC_3(k) = \ln\left(\sum_{i=k+1}^{h} \varrho_i\right) + k\left(\frac{\ln h}{h}\right).$$

Bai and Ng (2002) show that the probabilities of selecting the true number for all criteria go to unity as n, $T \rightarrow \infty$. However, in a finite sample, these criteria select somewhat different factor numbers. To see this, take the actual example. In the case of the burglary crime panel in Table 3.1, we have $n = 50$ and $T = 49$ (lost one sample due to the first differencing); the penalty function values for IC_1, IC_2, and IC_3 become 0.102, 0.157, and 0.079, respectively. See Figure 3.2. Evidently, the value of IC_2 is always higher than those of IC_1 and IC_3. For each criterion, the shape of the minimum k is magnified. For example, the large filled circle indicates that IC_2 is minimized at $k = 1$. As shown in Figure 3.2, the IC_2 chooses $k = 1$ for the optimal lag also; meanwhile, the IC_3 selects $k = 2$.

Hallin and Liska (2007, HL hereafter) point out this problem of Bai and Ng's IC criteria. The basic idea is simple. Instead of $k \times p(n, T)$, a more general IC criterion can be written as $ck \times p(n, T)$ for any finite $c > 0$. In a finite sample,

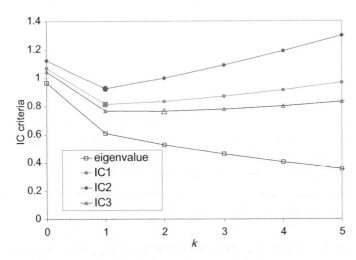

FIGURE 3.2 IC criteria with the burglary crime panel data

however, the selected factor number is heavily dependent on the value of c. HL's method is for the selection of c by using various subsamples.

Ahn and Horenstein's (2013, AH hereafter) criteria are free from the choices of the threshold function $p(n, T)$. They proposed the following two criteria:

$$ER(k) = \max_{0 \le k \le k_{max}} \varrho_k/\varrho_{k+1}, \quad GR(k) = \max_{0 \le k \le k_{max}} \ln\left[1 + \varrho_k/V_k\right]/\ln\left[1 + \varrho_{k+1}/V_{k+1}\right],$$

where $V_k = \sum_{i=k+1}^h \varrho_i$, ER stands for 'Eigenvalue Ratio' and GR stands for 'Growth Ratio.' AH's criteria requires us to know the eigenvalue for $k = 0$, which does not exist. They suggest the following 'mock' eigenvalue:

$$\varrho_0 = \sum_{i=1}^h \varrho_i / \ln(h). \tag{3.5}$$

Onatski (2009, 2010) proposes two methods for consistent factor number estimation. Onatski's (2009) test requires the assumption of Gaussian idiosyncratic errors. Onatski's (2010) criteria does not require Gaussianality, however. Onatski's (2010) estimator is defined as

$$\hat{k}(\delta) = \max\left\{i \le k_{max} : \varrho_i - \varrho_{i+1} \ge \delta\right\}, \tag{3.6}$$

where δ is a fixed positive number. See Onatski (2010) for a detailed procedure on how to calibrate δ.

Hl's, AH's, and Onatski's methods have not been used much compared with Bai and Ng's (2002) in the literature. In fact, there are not enough Monte Carlo simulation studies, except for Choi and Jeong (2018), to compare the finite sample performance among these methods. Even though HL, AH, and Onatski suggested that their methods have some benefits, the use of IC_2 seems to be much more robust with various data sets in my short experience. Regardless of which method is used, applied researchers should provide a subsample analysis like Figure 3.1 to prove the robustness of the criterion they use.

3.3   Standardization and prewhitening

Greenaway-McGrevy, Han, and Sul (2012a, 2012b; GHS hereafter) discuss the importance of the standardization and the prewhitening methods. To see this issue intuitively, consider the following two extreme examples. Assume that there is no common factor: $y_{it} = y_{it}^o$. Let $n = 3$ and consider that the following two covariance matrices of the idiosyncratic terms, y_{it}^o, are given by

$$\Sigma_1 = \begin{bmatrix} 1 & 0 & 0 \\ 0 & 1 & 0 \\ 0 & 0 & 1 \end{bmatrix}, \text{ and } \Sigma_2 = \begin{bmatrix} 100 & 0 & 0 \\ 0 & 1 & 0 \\ 0 & 0 & 1 \end{bmatrix}.$$

The eigenvalue of Σ_1 is 1 (only one non-zero eigenvalue so that the factor number is equal to zero); meanwhile, the eigenvalues of Σ_2 are 100 and 1 (two non-zero eigenvalues so that the factor number is equal to one). That is, if one series has a relatively huge variance, then the number of common factors (or the number of non-zero eigenvalues minus one) is over-estimated. Note that the eigenvalue of $c\Sigma_1$ is always equal to c with any $c > 0$. In general, y_{it}^o is independently distributed as $d\left(0, \sigma_{o,i}^2\right)$. Then

$$y_{it}^o \sim ind\left(0, \sigma_{o,i}^2\right), \quad \sigma_{o,i}^{-1} y_{it}^o \sim ind(0, 1).$$

That is, by standardizing its own standard deviation, the correct factor number can be estimated.

Since the variance of the idiosyncratic component is unknown, y_{it} is standardized rather than y_{it}^o. When the heterogeneity of the variances comes from the factor loadings (some outliers), the standardization may lead to the over-estimation. Alternatively, if the variance heterogeneity comes from the idiosyncratic errors, then the standardization is required for the consistent estimation of the factor number. Therefore, GHS suggest the following minimum rule. Let $\#\{y_{it}\}$ be the estimated factor number with y_{it}. Then the estimated factor number, $\hat{k}$, becomes

$$\hat{k} = \min \left[\#\{y_{it}\}, \#\{y_{it}^+\}\right], \tag{3.7}$$

where $y_{it}^+ = y_{it}/\hat{\sigma}_i$ with $\hat{\sigma}_i^2 = (T-1)^{-1} \sum_{t=1}^{T} \left(y_{it} - T^{-1} \sum_{t=1}^{T} y_{it}\right)^2$.

The serial dependence makes a similar result. As we did before, assume that there is no common factor: $y_{it} = y_{it}^o$. Suppose that y_{1t}^o follows the autoregressive process with order 1 – AR(1) but the rest of them are $iid(0, 1)$. That is, $y_{1t}^o = \rho y_{1t-1}^o + e_{1t}$. Then the variance of y_{1t}^o is given by $\sigma_{e1}^2/(1-\rho^2)$. As ρ approaches unity, the variance of y_{1t}^o diverges infinity. Meanwhile, the rest of the variances of y_{it}^o with $i > 1$ are just unity. Naturally, the dominant eigenvalue is equal to the variance of y_{1t}^o. To avoid possible over-estimation of the factor number, the prewhitening procedure is necessary. Contrast to the standardization, however, the prewhitening should be done homogeneously across i if it is more than or equal to one factor. When $y_{it} \neq y_{it}^o$ because of non-zero common factors, the individual prewhitening may lead to possible over-estimation. To see this, assume that $y_{it}^o \sim iid(0,1)$ but F_t follows AR(1). Then the serial dependence depends on the value of the factor loading. In a single factor case, we have

$$\mathbb{E}y_{it}y_{it-1} = \lambda_i^2 \mathbb{E}(F_t F_{t-1}).$$

Let $\hat{\rho}_i$ be the estimated AR(1) coefficient. Then the prewhitened series is given by

$$y_{it} - \hat{\rho}_i y_{it-1} = \lambda_i(F_t - \hat{\rho}_i F_{t-1}) + y_{it}^o - \hat{\rho}_i y_{it-1}^o. \tag{3.8}$$

Evidently, since $\hat{\rho}_i \neq \rho$ for all i, the prewhitened series of y_{it} has two common factors – a single dynamic factor though. If $\hat{\rho}_i$ approaches unity, the variance of the prewhitened idiosyncratic term becomes relatively larger than the rest of the variances. Hence it is very important to impose a homogeneity assumption. If $\hat{\rho}_i = \hat{\rho}$, then

$$y_{it} - \hat{\rho}y_{it-1} = \lambda_i(F_t - \hat{\rho}F_{t-1}) + y_{it}^o - \hat{\rho}y_{it-1}^o \tag{3.9}$$

so that regardless of the value of ρ, the relative variances of the prewhitened idiosyncratic components are not changed and the factor number does not change.

There are various prewhitening methods. Among them, the most convenient one is the first difference. However, to recover the common factors, the re-coloring is required. That is, the cumulative sum of the estimated common factors to the first differenced series becomes the estimated common factors to the original series.

3.4 Practice: factor number estimation

This section provides detailed instructions on how to run STATA, GAUSS, and MATLAB for estimating the number of common factors. It would be useful to learn computer languages at this time if you can. In fact, it is not hard to learn. Usually, a typical PhD student learns either GAUSS or MATLAB within a week.

3.4.1 STATA practice with crime rates

In this subsection, we will learn how to run STATA codes for the estimation of the number of common factors.

First, you need to download BN.ado and 'crime.csv' files from the book website at http://www.utdallas.edu/~d.sul/book/panel.htm. Note that 'crime.csv' includes 9 crime rates per 100,000 population for 50 states (including Alaska and Hawaii) from 1965 to 2014. The data come from uniform crime reporting statistics. Here is a screen shot of the actual data file (Figure 3.3).

A1			f_x	state_name								
A	B	C	D	E	F	G	H	I	J	K	L	M
1 state_name	id	year	Violent	murder	robbery	rape	assault	property	burglary	larceny	motorv	
2 Alabama	1	1965	199.8	11.4	28.7	10.6	149.1	1392.7	199.8	812.1	106.9	
3 Alabama	1	1966	230.3	10.9	32	9.7	177.7	1528	230.3	869.6	131	
4 Alabama	1	1967	238.6	11.7	33	10.5	183.5	1612.4	238.6	895	146	
5 Alabama	1	1968	232.4	11.8	41	11.1	168.5	1766.6	232.4	967.7	170.7	
6 Alabama	1	1969	250.4	13.7	41	14	181.7	1876.2	250.4	1037.8	171.2	
7 Alabama	1	1970	295.7	11.7	50.3	18.5	215.2	2183.8	295.7	1184	223.5	

FIGURE 3.3 Actual data set: crime.csv

STATA practice 3.1 Estimation of the factor number with crime rates (STATA EX 3-1)

STATA Codes	Notes
insheet using "crime.csv", comma	load the data (or you can import the data)
xtset id year	declare panel data
gen lmur = ln(murder)	taking natural log
gen dlmur = lmur - L.lmur	taking the first difference
egen sd_dlmur = sd(dlmur), by(id)	estimate standard error for each state
gen dlmur_s = dlmur / sd_dlmur	standardization
keep dlmur_s id year	delete other variables except for dlmur
reshape wide dlmur_s, i(id) j(year)	required procedure for BN.ado
order _all, alphabetic	required procedure for BN.ado
BN dlmur_s1966-dlmur_s2014, kmax(8)	run BN.ado with kmax = 8

STATA EX 3-1 provides line-by-line instruction how to run STATA

Note that in the last line, you need to use `dlmur_s1966` not `dlmur_s1965`. Due to the first difference, `dlmur_s1965` includes only zero. If you got the following error message, then you need to change the working directory (go to file and then click "change working directory") where 'BN.ado' and the data files are located.

```
.
. BN dlmur_s1966-dlmur_s2014, kmax(8)
unrecognized command: BN
r(199);
```

The final output file must be like this.

```
.
. BN dlmur_s1966-dlmur_s2014, kmax(8)
Use Bai&Ng's IC2
   Bai&Ng's   IC1   :  1
   Bai&Ng's   IC2   :  1
   Bai&Ng's   IC3   :  8
```

Here, IC_1 and IC_2 select one factor; meanwhile, IC_3 selects the maximum factor number. Of course, as I suggested, ignore IC_1 and IC_3.

Next, you need to verify whether or not your result is robust across various subsamples. To fulfill this task, you need to add one or two more lines before the 'xtset' command line. For example, you can drop the sample at year 1965 and year 2014. See the STATA Practice 3.2.

You need to consider various subsamples. There are two ways, broadly. First consider a fixed window width. In this example, the total number of time series (T) is 50. Let the window width be 49. Then you can consider the following two subsamples: From 1966 to 2014, or from 1965 to 2013. If the window width

STATA practice 3.2 Robust check with subsamples (STATA EX 3-2)

STATA Codes	Notes
insheet using "crime.csv", comma	load the data (or you can import the data)
drop if year < 1966	consider the subsample from 1966 to 2014
drop if year > 2013	consider the subsample from 1966 to 2013
xtset id year	declare panel data
⋮	
reshape wide dlmur_s, i(id) j(year)	required procedure for BN.ado
order _all, alphabetic	required procedure for BN.ado
BN dlmur_s1967-dlmur_s2013, kmax(8)	sample changes

STATA practice 3.3 Role of prewhitening (PCE data); before prewhitening (STATA EX 3-3)

STATA Codes	Notes
insheet using "pce.csv", comma	load the data (or you can import the data)
xtset id year	declare panel data
gen dp = (pee - L. pee)/L. pce	taking the growth rate -> inflation now
egen sd_dp = sd(dp), by(id)	estimate standard error for each item
gen dps = dp / sd_dp	standardization
⋮	
BN dps1979-dps2016, kmax(8)	run BN.ado with kmax = 8

reduces to 48, then you can consider the following three subsamples: From 1965 to 2012, from 1966 to 2013, and from 1967 to 2014. The second method is called 'recursive subsampling.' You fix the last year, but reduce the initial year. That is, you consider the following subsamples: From 1965 to 2014 (full sample), from 1966 to 2014, from 1967 to 2014, etc. You need to make sure that IC_2 selects the same number of – common factors across all subsamples.

3.4.2   STATA practice with price indices

The next panel data we will analyze is a personal consumption expenditure (PCE) price index that has been produced by the Bureau of Economic Analysis (BEA). The 'pce.csv' includes annual PCE prices for 46 detailed items from 1978 to 2016 ($n = 46$, $T = 39$). STATA Practice 3.3 provides the example STATA codes with 46 inflation rates before prewhitening. Even though price indexes have exponentially growing components, you should not take a logarithm since your interest is not in price indices themselves but in inflation

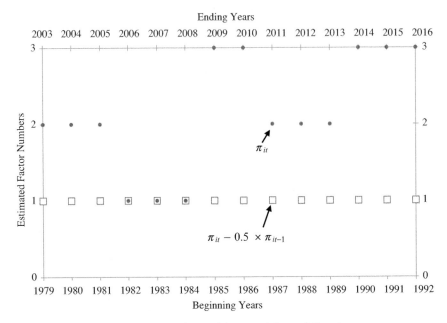

FIGURE 3.4 Estimated factor numbers with π_{it} and $(\pi_{it} - 0.5\pi_{it-1})$

rates. Of course, the log difference is not exactly the growth rate but a good proxy. Hence you need to take the growth rates of the price indexes. Next, you need to standardize the inflation rates and then estimate the number of the common factors. BN's IC_2 shows that the inflation rates have two common factors. When you repeat this exercise with various subsamples, you will get somewhat different results. Figure 3.4 shows the estimated factor numbers before and after prewhitening over 14 subsamples with 25 years of rolling windows. The dark circle indicates the selected factor number. Evidently, depending on the subsample periods, the estimated factor numbers have been fluctuating, which does not imply that the true factor numbers are fluctuating over time, but the estimated ones are not robust.

```
STATA Result:
. BN dlps1979-dlps2015, kmax(8)
Use Bai&Ng's IC2
Bai&Ng's IC1 : 8
Bai&Ng's IC2 : 2
Bai&Ng's IC3 : 8
```

Usually, inflation rates for durable goods are highly persistent since by definition durable goods last a long time. The extreme case is housing prices and the cost of higher education. The fitted estimate of the AR(1) coefficient with housing

STATA practice 3.4 Role of prewhitening (PCE data); after prewhitening (STATA EX 3-4)

STATA Codes	Notes
insheet using "pce.csv", comma	load the data (or you can import the data)
xtset id year	declare panel data
gen dp = (pee - L.pee)/L. pce	taking the growth rate -> inflation now
gen dpp = dp - L.dp*0.5	prewhitening with 0.5
egen sd_dpp = sd(dpp), by(id)	estimate standard error for each item
gen dpps = dpp / sd_dpp	standardization
⋮	
BN dpps1980-dpps2015, kmax(8)	lost one more obs due to prewhitening

prices is around 0.95 and that with the cost of higher education is around 0.96, respectively. Meanwhile, the fitted AR(1) coefficient with food is only around 0.15. As we studied in the previous section, the factor number may be over-estimated because of some highly persistent items. To verify this, you need to do prewhitening with inflation rates. STATA Practice 3.4 provides STATA codes for prewhitening procedure with detailed notes. Note that we lost one more sample due to the prewhitening; hence, the data starts from 1980. (See the last line in STATA Practice 3.4)

The result shows like this:

```
STATA Result:
Bai&Ng' s IC1 : 8
Bai&Ng' s IC2 : 1
Bai&Ng' s IC3 : 8
```

Figure 3.4 also shows that the estimate factor numbers after prewhitening. Regardless of subsample periods, only the estimated number is single.

Next, we will study how to use GAUSS and MATLAB codes. If you are a STATA user, just try reading the next subsection and compare how to utilize them to speed up your computation.

3.4.3 Practice with GAUSS

Note that there is little difference between GAUSS and MATLAB in terms of programming languages. We first provide GAUSS codes to replicate what we did with STATA. First, you need to open 'BN.pgm' and copy the entire text into the end of the following program in GAUSS Practice 3.5. 'BN.pgm' contains a procedure (called BN) which is the subroutine program for the Bai and

GAUSS practice 3.5 Exercise with PCE inflations (GAUSS EX 3-5)

	GAUSS Codes	Notes
1	`new;`	clear memory
2	`cls;`	clear screen
3	`t = 39; n=46;`	sample size
4	`load p[t,n+1] = n46_t39.csv;`	load a $T \times n$ data
5	`pi = p[., 2:n+1];`	delete the first column
6	`dp=(p1[2:t,.]-p1[1:t-1,.])./p1[1:t-1,.];`	dp = inflation
7	`dpp=dp[2:rows(dp),.] - dp[1:rows(dp)-1,.].*0.5;`	prewhitening
8	`dps=dp./sqrt(diag(vcx(dp))');`	standardization for dp
9	`dpps=dpp./sqrt(diag(vcx(dpp))');`	standardization for dpp
10	`bn(dps,8)~bn(dpps,8);`	IC_2 for dps and dpps
11	`proc BN(x,kmax)`	copy from BN.pgm

Ng's IC_2 criterion. Next, copy csv files for GAUSS. Note that anything, including numbers and characters between two '@'s, is treated as a statement. If you open the 'n46_t39.csv' file, then you can find '@' in cell A1 and in cell AV3. GAUSS will not read them from A1 to AV3. You need to assign a panel data variable ($T \times n$ matrix) to a separate csv file. Just by looking at the GAUSS program codes in GAUSS Practice 3.6, you probably understand what is going on. If you execute this file, then you will get two numbers (two IC_2s for the inflation and for the prewhitened inflation).

Here are more explanations for each line.

- Line 1: New; It's a new file. Clear all memories. You need to add the semicolon in the end of command.
- Line 4: Read `n46_t39.csv` file and name it p. The total number of columns in the csv file is 47. The variable p includes the year and 46 PCE indexes.
- Line 5: Assign the data from the second column to the last column of p as p1. Note that '[.,2:n+1]' implies the use of the data from the entire row (.) but from the second to n + 1 columns. See the help statement for matrix manipulation.
- Line 8: `sqrt(diag(vcx(dp))')`. Note that `vcx(dp)` is the covariance matrix of dp. `diag(·)` means to take the diagonal element. `sqrt(·)` implies the square root of the element. 'x'' implies a transpose of x. Hence `sqrt(diag(vcx(dp))')` implies the ($n \times 1$) vector of the standard error of dp.
- Line 8: './' stands for division of element by element. See the help statement for ExE operators.

GAUSS practice 3.6 Subsample analysis (GAUSS EX 3-6)

GAUSS Codes	Notes
1 new;	clear memory
⋮	
6 dp=(p1[2:t,.]-p1[1:t-1,.])./p1[1:t-1,.];	dp = inflation
7 for i(1,14,1)	do loop starts, i=1 to 14.
8 xx=dp[i:i+24,.];	construct a subsample with 25 years
9 dx=xx[2:rows(xx),.]-xx[1:rows(xx)-1,.].*0.5;	prewhitening
10 xxs=xx./sqrt(diag(vex(xx))');	standardization for xx
11 dxs=dx./sqrt(diag(vcx(dx))');	standardization for dx
12 i~bn(dxs,8)~bn(xxs,8);	print out i and IC_2S
13 endfor;	end of the do loop
⋮	

Next, we will study how to do subsample analysis by using a do-loop. GAUSS Practice 3.6 provides GAUSS example code for the do loop. If you execute GAUSS EX 3-6, then you will get the following output.

```
1.0000000    1.0000000 2.0000000
2.0000000    1.0000000 2.0000000
3.0000000    1.0000000 2.0000000
                ⋮
14.000000    1.0000000 3.0000000
```

We will study more about how to program in GAUSS in the next chapter. Next, we will study MATLAB codes.

3.4.4 Practice with MATLAB

There are many good websites for the education of MATLAB. Also, MATLAB itself provides thousands of library and specific functions. Due to this convenience, most statisticians, natural scientists, and other social scientists use MATLAB. Here I provide a very basic comparison between GAUSS and MATLAB. To execute the MATLAB program, you need to copy BN.m and data files for MATLAB. Open one of the csv files and compare it to one of the GAUSS csv files. The only difference is the decoration. In MATLAB, any numbers or commands after '%' are treated as statements. In the following, I translate GAUSS codes in GAUSS Practice 3.5 into MATLAB.

(MATLAB EX 3-5)

```
clear;
load MATn46_t39.csv;
p = MATn46_t39;
T = size(p,1); n = size(p,2);
p1 = p(:,2:n);
n=n-1;
dp = (p1(2:T,:) - p1(1:T-1,:))./p1(1:T-1,:);
dpp = dp(2:T-1,:)-dp(1:T-2,:).*0.5;
dps = dp./(ones(T-1,1)*(sqrt(var(dp))));
dpps = dpp./((ones(T-2,1)*sqrt(var(dpp))));
[BN(dps,8) BN(dpps,8)]
```

The next codes are corresponding to GAUSS Practice 3.6.

(MATLAB EX 3-6)

```
clear;
load MATn46_t39.csv;
p = MATn46_t39;
T = size(p,1); n = size(p,2);
p1 = p(:,2:n);
n=n-1;
dp = (p1(2:T,:) - p1(1:T-1,:))./p1(1:T-1,:);
for i=1:14;
  xx = dp(i:i+24,:);
  dx = xx(2:25,:)-xx(1:24,:)*0.5;
  xxs = xx./(ones(25,1)*sqrt(var(xx)));
  dxs = dx./(ones(24,1)*sqrt(var(dx)));
[i BN(dxs,8) BN(xxs,8)]
end
```

4

DECOMPOSITION OF PANEL

Estimation of common and idiosyncratic components

In this chapter, we study how to estimate the common factors and factor loadings. Once the common components are estimated, the idiosyncratic components are extracted from the estimated common factors. Before we get into the econometric theory, we will study how to measure the accuracy of an estimator first.

4.1 Measurement of accuracy: order in probability

The uncertainty between a true parameter and its estimate is usually reduced as the number of observations used in the estimation increases. The asymptotic theory proves how far the distance between the estimate and the true parameter is. Usually, the accuracy is expressed as a function of the number of observations. As more observations are available, the estimator becomes more accurate. Here we study two definitions, which will be used very often in the rest of this book.

Suppose that x is just a sequence of a finite numeric numbers; then x can be expressed as $O(1)$. Here are some examples.

$$n^{1/2} = O(n^{1/2}), \ \ 4 = O(1), \ \ 0 = O(1), \ \ \ln n = O(\ln n), \ \ \rho^n = O(\rho^n) \qquad (4.1)$$

A formal definition goes like this. As $n \to \infty$, $\lim_{n \to \infty} x/n = c < \infty$, then $x = O(n)$. Of course, x can be written as $O(n^2)$ if $x = O(n)$ since $\lim_{n \to \infty} x/n^2 = 0$. We will extend this definition to random variables.

Let x_i be an iid random variable, or write it as $x_i \sim iid(0, \sigma^2)$. Another way to express x_i is as follows:

$$x_i \sim iid(0, \sigma^2), \ \text{ or } x_i = O_p(1) \text{ if } \sigma^2 < \infty. \qquad (4.2)$$

If the variance of x_i is shrinking at the $\sqrt{n}$ rate as n increases, then

$$x_i \sim iid(0, \sigma^2/n) \Leftrightarrow \sqrt{n}x_i \sim iid(0, \sigma^2) \Rightarrow \sqrt{n}x_i = O_p(1) \Leftrightarrow x_i = O_p(n^{-1/2}). \quad (4.3)$$

Here we use the following fact:

$$x_i = n^{-1/2}O_p(1) = O(n^{-1/2})O_p(1) = O_p(n^{-1/2}).$$

Usually, an estimator has an asymptotic (or limiting) distribution. Let $\hat{\mu}$ be an estimator and assume that its limiting distribution is a normal distribution with the asymptotic variance of σ_μ^2/n. Alternatively, we can write it as

$$(\hat{\mu} - \mu) \to^d \mathcal{N}\left(0, \sigma_\mu^2/n\right). \quad (4.4)$$

Then we can express it as

$$\hat{\mu} - \mu = O_p(n^{-1/2}), \quad \text{or} \quad \sqrt{n}(\hat{\mu} - \mu) = O_p(1). \quad (4.5)$$

That is, the distance between $\hat{\mu}$ and μ is expressed as $O_p(n^{-1/2})$.

Next, we will learn some rules for O_p and O.

1 $O_p(n^\alpha) + O(1) = \begin{cases} O_p(n^\alpha) & \text{if } \alpha \geq 0, \\ O_p(1) & \text{if } \alpha < 0. \end{cases}$

2 $O_p(n^\alpha)O(1) = O_p(1)O(n^\alpha) = O_p(n^\alpha)$ for all α.

3 $O_p(n^\alpha) + O_p(n^\beta) = O_p(n^\gamma)$ where $\gamma = \min[\alpha, \beta]$.

4.2 Estimation of the common factors

There are three ways to estimate the common factors. Breitung and Choi (2013) provide an excellent survey on this topic. Here we study only two methods popularly used in practice: Principal Component (PC) estimation and the simple cross-sectional average (CSA). See Bai (2003, 2004) for the statistical inference on the estimated stationary and nonstationary common factors in detail, respectively.

Before we study the estimation methods, we need to know which parameters we are estimating. For example, consider a single factor case.

$$y_{it} = a_i + \alpha_i \theta_t + y_{it}^o$$

Unless $\lambda_i = 1$ for all i, the common component can be rewritten as

$$\alpha_i \theta_t = (\alpha_i \sigma_\theta)(\sigma_\theta^{-1}\theta_t) = \lambda_i F_t, \quad (4.6)$$

where the variance of F_t always becomes unity. That is, the PC method imposes the following restriction of the variance of F_t for the identification.

$$T^{-1}\sum_{t=1}^{T} F_t^2 = 1 \quad (4.7)$$

In the case of multiple factors, the identification restriction becomes

$$T^{-1} \sum_{t=1}^{T} F'_t F_t = \mathbf{I}_r, \tag{4.8}$$

where r is the number of common factors.

If F_t is nonstationary, then the following restriction is imposed instead.

$$T^{-2} \sum_{t=1}^{T} F'_t F_t = \mathbf{I}_r$$

However, this restriction does not make any difference for the actual estimation. Now we are ready to study how to estimate the common factors.

4.2.1 Cross-sectional average (CSA) approach

When $r = 1$ (the single factor case), the sample CSA approximates the common factor very well.

$$\hat{F}^c_t = \frac{1}{n} \sum_{i=1}^{n} y_{it} = \bar{a}_n + \bar{\lambda}_n F_t + \frac{1}{n} \sum_{i=1}^{n} y^o_{it}, \tag{4.9}$$

where $\bar{a}_n$ and $\bar{\lambda}_n$ are the sample means of a_i and λ_i, respectively. Since y^o_{it} has a zero mean for each i, the sample average converges zero in probability as long as y^o_{it} is not integrated. For example, if y^o_{it} follows a random walk process ($y^o_{it} = y^o_{it-1} + \varepsilon_{it}$) we state that y^o_{it} is integrated of order one, or $I(1)$. If y^o_{it} follows an AR(1) process – $y^o_{it} = \rho y^o_{it-1} + \varepsilon_{it}$ with $|\rho| < 1$ – then y^o_{it} is not integrated. Or, simply, we write it as $y^o_{it} \sim I(0)$. Nonetheless, when y^o_{it} is $I(0)$, the approximation error to F_t is then

$$\hat{F}^c_t = \bar{a}_n + \bar{\lambda}_n F_t + O_p(n^{-1/2}) \tag{4.10}$$

so that as $n \to \infty$, $\hat{F}^c_t$ converges $a + \lambda F_t$ where a and λ are the true value of the means of a_i and λ_i regardless of the size of T. Hence even when T is small, the consistency of $\hat{F}^c_t$ is only depending on the size of n. Some theoretical econometricians criticize this method since $\hat{F}^c_t$ converges a if $\lambda = 0$. Of course, this is a very rare case. In practice, such a possibility can be ruled out completely. However, it is not always that this method is superior to the PC estimation. If the number of common factors is more than one, then the efficiency gain drops significantly.

We consider the case of $r = 2$. In this case, the first and second common factors can be approximated by two sub-cross-sectional averages. Note that the overall sample cross-sectional average leads to

$$\hat{F}^c_t = \frac{1}{n} \sum_{i=1}^{n} y_{it} = \bar{a}_n + \bar{\lambda}_{1n} F_{1t} + \bar{\lambda}_{2n} F_{2t} + O_p(n^{-1/2}). \tag{4.11}$$

Since two factors are unknown, the simple cross-sectional average is not consistently estimating either the first or second factor. However, when the role of the second factor compared to that of the first factor is limited – in other words, the variance of λ_{1i} is much larger than that of λ_{2i} – the sample cross-sectional average looks like the PC estimator for the first factor. We will show graphical evidences in a while.

To identify F_{1t} and F_{2t}, one needs at least two cross-sectional averages for the exact identification. Let $n_1 = n_2 = n/2$. Then randomly assign y_{it} into two groups (S_1 and S_2) without overlapping.

$$\hat{F}^c_{1t} = \frac{1}{n_1}\sum_{i\in S_1}^{n_1} y_{it}, \quad \hat{F}^c_{2t} = \frac{1}{n_2}\sum_{i\in S_2}^{n_2} y_{it} \tag{4.12}$$

Then as $n_1, n_2 \to \infty$, the sample cross-sectional averages estimate a linear projection of the statistical common factors consistently. That is,

$$\hat{F}^c_{1t} = \bar{a}_{n_1} + \bar{\lambda}_{1,n_1} F_{1t} + \bar{\lambda}_{2,n_1} F_{2t} + O_p(n_1^{-1/2}),$$
$$\hat{F}^c_{2t} = \bar{a}_{n_2} + \bar{\lambda}_{1,n_2} F_{1t} + \bar{\lambda}_{2,n_2} F_{2t} + O_p(n_2^{-1/2}).$$

If $\bar{\lambda}_{1,n_1} = \bar{\lambda}_{1,n_2}$ and $\bar{\lambda}_{2,n_1} = \bar{\lambda}_{2,n_2}$, then F_{1t} and F_{2t} cannot be identified. Hence if $\hat{F}^c_{1t}$ is very similar to $\hat{F}^c_{2t}$, then both of them need to be re-estimated with different subgroups. The easiest way is sorting $\hat{\lambda}_{1i}$ – which is the estimated slope coefficient on $\hat{F}^c_{1t}$ – from the smallest and largest, and then form subgroups based on the rank of $\hat{\lambda}_{1i}$. Once $\hat{F}^c_{1t} \neq \hat{F}^c_{2t}$, then run the following regression for each i.

$$y_{it} = a_i + a_{1i}\hat{F}^c_{1t} + a_{2i}\hat{F}^c_{2t} + \text{error} \tag{4.13}$$

And then form two different subgroups based on the value of α_{1i} or α_{2i}, and re-estimate $\hat{F}^c_{1t}$ and $\hat{F}^c_{2t}$. The second stage CSAs usually provide a more distinct difference between $\hat{F}^c_{1t}$ and $\hat{F}^c_{2t}$.

Overall, the sample CSAs are good proxies of the common factors, but if the factor number increases, then the accuracy drops down. I will show it later, but there are more benefits empirically though. Also the ranking of λ_i is important.

4.2.2   Principal component estimator

Next, consider the PC estimators, which can be more accurate than the sample CSA if the number of common factors is more than one. The PC estimator can be thought as the minimizers of the following sum of squares errors.

$$\arg\min_{\lambda_i,F_t} \sum_{i=1}^{n}\sum_{t=1}^{T} (y_{it} - \lambda'_i F_t)^2, \tag{4.14}$$

where the fixed effects a_i are ignored. From the first order conditions in (4.14), the optimal solutions can be obtained. The estimators of the common factors become the eigenvectors corresponding to the r largest eigenvalues of the covariance matrix of y_{it}. The solution is exactly similar to the estimated eigenvalues of an $n \times n$ covariance matrix of y_{it}, where each element becomes $T^{-1} \sum_{t=1}^{T} \tilde{y}_{it} \tilde{y}_{jt}$ and where $\tilde{y}_{it}$ is the deviation from its time series mean. In this case, the rth largest eigenvectors of the $n \times n$ covariance matrix become the PC-estimated factor loadings. If a $T \times T$ covariance matrix is used where each element becomes $n^{-1} \sum_{i=1}^{n} y_{it} y_{is}$, then the rth largest eigenvectors become the PC-estimated common factors. Next, by running y_{it} on the estimated common factors, $\hat{F}_t$ for each i, the factor loadings can be estimated. Once the factor loadings are estimated, the common factors are obtained by running y_{it} on the estimated factor loadings λ_i over each t. The resulting estimators are called PC estimators.

As we studied earlier, the factor loadings and common factors cannot be identified separately. For the case of multiple factors, we have

$$y_{it} = \lambda_i' F_t + y_{it}^o = \lambda_i' H^{-1\prime} H F_t + y_{it}^o,$$

with any invertible matrix of H. The consistency of the PC estimator (and the consistency of the CSA estimators as well) is measured by HF_t rather than just F_t.

Bai (2003) showed that the PC estimator, $\hat{F}_t$, has the following statistical accuracy.

$$\hat{F}_t - HF_t = O_p(n^{-1/2}) + O_p(T^{-1}). \tag{4.15}$$

This condition implies that if $\sqrt{n} > T$, then the PC estimator is less accurate than the sample CSA.

Statistically, it is not discussed, but the PC estimator for the first dominant factor is more accurate than the PC estimator for the second factor. The underlying reason goes like this. If the signal from the common component is strong, then, generally, the PC estimator becomes accurate. Obviously, the first eigenvalue is larger than the second eigenvalue so that the accuracy of the PC estimator for the first factor is higher than that of the second factor.

Due to the same reason, usually, the sample cross-sectional average, $\hat{F}_t^c$, looks very similar to the PC estimate of the first common factor. To see this, assume that the two true common factors to y_{it} influence equally on y_{it}. Let $\theta_{1t} \sim iid\mathcal{N}(0,1)$, $\theta_{2t} \sim iid\mathcal{N}(0,1)$, $\alpha_{1i} \sim iid\mathcal{N}(1,1)$, $\alpha_{2i} \sim iid\mathcal{N}(1,1)$, but $\theta_{2t} = \phi\theta_{1t} + v_{2t}$. If $\phi > 0$, then y_{it} can be written as

$$y_{it} = a_i + (\alpha_{1i} + \phi\alpha_{2i})\theta_{1t} + (\alpha_{2i}/c)(cv_{2t}) + y_{it}^o \tag{4.16}$$

so that $F_{1t} = \theta_{1t}$, $F_{2t} = cv_{2t}$, where $c = 1/(1 - \phi^2)$, $\lambda_{1i} = \alpha_{1i} + \phi\alpha_{2i}$, and $\lambda_{2i} = \alpha_{2i}(1 - \phi^2)$. In this case, $\mathbb{E}\lambda_{1i} = 1 + \phi$, but $\mathbb{E}\lambda_{2i} = 1 - \phi^2$. As $n \to \infty$, the sample cross-sectional average is then given by

$$\hat{F}_t^c = a_n + (1 + \phi)\theta_{1t} + (1 - \phi^2)F_{2t} + O_p(n^{-1/2}). \tag{4.17}$$

Meanwhile, the PC estimate for the first common factor becomes

$$\hat{F}_{1t} = \theta_{1t} + O_p(n^{-1/2}) + O_p(T^{-1}). \tag{4.18}$$

As the correlation between the true factors θ_{1t} and θ_{2t} increases, the distance between $\hat{F}_{1t}$ and $\hat{F}_{2t}$ is getting smaller. Note that if $\phi < 0$, then θ_{2t} becomes the dominant statistical factor.

4.2.3 Comparison between two estimators for the common factors

Only when the identification is satisfied is it possible to compare the two estimators: PC and CSA estimators. Here I provide simple Monte Carlo simulation results based on the following data generating process.

$$y_{it} = \lambda_{1i} F_{1t} + y^o_{it},$$

where $y^o_{it} \sim iid\mathcal{N}(0, \sigma^2)$, $F_{1t} \sim iid\mathcal{N}(0, 1)$, and $\lambda_{1i} \sim iid\mathcal{N}(1, 1)$. Note that the value of σ^2 controls for the signal value. As this value decreases, the eigenvector can be estimated more accurately. Here I consider only a single factor case. Otherwise, it is impossible to distinguish whether or not both CSA and PC estimators are estimating the true factor. We will see shortly what both estimators estimate when there is more than a single factor.

Figure 4.1 shows the mean squares errors (MSE) of the PC and CSA estimators with $\sigma = 1$ and $\sigma = 5$. For both cases, I set $n = 100$. The number of the simulation size is 5,000. Evidently, the MSE of the CSA estimator is not dependent on T but only dependent on the value of σ: As the noisy ratio (or the value of σ) increases, the MSE of the CSA estimator increases. Meanwhile, the MSE of the

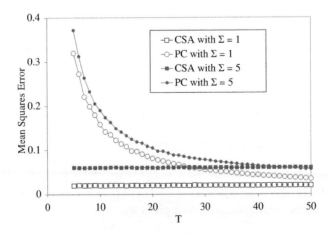

FIGURE 4.1 Mean squares errors of PC and CSA estimators ($n = 100$)

PC estimator is dependent both on the size of T and the value of σ. As T increases or the value of σ decreases, the MSE of the PC estimator becomes smaller. Overall, unless the value of σ is not much large, the CSA estimator is usually more efficient than the PC estimator.

There is another advantage of the CSA estimator. Suppose that we don't know whether or not y_{it}^o is $I(1)$. If y_{it}^o is $I(1)$, then the first differenced series should be used for the estimation. Then the level common factor is estimated by taking the cumulative sum of the estimated common factor with the first differenced data. Consider the CSA estimator first. Let

$$\hat{f}_t^c = \frac{1}{n} \sum_{i=1}^n \Delta y_{it},$$

then we have

$$\hat{F}_t^{c*} = \sum_{s=1}^t \hat{f}_s^c = \sum_{s=1}^t \frac{1}{n} \sum_{i=1}^n \Delta y_{is} = \hat{F}_t^c - \hat{F}_1^c,$$

where $\hat{F}_t^c = n^{-1} \sum_{i=1}^n y_{it}$. Hence after eliminating the time series mean, the CSA estimator using the cumulative first differenced series becomes exactly identical with the CSA estimator using the level data. Meanwhile, the cumulative sum of the PC estimator with Δy_{it} is not at all the same as that with y_{it}. The underlying reason is straightforward. The PC estimator with the level data is the minimizer of the sum of the squared errors given in (4.14), which is far different from the cumulative sum of the minimizer of the sum of the squared but first differenced errors. To be specific, consider the following example.

$$y_{it} = a_i + \lambda_i F_t + y_{it}^o \text{ with } F_t = t - \frac{1}{T} \sum_{t=1}^T t + G_t$$

so that the first difference becomes

$$\Delta y_{it} = \lambda_i + \lambda_i \Delta G_t + \Delta y_{it}^o.$$

The cumulative sum of ΔG_t will not be the same as $F_t - F_1$ but becomes $G_t - G_1$. That is, the trending part in the common factor is permanently missing by taking the first difference.

Figure 4.2 shows the four estimators of the common factor for the violent crime. As we just discussed, the cumulative CSA with Δy_{it} must be identical to the CSA with y_{it} (only mean difference but here the heterogeneous mean is adjusted). Also the PC estimator with the level data is very similar to the CSA estimator. Meanwhile, the cumulative sum of the PC estimator with Δy_{it} looks very different from the rest of the series. As we studied earlier, the overall trend in the level data cannot be seen in the cumulative sum of the PC estimator. Hence it is important to use the prewhitening method to determine

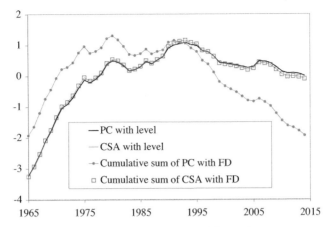

FIGURE 4.2   The estimated common factor with violent crime

the number of common factors, but do not use the cumulative sum to estimate the common factors. We will investigate this issue further in the practice section.

4.3   Estimation of the idiosyncratic components

The estimation of the common components is equivalent to the estimation of the idiosyncratic components. However, the estimation of the common factors is very different from the estimation of the common components. In this section, we will study the difference. Denote C_{it} as $\lambda_i' F_t$. And let $\hat{C}_{it}^c$ be the estimated common components by using the CSA estimators of the common factors, $\hat{F}_t^c$. Similarly, let $\hat{C}_{it}$ be the estimated common components by using the PC estimator, $\hat{F}_t$.

The PC and CSA estimators for C_{it} become

$$\hat{C}_{it} = \hat{\lambda}_i' \hat{F}_t, \; \& \; \hat{C}_{it}^c = \hat{\lambda}_i^{c'} \hat{F}_t^c, \tag{4.19}$$

where $\hat{\lambda}_i$ and $\hat{\lambda}_i^c$ are the PC and CSA estimators for the factor loadings λ_i, respectively. For example, $\hat{\lambda}_{1i}^c$ and $\hat{\lambda}_{2i}^c$ (in the case of two factors) are obtained by running the following regression for each i.

$$y_{it} = a_i + \lambda_{1i} \hat{F}_{1t}^c + \lambda_{2i} \hat{F}_{2t}^c + u_{it}. \tag{4.20}$$

The resulting LS estimators for λ_{1i} and λ_{2i} becomes the CSA estimators, and the regression residuals $\hat{u}_{it}$ become the estimates of the idiosyncratic components. This method, however, is less efficient than the PC estimators unless the ranking of λ_i is known. If the ranking of λ_i is known, then forming subgroups becomes easy, and the resulting $\hat{F}_{1t}^c$ must be different from $\hat{F}_{2t}^c$.

The PC estimators in (4.14) are the optimal minimizers of the idiosyncratic components. Even though the PC estimators for the common factors may be less efficient than the CSA estimators, the PC estimators for the idiosyncratic components or the common components are the most efficient.

Bai (2003) provides the following asymptotic result: Under suitable regularity conditions, the PC estimators, $\hat{C}_{it}$, have the following asymptotic distribution.

$$\delta_{nT}(\hat{C}_{it} - C_{it}) \to^d \mathcal{N}(0, \Omega_c^2), \tag{4.21}$$

where $\delta_{nT} = \min\left[\sqrt{n}, \sqrt{T}\right]$, and Ω_c^2 is the asymptotic variance. See Bai (2003) for the detailed expression of Ω_c^2. The result in (4.21), at first glance, looks strange since C_{it} is varying over t across i. Hence by using $n \times T$ observations, deriving the inference of the $n \times T$ observations of C_{it} sounds very wrong. However, as it is shown in (4.19), the total number of unknown parameters in C_{it} is just $(n + T)$ rather than $n \times T$. Note that it is not hard to show that the limiting distribution of the CSA estimator, $\hat{C}_{it}^c$, is similar to (4.21). The convergence rate is δ_{nT}, which is the minimum value between $\sqrt{n}$ and $\sqrt{T}$. However, this result should be interpreted in the asymptotic sense. Only when both n and T are large can the accuracy of the PC estimator depend on δ_{nT}. In a real situation, one should always choose a large T panel, unless there is no serial dependence. If F_t is more persistent, then the estimation of λ_i by running y_{it} on a constant and the estimated factors becomes more accurate simply because more persistent regressors usually lead to more accurate estimation of the slope coefficients. Meanwhile, λ_i is cross-sectionally independent. Hence the accuracy of the estimation of F_t by running y_{it} on a constant, and the estimated factor loadings for each t are not directly related to the serial dependence of the common factors, F_t.

4.4 Variance decomposition

Once the factor number and the common factors are estimated, it is always useful to check how much the estimated common factors explain the variation of the panel data of interest. It is important to note that the idiosyncratic term must be stationary. Let y_{it}^+ be the standardized sample of the panel data y_{it}. See (3.2) for the precise definition. If the panel data is persistent, then the prewhitened or differenced data should be used. Here we assume that y_{it} is not serially correlated much. Note that the standardized sample, $\tilde{y}_{it}^+$, can be rewritten as

$$\tilde{y}_{it}^+ = \frac{\tilde{y}_{it}}{\hat{\sigma}_i} = \frac{1}{\hat{\sigma}_i}(\lambda_i'\tilde{F}_t + \tilde{y}_{it}^o),$$

where '~' stands for the deviation from its time series mean, and $\hat{\sigma}_i^2$ is the variance of $\tilde{y}_{it}^+$. Let $V(x_{it})$ be the true time series variance of x_{it}. That is, $V(x_{it}) =$

$\mathbb{E}T^{-1}\sum_{t=1}^{T}\left(x_{it}-T^{-1}\sum_{t=1}^{T}x_{it}\right)^{2}$. Then in a single-factor case, the variance of y_{it}^{+} can be decomposed into

$$V\left(\tilde{y}_{it}^{+}\right)=1\simeq \underbrace{\lambda_{i}^{2}/\sigma_{i}^{2}}_{\substack{\text{The part explained}\\\text{by common factors}}}+\underbrace{V\left(\tilde{y}_{it}^{o}\right)/\sigma_{i}^{2}}_{\substack{\text{The part explained}\\\text{by idiosyncratic errors}}},$$

(4.22)

since $V\left(\tilde{F}_{t}\right)=1$ always, and the covariance between the common factor and the idiosyncratic components must be tiny by definition. The equation in (4.22) is called 'variance decomposition' equation, which shows how much the common factors explain the time-varying fluctuation of the panel data of interest. As I pointed out in the beginning of this book, many empirical studies have attempted to eliminate the cross-sectional dependence from the panel data of interest rather than explain the cross-sectional dependence. If this dependence is small enough to ignore, then the first part in (4.22) must be small as well.

Alternatively, one can decompose the panel information by running the following regression.

$$\tilde{y}_{it}=a_{i}+\lambda_{i}\tilde{F}_{t}+u_{it},$$

(4.23)

where $u_{it}=\tilde{y}_{it}^{o}$. Then the goodness of fitness statistic for the ith individual, R_{i}^{2}, is given by

$$R_{i}^{2}=1-\left[\hat{\sigma}_{u}^{2}/\hat{\sigma}_{i}^{2}\right]=1-\left[V(\hat{u}_{it})/V(\tilde{y}_{it})\right]\simeq \lambda_{i}^{2}/\sigma_{i}^{2}.$$

(4.24)

That is, the R_{i}^{2} statistic from running $\tilde{y}_{it}$ on the estimated common factors $\tilde{F}_{t}$ becomes the explained fraction by the common factors. Naturally, as more common factors are included in (4.23), R_{i}^{2} is increased and approached to unity. Hence the selection of the proper number of the common factors is important.

Table 4.1 reports the estimated variations of the two growth rates of the crime rates – property and murder rates – due to the common factors. Since the crime rates show high persistency, the first differenced (logged) data is used for the calculation. As it is shown in Table 3.1 in chapter 3, all crime rates have only a single factor. The first column lists the names of each of five states where the estimated variations of the property crime by the common factor is largest and smallest. For example, 85% of the property crime in Connecticut can be explained by the unknown single common factor. Only the 15% of the property crime in Connecticut is due to a state-specific reason. Meanwhile, only the 22% of the property crime in Montana is explained by the common factor.

The second column lists the names of each of the five largest states where the estimated variations of the murder rates by the common factor are largest and smallest. Interestingly, the murder rates listed for five states – Montana through North Dakota – are totally independent from the national trend (or common factor). Meanwhile, only in two states – Texas and California – does

TABLE 4.1 Variance decomposition with growth rates of crimes

	Property	Murder		Property	Murder
Connecticut	0.847	0.266	Texas	0.597	0.623
New Jersey	0.831	0.486	California	0.656	0.537
Ohio	0.824	0.489	Ohio	0.824	0.489
Illinois	0.812	0.371	New Jersey	0.831	0.486
North Carolina	0.808	0.304	New York	0.629	0.418
⋮	⋮	⋮	⋮	⋮	⋮
Mississippi	0.378	0.236	Montana	0.222	0.025
North Dakota	0.363	0.021	New Hampshire	0.557	0.025
Vermont	0.308	0.024	Vermont	0.308	0.024
Alaska	0.231	0.036	Maine	0.546	0.023
Montana	0.222	0.025	North Dakota	0.363	0.021

the common factor explain more than 50% of the variations of the murder rates. Compared with the property crime, the murder rates are less cross-sectionally dependent.

Figure 4.3 shows the average of the explained variations in (4.22) by the common factor to various crime rates across states. Interestingly, the single common factor of property crime, including larceny, explains almost 60% of variation; meanwhile, the single common factor of extreme violent crime, such as murder, explains less than 20% of variation. The common factor of the rape crime explains more than 20% but less than 30%. The common factor of assault is higher than that of rape, but it is lower than that of burglary and robbery. Therefore, even though each crime rate has a single common factor, the influence on this factor – if the underlying factor is the same for all crime rates – to each crime is very different.

4.5 Cross-sectional dependence and level of aggregation

The most disaggregate panel data are panel of household survey data. National longitudinal survey (NLS) conducted by BLS is a well-known example. NLS consists of five panel data sets. Among them, two national longitudinal surveys of youth 1979 and 1997 (called NLSY79 and NLSY97) have been popularly used. The Panel Study of Income Dynamics (PSID) by the University of Michigan has been used popularly as well. British Household Panel Study, Household Income and Labor Dynamics in Australia, Korea Labor Income Panel Study (KLIPS), Canadian Survey of Labor and Income Dynamics, and German Socioeconomic Panel have provided household survey data.

The question of interest is, then, whether or not a micro-disaggregate panel data is cross-sectionally dependent. Unfortunately, the number of time series observations is not big enough to select the optimal number of the common

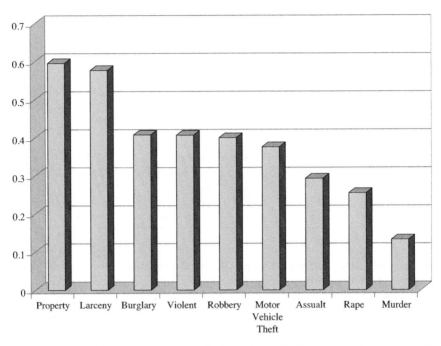

FIGURE 4.3 Explained growth rates of crimes by a single common factor over 48 contiguous states

factors. However, it is not impossible to conjecture how much the common factors influence on the household level data. First, I discuss a simple but straightforward conjecture and then provide the empirical evidence.

4.5.1 General static factor structure

Assume that the ith household income, y_{it}, follows the following factor structure.

$$y_{it} = a_i + \alpha_i'\theta_t + y_{it}^o. \tag{4.25}$$

Next, consider a state-level aggregation. The per capita household income in the jth state is written as

$$\frac{1}{n_j}\sum_{i\in C_j}^{n_j} y_{it} = \bar{a}_{n_j} + \bar{\alpha}_{n_j}'\theta_t + \frac{1}{n_j}\sum_{i\in C_j}^{n_j} y_{it}^o, \tag{4.26}$$

where C_j is the set of the household in the jth state, $\bar{a}_{n_j}$ is the sample cross-sectional mean of a_i for $i \in C_j$, and $\bar{\alpha}_{n_j}$ is the vector of the sample cross-sectional means of α_i. The last term in (4.26) is converging zero in probability as $n_j \to \infty$

because y_{it}^o has a zero mean with a finite variance. Denote the state-level data, y_{jt}, as

$$y_{jt} = \frac{1}{n_j} \sum_{i \in C_j}^{n_j} y_{it}, \ \& \ y_{jt}^o = \frac{1}{n_j} \sum_{i \in C_j}^{n_j} y_{it}^o, \tag{4.27}$$

and rewrite (4.26) as

$$y_{jt} = a_j + a_j'\theta_t + y_{jt}^o. \tag{4.28}$$

All household-level data are not observable, but the state-level data are observable. From the state-level data, the variance ratio of the common components $(a_j'\theta_t)$ to the idiosyncratic term (y_{jt}^o) can be calculated. Obviously, this estimate is not either zero or infinity. Let

$$\zeta_t = V(a_j'\theta_t)/V(y_{jt}^o), \text{ with } 0 < \zeta_t < \infty \text{ for all } t. \tag{4.29}$$

The result in (4.29) is not an assumption but a fact. Then what are the implications of the result in (4.29)? First, recall (4.27). The variance of y_{jt}^o must be equal to

$$\mathbb{E}(y_{jt}^o)^2 = \mathbb{E}\left(\frac{1}{n_j} \sum_{i \in C_j}^{n_j} y_{it}^o\right)^2 = \frac{1}{n_j}\left[\frac{1}{n_j} \sum_{i \in C_j}^{n_j} \sigma_{i,o}^2\right] = \frac{\sigma_{j,o}^2}{n_j}, \tag{4.30}$$

where $\sigma_{i,o}^2 = \mathbb{E}(y_{it}^o)^2$, and $\sigma_{j,o}^2$ is the mean of $\sigma_{i,o}^2$ for the jth state. If $\sigma_{j,o}^2$ is a finite, then as $n_j \to \infty$, the variance of y_{jt}^o must approach to zero. Obviously, it is not true since the variance of y_{jt}^o is constant, as shown in (4.29). Then the only possibility must be $\sigma_{i,o}^2$ should be a very large number relative to the variance of the common components. In other words,

$$V(y_{it})/V(y_{it}^o) = V(a_i'\theta_t)/V(y_{it}^o) + 1 \simeq 1. \tag{4.31}$$

That is, the role of the common factors on the individual household level data is very limited. Hence the cross-sectional correlation among disaggregate household level panel can be ignored. This implication is somewhat obvious and intuitively correct.

Next, there is another important implication from (4.29). Suppose that individuals in a state are not much different from individuals in other states on average. That is, assume that $\alpha_i = (\alpha_{1i}, \ldots, \alpha_{ri})$ have finite means $\alpha = (\alpha_1, \ldots, \alpha_r)$ for $i = 1, \ldots, n$, where n is the total number of households in the United States. That is,

$$\alpha_i \sim iid(\alpha, \Sigma_\alpha^2). \tag{4.32}$$

Then it is not hard to conjecture that the cross-sectional mean of α_i in the jth state must not be much different from that in the sth state as long as n_j and n_s are large enough. That is,

$$\text{plim}_{n_j \to \infty} \frac{1}{n_j} \sum_{i \in C_j} \alpha_i = \text{plim}_{n_s \to \infty} \frac{1}{n_s} \sum_{i \in C_s} \alpha_i = \alpha. \qquad (4.33)$$

This implies that $\alpha_j = \alpha$ for all j, and the number of common factors at the state level must be single. That is,

$$\alpha_j' \theta_t = \alpha_{1j} \theta_{1t} + \cdots + \alpha_{rj} \theta_{rt} = \alpha_1 \theta_{1t} + \cdots + \alpha_r \theta_{rt} = \theta_t^*, \qquad (4.34)$$

where θ_t^* is the state level common factor. Note that factor loadings are not varying across j, the sum of several common factors can be written as a single factor.

The result in (4.34) is, of course, depending on the assumption in (4.32). If the mean of α_i in one state is different from that in other states, the result in (4.33) does not hold so that the number of the common factors to the aggregated panel remains the same as that of the disaggregated panel in (4.25). Table 3.1 shows, however, that the assumption in (4.32) seems to work very well. All selected factor numbers are single for all crime rates at the state level. Similarly, all aggregated-level data (state or city level) must have a single common factor as long as the aggregation is not composite. For example, the unemployment rates panel across states should have a single factor. However, housing price index panel may not have a single factor because, depending on the states, the assumption in (4.32) does not hold more likely. It is possible that housing prices in California are more dependent on the US macro policy than those in Iowa or Alaska. Meanwhile, with financial variables, such as exchange rates, interest rates, stock prices and money supply growth rates, the assumption in (4.32) cannot be applied since these variables cannot be viewed as cross-sectionally aggregated variables.

Figure 4.4 shows more direct estimation evidence of the positive relationship between the degree of the cross-sectional dependence and the level of aggregation. BEA reports per capita personal income for each county from 1969. Per capita annual personal incomes for total 3,089 counties are available from 1969 to 2013, a total of 45 years. Average populations are calculated for each country over 45 years as well. After sorting counties by their population averages, I formed a total of 62 subgroups. The first subgroup includes 50 counties of which population averages are the lowest. The next 50-lowest counties are assigned as the second subgroup, and so on. The last subgroup (62nd) consists of 39 counties of which the populations are largest. For each subgroup, the sample cross-sectional correlations are calculated. The total number of sample cross-sectional correlations is 1,225. Figure 4.4 plots the lower 5% and upper 95% of the sample correlations. Evidently, as the population average (n_j) is larger, the average correlation, which can be thought of as the degree of cross-sectional dependence, is higher. As it shown in (4.30), with given σ_{jo}^2, as n_j

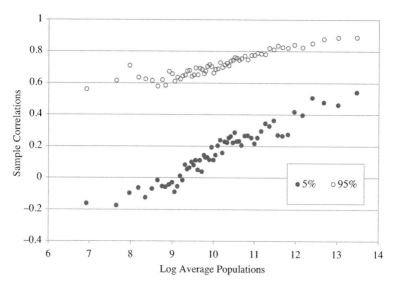

FIGURE 4.4 Cross-sectional correlations and the level of aggregation

increases, the relative variances of the idiosyncratic components in the aggregated panels are decreasing over n_j.

Lastly, the number of common factors to the panel of 1,875 households' annual wage from KLIPS from 1998 to 2014 (total 17 time series observations) is examined. The IC_2 selects zero common factors after standardizing the first differenced in the log annual wage. Since the number of time series observations is small, this result is not much reliable. The lower 5% and upper 95% of the sample cross-sectional correlations are also calculated. They are −0.36 and 0.38. Naturally, it is hard to believe that there is any significant cross-sectional correlation in a household-level panel data. Of course, it does not mean that there are no common factors, but the factor loadings are so tiny that the common factors are influencing little on the household-level annual wage.

4.5.2   Hierarchical factor structure

Even though (4.25) looks reasonable, there are some cases where (4.25) does not hold. For example, consider real GDP per capita across countries. The level of the aggregation in real GDP per capita data is the highest possible. But as Phillips and Sul (2007, 2009) show, real GDP per capita do not share the same common factors. Instead, real GDP per capita in each country may have a different factor structure: the hierarchical model. Assume that a random variable $y_{ij,t}$ has the following hierarchical factor representation.

$$y_{ij,t} = \mu_{yij} + \delta_{Wij}F_{wt} + \delta_{Fij}F_{jt} + y^o_{ij,t}, \tag{4.35}$$

where $j = 1, ..., J, i = 1, ..., n$ and j, i stand for country and individual, respectively. The common factor, F_{wt}, is the global factor; meanwhile, F_{jt} is a country-specific common factor. The total number of common factors becomes $1 + J$ for the individual level. Here we assume that in each country, the total number of individuals is the same. Next, consider the country-level aggregation.

$$y_{jt} = \mu_j + \delta_{Wj} F_{wt} + \delta_{Fj} F_{jt} + o_p(1),$$

where y_{jt}, μ_j, δ_{Wj}, and δ_{Fj} are the cross-sectional averages of y_{ijt}, μ_{yij}, δ_{Wij}, and δ_{Fij}, respectively. The last $o_p(1)$ term is the cross-sectional average of $y_{ij,t}^o$ over i so that as $n \to \infty$, this term converges to zero in probability. Now $\delta_{Fj} F_{jt}$ becomes the idiosyncratic term for the country-level aggregation so that the total number of common factors becomes one.

4.6 Practice: common factors estimation

Here GAUSS Practice is provided first. MATLAB follows next and then STATA Practice is given in the end. Please read GAUSS Practice first even if you are not a GAUSS user. You don't need to pay attention on how to program in GAUSS, but you need to learn what you should do to estimate the PC factors 'correctly.'

4.6.1 GAUSS practice I: principal component estimation

The 'ex_gauss.pgm' includes the procedure 'pc'. The usage of the 'pc' procedure is as follows.

```
{f,l,v,c} = pc(x,k)
```

There are two inputs: x is a $T \times n$ panel data of interest, k is the number of the common factors. The 'pc' generates four output variables: f is the $(T \times k)$ PC estimated vector of the common factors, l is the $(n \times k)$ PC-estimated vector of factor loadings, v is the $(N \times 1)$ vector of R_i^2 in (4.24) or the total explained fraction by the common factors, and c is the sum of the fixed effect and the estimated idiosynratic components.

In the following, I provide the example GAUSS codes to estimate the common factor and factor loading with 46 PCE inflation rates.

GAUSS EX 4-1
```
new; cls; t = 39; n=46;
load p[t,n+1] = n46_t39.csv;
dp = (p[2:t,2:n+1] -p[1:t-1,2:n+1] )./p[1:t-1,2:n+1] ;
dp1 = dp[2:rows(dp),.] -dp[1:rows(dp)-1,.] ;
ddp = dp1./sqrt(diag(vcx(dp1))' );
k = bn(ddp,8) ;
pdp = dp./sqrt(diag(vcx(dp))' );
{f,l,el,v} = pc(pdp,k) ;
```

Here you need to use the prewhitened (or double differenced) inflation rates to determine the factor number. Once you get the factor number with the prewhitened panel data, you should use the standardized inflation rates (not double differenced series) to estimate the common factor. As it is shown in Figure 4.2, the cumulative sum of the estimated PC factor with the double differenced data lost the trending behavior of the inflation rate completely. In the next subsection, we will study why the standardization is so important to estimate the common factors.

4.6.2   GAUSS practice II: standardization and estimation of PC factors

As we studied in Section 3.3, we should standardize a panel data before estimating the factor number. Furthermore, the standardization is also influencing the PC estimation of the common factors. Figure 4.5 shows an actual example to demonstrate the importance of the standardization. The 'int99.cvs' includes the one-month interest rates for 28 industrial countries from 1999.M1 to 2015. M11. Here are the GAUSS codes used to make Figure 4.5.

GAUSS EX 4-2
```
new; cls;
t = 203; n = 28;
load dat[t,n+1] = int99.csv;
sq = dat[.,2:n+1] ; kk = diag(vcx(sq)) ; k1 = maxindc(kk);
{f1,l1,v1,e1} = pc(sq,1);
```

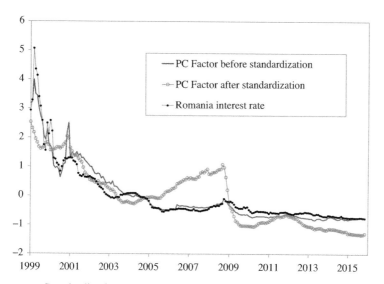

FIGURE 4.5 Standardization and the common factors estimation

```
sq1 = sq./sqrt(diag(vcx(sq))');
{f2,12,v2,e2} = pc(sq1,1);
ff = -f1~-f2~sq[.,k1];
ff = ff - meanc(ff)'; ff = ff./sqrt(diag(vcx(ff))');
ff;
```

Note that as is shown in the earlier example (in line 10), the plotted series are demeaned and standardized. The panel data 'sq' is not standardized. The 'sq1' is the standardized panel data. The 'f1' and 'f2' are the estimated PC common factors with 'sq' and 'sq1', respectively. The 'k1' shows which country has the most volatile interest rate. Among 28 countries, Romania has the most volatile rate during the period between 1999.M1 and 2015.M11. As Figure 4.5 shows, evidently, the estimated PC factor with the non-standardized panel data is very closed to the interest rate in Romania. After standardizing the panel data, the estimated PC factor is very different.

4.6.3 MATLAB practice

The 'pc.m' is the MATLAB function for the PC estimation. The usage of this function is exactly the same as 'pc' procedure in GAUSS.[1] To use this function, you need to type

```
[f,l,v,c] = pc(x,k)
```

See GAUSS EX 4-1 for the definitions of f, l, v, and c. In the following, MATLAB version codes for GAUSS EX 4-1 and GAUSS EX 4-2 are presented.

MATLAB EX 4-1
```
clear;
load MATn46_t39.csv; p = MATn46_t39;
[T,n] = size(p); p1 = p(:,2:n); n=n-1;
dp = (p1(2:T,:) - p1(1:T-1,:))./p1(1:T-1,:);
dp1 = dp(2:T-1,:) - dp(1:T-2,:);
ddp = dp1./(ones(T-2,1)*(sqrt(var(dp1))));
k = BN(ddp,8);
pdp = dp./(ones(T-1,1)*(sqrt(var(dp))));
[f l e1 v] = pc(pdp,k);
```

MATLAB EX 4-2
```
clear;
load MATint99.csv; dat = MATint99; [T,n] = size(dat);
sq = dat(:,2:n); kk = var(sq)'; k1 = find(kk==max(kk));
[f1,l1,v1,e1] = pc(sq,1);
sq1 = sq./(ones(T,1)*sqrt(var(sq)));
```

```
    [f2,12,v2,e2] = pc(sq1,1);
    ff =[-f1 -f2 sq(:,k1)];
    ff = ff - ones(T,1)*mean(ff); ff = ff./(ones(T,1)*sqrt
(var(ff)));
    ff
```

4.6.4 STATA practice

Download 'pc.ado' to the directory where your data sets are. Here are examples for how to use this function. In STATA Practice 3.3, you can add the following command right after the BN command line.

STATA EX 4-1
```
clear
insheet using "pce.csv", comma
xtset id year
gen p = pce
gen dp = (p - L.p) / L.p
egen sd_dp = sd(dp), by(id)
gen dps = dp / sd_dp
gen dp2 = dp - L.dp
egen sd_dp2 = sd(dp2), by(id)
gen dp2s = dp2 / sd_dp2
keep dps dp2s id year
reshape wide dps dp2s, i(id) j(year)
order _all, alphabetic
BN dp2s1980-dp2s2016, kmax(8)
pc dps1979-dps2016, k(1)
```

The 'pc.ado' provides the same four output variables as MATLAB or GAUSS 'pc' subroutine do: Common factors (f), factor loadings (l), total fraction explained by the common factors (v), and the sum of the idiosyncratic and fixed effect (e). To print out a variable, you need to add two more lines. For example, if you want to print out the estimated common factor, then you need to add the following two lines.

```
matrix f = r(f)
matrix list f
```

For the variance decomposition, you need to add

```
matrix v = r(v)
matrix list v
```

If you want to use the variable for another procedure or program, then you need to add the following commands.

```
matrix e = r(e)
svmat e
forvalue i=1/38 {
   local j = 1978+'i'
   rename e'i' e'j'
   }
```

The second line 'svmat e' makes a matrix e1 through e38 (total 38 times series observations). However, if the variable dps starts from 1979, you need to change the year. The do loop (forvalue i = 1/38) makes such changes.

Note

1 Note that a subroutine program is called a function in MATLAB, a procedure in GAUSS, and a program in STATA.

5

IDENTIFICATION OF COMMON FACTORS

True latent factors are usually unknown to researchers. PC-estimated factors are purely statistical factors, which are independent of each other. These estimated factors are not usually the true latent factors. Empirical researchers have used the following two general identification strategies. First, earlier researchers are forced to settle for simply describing the factors using their shape, correlation to observed series, and factor loadings. This approach provides a somewhat ambiguous, but intuitive, identification. Particularly, this approach has been used for the reduction of dimensionality: Suppose that there are too many explanatory variables compared with the sample size. In this case, one can use the PC estimators of common factors with all variables. Assume that there are two common factors. Then via the variance decomposition, one may attempt to find a set of variables that are highly correlated with the estimated first statistical factor. From their names or the characteristics of the explanatory variables in the set, researchers may be able to subtract some common information about the nature of the first factor. Next, after excluding the variables in the first set, one may attempt to find the second set of explanatory variables that are highly correlated with the second PC estimator. Again, from the common characteristics among the second set, one may be able to identify the nature of the second factor. This approach, however, requires the restriction that the latent factors are independent of each other. Otherwise, the statistical factors are not equal to the latent factors so that the identification becomes failed.

The other approach is a pure statistical method to identify unknown factors. So far, there are two methods available: Bai and Ng (2006) and Parker and Sul (2016). Let θ_t be a $(r \times 1)$ vector of the unknown but true latent factors and P_t be a $(m \times 1)$ vector of observed and potential factors. Bai and Ng (2006) propose several tests to check whether or not a linear combination among the

PC estimates of θ_t is identical to the potential factors P_t: Their methods require some restrictive assumptions. Alternatively, Parker and Sul (2016) propose a more direct identification procedure. The identification strategy does not require any restrictions for the PC estimators. We first study Parker and Sul's (2016) method, and then discuss Bai and Ng's (2006) approach next.

5.1   Difference between statistical and latent factors

Before we discuss how to identify unknown latent factors, we need to distinguish statistical factors from unknown latent factors. Define $\theta_t = [\theta_{1t}, \ldots, \theta_{rt}]$ as a $(1 \times r)$ vector of the true underlying (or latent) common factors at time t. They are not the statistical factors in the sense that θ_{jt} is possibly correlated with θ_{st} for $j \neq s$. The common components, $\alpha_i'\theta_t$, can be rewritten as

$$\alpha_i'\theta_t = \lambda_i'F_t. \tag{5.1}$$

To be specific, consider the case of $r = 2$. Assume that the true underlying factors can be rewritten as

$$\begin{bmatrix} \theta_{1t} \\ \theta_{2t} \end{bmatrix} = \begin{bmatrix} b_{11} & b_{12} \\ b_{21} & b_{22} \end{bmatrix} \begin{bmatrix} F_{1t} \\ F_{2t} \end{bmatrix}, \tag{5.2}$$

where F_{1t} and F_{2t} are statistical factors so that they are independent of each other and have the unitary variance. That is, $T^{-1}\sum_{t=1}^{T} F_{1t}^2 = T^{-1}\sum_{t=1}^{T} F_{2t}^2 = 1$.

The PC estimates always generate the following orthogonal condition: $T^{-1}\sum_{t=1}^{T} F_{1t}F_{2t} = 0$. Then from (5.1) and (5.2), the following equality holds.

$$F_t = B^{-1}\theta_t, \quad \lambda_i = B'\alpha_i, \tag{5.3}$$

where B is the coefficient matrix in (5.2). Unless $b_{12} = b_{21} = 0$, $\theta_t \neq F_t$. In other words, the traditional method – plotting PC estimates for the statistical common factors and trying to explain what they are – is not helpful at all to identify the unknown latent factor θ_t. Only when $r = 1$ (single factor case) does the statistical factor become identical to the latent factor after standardization.

To demonstrate the difference between the latent and statistical factors, let's take the following exercise. Let

$$B = 5 \times \begin{bmatrix} 0.5 & -0.1 \\ 0.5 & 0.2 \end{bmatrix}$$

and generate pseudo latent factors from (5.2), where F_{1t} and F_{2t} are generated from

$$F_{jt} = 0.8F_{jt-1} + v_{jt} \text{ and where } v_{jt} \sim iidN(0, 1/25) \text{ for } j = 1, 2$$

so that the variance of F_{jt} becomes always unity for $j = 1, 2$. Then the simulated panel (100×50) is generated by $\alpha_i'\theta_t + y_{it}^o$, where $\alpha_{1i} \sim iidN(1, 1)$ and

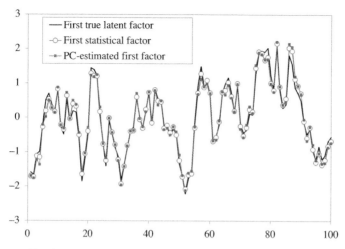

FIGURE 5.1   First latent, statistical, and PC-estimated factors ($n = 50$; $T = 100$)

$a_{2i} \sim iid\mathcal{N}(1, 1)$, $y_{it}^o \sim iid\mathcal{N}(0, 1)$. Since $b_{11} > |b_{12}|$ and $b_{21} > b_{22}$, F_{1t} becomes the dominant or first statistical factor. In the opposite case, F_{2t} becomes the eigenvector associated with the largest eigenvalue.[1]

Figure 5.1 shows a random realization of the first true latent, statistical, and PC-estimated factors. Since $|b_{12}|$ is relatively small to $|b_{11}|$, the first statistical factor looks much similar to the first latent factor. Naturally, the PC-estimated first factor is also similar to the true latent factor. If $|b_{12}|$ is getting larger or approaches to $|b_{11}|$, the correlation between the first latent and statistical factors is getting small enough. In this case, the first latent factor does not look like the first statistical factor at all. Also, note that the simple cross-sectional average does not look like the first true latent factor either. Nonetheless, if $|b_{12}| \simeq 0$ or small enough, then the first latent factor is close to the first statistical factor. Then by matching the PC estimated first factor with other potential variables, one might be able to get or identify the first latent factor. Of course, such arbitrary method becomes valid only when $|b_{21}| \simeq 0$ like in Figure 5.1. Otherwise, this arbitrary method leads to a spurious result.

Figure 5.2 shows the second latent, statistical, and PC-estimated factors. Since $|b_{21}| > |b_{22}|$, the second true latent factor looks more like the first statistical factor rather than the second statistical factor. Nonetheless, the PC-estimated second factor is roughly similar to the second statistical factor. This result is natural since the signal from the second factor is much weaker than that from the first factor so that the estimation is affected by the signal ratio. Clearly, as shown in Figure 5.2, if one tries to match the PC-estimated second factor with potential variables, then one must get a spurious result since the PC-estimated second factor is far from the second latent factor.

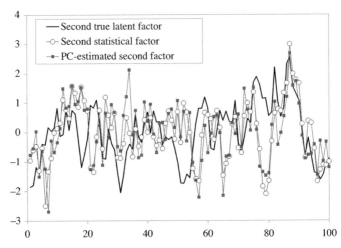

FIGURE 5.2 Second latent, statistical, and PC-estimated factors ($n = 50$; $T = 100$)

Due to this reason, one should not attempt to explain or match the estimated PC factors with other potential variables. Statistical factors are illusive. Under certain circumstances, only the first PC-estimated factor looks similar to the first latent factor. In the next section, we will study the basic econometric theory of how to identify the unknown latent factor.

5.2 Asymptotically weak factors approach

Parker and Sul's (2016) method is based on the notion of an 'asymptotically weak factor.' A panel data has asymptotically weak factors if the common components asymptotically vanish. Statistically, the notion of asymptotically weak factors is defined as follow:

> y_{it} has asymptotically weak factors if and only if the common components
> $$\lambda_i' F_t = O_p\left(C_{nT}^{-1}\right), \text{ where } C_{nT} = \min\left[\sqrt{n}, \sqrt{T}\right].$$

Here I provide an example first. Consider the case of the PCE panel. Inflation rates have a single factor π_t. Let λ_i be the i-th factor loading.

$$\pi_{it} = \lambda_i \pi_t + \pi_{it}^o, \tag{5.4}$$

where π_{it} has a strong (or not weak) factor. Meanwhile, the estimates of the idiosyncratic component, $\hat{\pi}_{it}^o$, have an asymptotically weak factor, even when π_{it}^o does not have any factors. To see this, assume that π_t is known to econometricians. Then we need to estimate factor loadings by running the regression in (5.4).

The residual or the estimated idiosyncratic term can be defined as

$$\hat{\pi}_{it}^o = \pi_{it} - \hat{\lambda}_i \pi_t = \pi_{it}^o + (\lambda_i - \hat{\lambda}_i)\pi_t = \pi_{it}^o + \kappa_i \pi_{it}. \tag{5.5}$$

Hence $\hat{\pi}_{it}^o$ has a factor structure: The common factor becomes π_t, but the factor loading becomes $\kappa_i = \lambda_i - \hat{\lambda}_i$. If so, can IC_2 detect this factor? Note that $\lambda_i - \hat{\lambda}_i = O_p(T^{-1/2})$. In other words, as $T \to \infty$, the randomness of $\hat{\lambda}_i$ around λ_i disappears at the $T^{1/2}$ rate. Alternatively from a central limit theorem, we can show that

$$\sqrt{T}(\hat{\lambda}_i - \lambda_i) \to^d N(0, \sigma_\lambda^2), \quad \text{or} \quad \sqrt{T}(\hat{\lambda}_i - \lambda_i) = O_p(1).$$

Even though $\hat{\pi}_{it}^o$ has the factor of π_t, the factor loadings are converging zero as both $n, T \to \infty$. Therefore, asymptotically, $\hat{\pi}_{it}^o$ is free from cross-sectional dependence, or does not have any significant factor. In other words, π_{it}^o has an asymptotically weak factor.

Even when π_t is unknown, we can apply the same logic here. Instead of π_t, we need to use $\hat{\pi}_t$. Then the estimated idiosyncratic term in (5.5) can be rewritten as

$$\hat{\pi}_{it}^o = \pi_{it} - \hat{\lambda}_i \hat{\pi}_t = \pi_{it}^o + (\lambda_i \pi_t - \hat{\lambda}_i \hat{\pi}_t). \tag{5.6}$$

From (4.21), we know that $\lambda_i \pi_t - \hat{\lambda}_i \hat{\pi}_t = O_p(C_{nT}^{-1})$. Hence $\hat{\pi}_{it}^o$ has an asymptotically weak factor.[2]

Let $\#(\cdot)$ be the number of common factors and the estimates of the factor number be $\hat{\#}(\cdot)$. Then the following result holds.

> If y_{it} has asymptotically weak factors, as $T, n \to \infty$ jointly,
> $$\lim_{n,T\to\infty} \Pr\left[\hat{\#}(y_{it}) = 0\right] = 1.$$

That is, the estimated factor number is more likely to be zero if y_{it} has only asymptotically weak factors. Parker and Sul (2016) use this fact to identify whether each potential factor becomes one of the latent common factors. First we consider a single-factor case.

5.2.1 Single-factor case

The true model is given by

$$y_{it} = a_i + \alpha_i \theta_t + y_{it}^o,$$

where θ_t is the true latent factor, and α_i is the true latent factor loading coefficient. As we discussed, the true latent factor and factor loading are not separately identfiable unless we have additional variables to identify them. Note that

$$y_{it} = a_i + (\alpha_i \sigma_\theta)(\sigma_\theta^{-1}\theta_t) + y_{it}^o = a_i + \lambda_i F_t + y_{it}^o, \tag{5.7}$$

where σ_θ^2 is the variance of θ_t so that the statistical factor, F_t, has the unitary variance.

Consider a group of potential common factors: $P_t = [P_{1t}, \ldots, P_{qt}]'$. Suppose that $P_{jt} = c\theta_t$ for all t and $0 < |c| < \infty$, then the residuals from the following regression have only an asymptotically weak factor, as we showed in (5.5).

$$y_{it} = a_i + \beta_i P_{jt} + v_{it}.$$

Define $\hat{v}_{it} = y_{it} - \hat{a}_i - \hat{\beta}_i P_{jt}$. As $n, T \to \infty$, the probability of selecting zero factor number with $\hat{v}_{it}$ becomes unity.

$$\lim_{n,T \to \infty} \Pr\left[\#(\hat{v}_{it}) = 0\right] = 1 \text{ if } P_{jt} = c\theta_t \tag{5.8}$$

It is important to note that P_{jt} can be different from θ_t for some periods. Let Ω_o be a fixed set of time periods. Assume that

$$y_{jt} = \begin{cases} \theta_t & \text{if } t \notin \Omega_o \\ \theta_t + \epsilon_{jt} & \text{if } t \in \Omega_o \end{cases} \quad \text{for } \epsilon_{jt} \sim d\left(0, \sigma_j^2\right). \tag{5.9}$$

Call the number of elements of Ω_o, p, which is fixed as $n, T \to \infty$. So y_{jt} is not the leader for a fixed but small p time period. In this case, the residuals in (5.16) should not have any significant factor.

If $P_{jt} = c\theta_t + u_t$, where u_t is a random error with a finite variance, then P_{jt} is not a true factor to y_{it} but is just correlated with y_{it}. Observe this.

$$\begin{aligned} y_{it} &= a_i + a_i c^{-1}(c\theta_t + u_t) - a_i c^{-1} u_t + y_{it}^o \\ &= a_i + \alpha_i^* P_{jt} + v_{it}, \end{aligned}$$

where $\alpha_i^* = a_i/c$ and $v_{it} = -\alpha_i^* u_t + y_{it}^o$. Since both α_i^* and u_t are just random variables with finite variances, v_{it} has a single factor. Naturally, the regression residuals, $\hat{v}_{it}$, have a single factor. As $n, T \to \infty$, IC_2 must pick the correct number of the common factors.

$$\lim_{n,T \to \infty} \Pr\left[\#(\hat{v}_{it}) = 1\right] = 1 \text{ if } P_{jt} = c\theta_t + u_t.$$

5.2.2 Multi-factor case

For a clear presentation, we consider the case $r = 2$ in this subsection, but the case of $r > 2$ is simply an extension of the the case of $r = 2$. When $r \geq 2$, the following two-step procedure is needed. The first step selects possibly many potential factors that can be closed to the true factor. Meanwhile, the second step narrows down the candidates.

The true model with $r = 2$ can be written as

$$y_{it} = a_i + \alpha_{1i}\theta_{1t} + \alpha_{2i}\theta_{2t} + y_{it}^o. \tag{5.10}$$

From (5.2), the true latent factors, θ_{1t} and θ_{2t}, can be rewritten as a linear combination of two statistical factors of F_{1t} and F_{2t}. From the direct calculation, we can rewrite (5.10) as

$$y_{it} = \begin{cases} a_i + c_{1i}\theta_{1t} + c_{2i}F_{1t} + y_{it}^o \\ a_i + d_{1i}\theta_{1t} + d_{2i}F_{2t} + y_{it}^o, \end{cases}$$

where c_{ji} and d_{ji} are functions of α_{ji}, b_{ji}, and λ_{ji} for $j = 1, 2$. For example, $c_{1i} = \lambda_{2i}\alpha_{1i}/(\lambda_{2i} - \alpha_{2i}b_{22})$. If $P_{jt} = \theta_{1t}$, then instead of θ_{1t}, one can replace by P_{jt}. Also, instead of F_{1t}, one can replace it by the PC estimator, $\hat{F}_{1t}$. Hence the first step is simply running the following two regressions.

$$y_{it}^+ = a_{1i} + \beta_{1i}P_{jt} + \lambda_{1i}\hat{F}_{1t} + u_{1,it}, \qquad (5.11)$$

$$y_{it}^+ = a_{2i} + \beta_{1i}P_{jt} + \lambda_{2i}\hat{F}_{2t} + u_{2,it}, \qquad (5.12)$$

where y_{it}^+ is standardized y_{it} by its standard deviation. Note that when $r > 2$, then total $(r - 1)$ PC estimates should be included in the regression. Then it is easy to see that as $n, T \to \infty$,

$$\Pr\left[\#\left(\hat{u}_{1,it}\right) = 0 \text{ or } \#\left(\hat{u}_{2,it}\right) = 0\right] = 1. \qquad (5.13)$$

If $P_{jt} \neq \theta_{1t}$, then as $n, T \to \infty$,

$$\Pr\left[\#\left(\hat{u}_{1,it}\right) = 0 \text{ or } \#\left(\hat{u}_{2,it}\right) = 0\right] = 0. \qquad (5.14)$$

Note that when the PC factors are estimated, the standardized samples, y_{it}^+, should be used. If a non-standardized sample (y_{it}) is used, then the regression residuals should be standardized.

Next, after collecting all potential observed factors with which the condition in (5.13) is satisfied, the following regression should be run for selecting the true factors. When $r = 2$, select a pair of potential factors (P_{jt} and P_{st}) and run the following regression.

$$y_{it}^+ = a_i + \beta_{1i}P_{jt} + \beta_{2i}P_{st} + u_{it}. \qquad (5.15)$$

If P_{jt} and P_{st} are the true factors, then the regression residuals $\hat{u}_{it}$ should have only asymptotically weak factors. In other words, the estimated factor number with $\hat{u}_{it}$ must be zero.

$$\#(\hat{u}_{it}) = 0.$$

Otherwise, one of them is not the true factor.

Lastly, you need to repeat the first and second steps over different subsamples. If you can't get any robust result, then you should search other potential variables.

5.2.3   Some tips to identify latent factors

Identifying common factors in practice is not easy at all. Here are some econometric suggestions to find out some of the potential variables. When the panel data of interest consists of prices – for example, stock market prices, PCE prices, exchange rates, interest rates etc. – a leadership model can be a good choice: A single price leader sets the market price, and the rest of the firms follow the leader's decision. In this case, P_{jt} become simple y_{jt}. Then for each j, one needs to run $n - 1$ regression and construct the $T \times (n - 1)$ matrix of the residuals from the following regression.

$$y_{it} = a_{i,j} + b_{i,j} y_{jt} + v_{i,j,t} \text{ for } i \neq j. \tag{5.16}$$

If y_{jt} is the true factor, θ_t, then IC_2 must not detect any common factor.

Gaibulloev, Sandler, and Sul (2013) used the regression in (5.16) to identify the common factor to the panel data of the transnational terrorism across 106 countries from 1970 to 2007. Regardless of the sample size and subsample periods, they found a single factor, and, more importantly, they identify that the transnational terrorism in Lebanon – where many resident terrorist groups have practiced small-scale terrorist incidents before they moved to a bigger-scale international terrorism – is the common driver of global transnational terrorist incidents. Greenaway-McGrevy, Mark, Sul, and Wu (2018, GMSW hereafter) used the price leadership model to find out the common factors to 27 bilateral exchange rates. We will study this paper in detail as a case study later.

Even when there is a single factor, multiple firms set the market price, and the rest of the firms follow their decision. Suppose that y_{jt} and y_{st} are jointly making decisions. Then the common-factor estimates must be explained by both y_{jt} and y_{st}. In the case of a single factor, one can run the following regression to get the fitted value.

$$\hat{F}_t = a + \beta_j y_{jt} + \beta_s y_{st} + u_{js,t}, \tag{5.17}$$

where $\hat{F}_t$ is either the cross-sectional average or the PC estimate. Let $\tilde{F}_{js,t}$ be the fitted value with the regressors of y_{jt} and y_{st}. If y_{jt} and y_{st} are truly leaders, then the slope coefficients on y_{jt} and y_{st} show relative importance. Furthermore, the residuals from the following regression must have only asymptocially weak factors.

$$y_{it} = a_i + a_i \tilde{F}_{js,t} + v_{i,js,t}$$

The total number of regressions in (5.17) becomes $n(n - 1)/2$. For trivariate case, the total number becomes $C(n, 3) = n(n - 1)(n - 2)/6$, and so on. As you consider more leaders, the number of cases increases exponentially. More importantly, the false identification rate is possibly increasing as well. Hence when you find a group of true leaders, you need to do the subsample analysis for the robust check (by repeating the procedure with various different subsamples). If the number of the common factors is more than one, then instead of P_{jt} in (5.11) and (5.12), you need to use $\tilde{F}_{js,t}$.

The leadership model does not work for all types of panel data. For example, the common factor to the panel data of violent crime rates cannot be explained by the leadership model. Crime rates in a few states can be responsible for the common factors to all of the states. A potential variable does not need to be a panel data, but just a federal or national aggregate. For example, US real income per capita, Gini coefficient, and federal demographic changes may be responsible for the common factor. In this case, instead of y_{jt} or y_{st}, you need to consider outside variables. However, the procedure to identify the common factors is exactly the same.

5.2.4 Application: testing homogeneity of factor loadings

Parker and Sul's (2016) method can be used for testing whether the factor loadings are homogeneous across i when there is a single factor in a panel data. If the common factors are multiple, then it implies that automatically the factor loadings are not homogeneous. Consider the following modification when the factor loadings are homogeneous.

$$y_{it} - \frac{1}{n}\sum_{i=1}^{n} y_{it} = \left(\lambda_i - \frac{1}{n}\sum_{i=1}^{n}\lambda_i\right)F_t + y_{it}^o - \frac{1}{n}\sum_{i=1}^{n}y_{it}^o.$$

Suppose that $\lambda_i = \lambda$ for all i. Then we have

$$y_{it} - \frac{1}{n}\sum_{i=1}^{n} y_{it} = y_{it}^o - \frac{1}{n}\sum_{i=1}^{n}y_{it}^o.$$

Hence, $y_{it} - \frac{1}{n}\sum_{i=1}^{n}y_{it}$ has no common factor.

In practice, a few λ_i can be heterogeneous. However, as long as the number of heterogeneous factor loadings is fixed but others are homogeneous, then $n \rightarrow \infty$,

$$\lambda_i \sim iid\left(\lambda, \sigma_\lambda^2 n^{-1/2}\right), \text{ or } \lambda_i - \lambda = O_p(n^{-1/2}).$$

Instead of λ, we can use the sample mean. That is,

$$\left(\lambda_i - n^{-1}\sum_{i=1}^{n}\lambda_i\right)F_t = O_p(n^{-1/2}).$$

In other words, $y_{it} - \frac{1}{n}\sum_{i=1}^{n}y_{it}$ has only a asymptotically weak factor. Hence the IC_2 will select a zero factor number in this case.

Similarly, one can test whether the year effects are good enough. Consider the case. The true data generating process is given by

$$y_{it} = \alpha_i + \lambda_i F_t + \mathbf{x}_{it}\beta + u_{it}, \text{ with } \lambda_i = \lambda,$$

but the regression is run

$$y_{it} = \alpha_i + F_t + \mathbf{x}_{it}\beta + u_{it},$$

TABLE 5.1 Selected factor number with various crime rates

	y_{it}				$y_{it} - n^{-1} \sum_{i=1}^{n} y_{it}$			
Differenced	*No*	*No*	*Yes*	*Yes*	*No*	*No*	*Yes*	*Yes*
Standardization	*No*	*Yes*	*No*	*Yes*	*No*	*Yes*	*No*	*Yes*
Violent	8	8	2	1	8	8	1	0
Murder	5	3	3	1	5	3	7	0
Robbery	7	7	3	1	7	8	2	0
Rape	7	6	1	1	6	5	1	0
Assault	6	8	1	1	6	6	0	0
Property	7	7	1	1	7	8	0	0
Burglary	8	8	2	1	8	8	1	0
Larceny Theft	6	7	1	1	6	8	0	0
Motor Vehicle Theft	8	8	1	1	8	8	0	0

where $\mathbf{x}_{it}$ is $(1 \times k)$ vector of explanatory variables. If F_t eliminates the cross-sectional dependence successfully (or $\lambda_i = \lambda$ for all i), then the regression residuals should not contain any strong factor. Hence if

$$\hat{\#}(\hat{u}_{it}) = 0.$$

Table 5.1 reports the empirical evidence of the homogeneous factor loadings. After eliminating the common time effects (or the cross sectional averages), the factor number is re-estimated with various samples. Definitely after common time effects are eliminated, the crime rates standardized and differenced show no evidence of cross-sectional dependence. This result is not surprising. We studied in the previous section (see Section 4.5 in Chapter 4), the factor loadings can be homogeneous if the level of the aggregation is high enough and the individuals do not have hierarchical factor structure.

5.3 Residual-based approach

In this section, we study Bai and Ng's (2006) residual based approach to identify the common factors. We consider a single-factor case as an example here. If P_{jt} is the true factor, then the following regression error must be zero.

$$P_{jt} = a + \beta_0 \theta_{1t} + u_t. \tag{5.18}$$

Bai and Ng (2006) test whether the residuals $\hat{u}_t$ are equal to zero statistically. Instead of θ_{1t}, one can use the PC estimator. Then the empirical regression becomes

$$P_{jt} = a + \beta_1 \hat{F}_{1t} + u_t^*,$$

where $u_t^* = u_t + \beta_1 (F_{1t} - \hat{F}_{1t})$, and $\beta_1 = \beta_0 B$.

Bai and Ng (2006) consider the following statistic for each j and t.

$$\tau_t(j) = \frac{\hat{P}_{jt} - P_{jt}}{\sqrt{V(\hat{P}_{jt})}}.$$ (5.19)

In their Monte Carlo simulation, they found that the performance of the max τ_t test works well. The max τ_t test is defined as

$$M(j) = \max_{1 \leq t \leq T} |\hat{\tau}_t(j)|,$$ (5.20)

where $\hat{\tau}_t(j)$ is obtained with the estimate of $V(\hat{P}_{jt})$. The problem is this test is too conservative. If $P_{jt} = \theta_{1t}$ for all t except for one period, then the max τ_t test rejects the null that P_{jt} is θ_t. Also another restriction is that u_t should not be serially correlated. Otherwise, the critical value for the max τ_t test is unknown asymptotically so that there is one need to use the bootstrap procedure to get the correct critical value.

Bai and Ng (2006) propose several other tests similar to (5.19), but again their test requires somewhat strong restrictions. However, Parker and Sul's (2016) identification procedure does not tell whether or not the potential P_{jt} is exactly a true factor or approximately a true factor. If $P_{jt} = \theta_{1t}$ always, then Bai and Ng's (2006) max τ_t test should not reject the null.

5.4   Empirical example: exchange rates

The cross-sectional co-movements among exchange rates was discussed by O'Connell (1988) but has primarily been treated as a nuisance parameter rather than a key determinant of the exchange rates. For example, Mark and Sul (2001) used the time-fixed effect (or year dummies) to eliminate the cross-sectional dependence, and Engel, Mark, and West (2007) used a common factor model, but didn't explain the source of the dependence. Recently, researchers have taken the role of cross-sectional dependence more seriously. Engel, Mark, and West (2015) find the principal components to remain significant after controlling for macroeconomic fundamental determinants and use them to predict future exchange rate of returns. Verdelhan (2015) also assumes a two-factor structure and argues that a dollar exchange rate of return and a carry exchange rate of return are exchange rate common factors. Verdelhan (2015) gives them a risk-based interpretation by showing that carry and dollar factors can account for two different cross-sections of currency risk premia. Greenaway-McGrevy et al. (2018, GMSW hereafter) use Parker and Sul's (2016) method to identify the US and Euro rates as the key determinants of the exchange rates. GMSW give the US and Euro factors as the risk factors Verdelhan claimed, but at the same time, they also interpret them as the geographical currency factors.

Here we replicate GMSW's work by using the same data set but use a different numeraire. Define s_{it}^j as logarithms of the price of the USD in country i currency with the j numeraire currency. The nominal exchange rate is the relative price of a currency against the numeraire, the log exchange rates with the New Zealand (NZ) dollar rate is defined as

$$s_{it}^{nz} = s_{it}^{us} - s_{nz,t}^{us}.$$

GMSW find two factors with s_{it}^{j}: The sample cross-sectional averages of the nominal exchange rates with USD ($s_{us,\ t}$) and Euro ($s_{eu,\ t}$) numeraires. That is,

$$s_{us,t} = \frac{1}{n}\sum\nolimits_{i=1}^{n} s_{it}^{us}, \quad s_{eu,t} = \frac{1}{n}\sum\nolimits_{i=1}^{n} s_{it}^{us} - s_{eu,t}^{us},$$

where both of them are linear combinations of the USD and Euro currency values. Nonetheless, since s_{it}^{nz} includes additional common time series, $s_{nz,t}^{us}$, we expect to find three factors. As GMSW did, the factor number with 27 bilateral exchange rates from 1999.M1 to 2015.M12 is determined by IC_2 criterion. All series are first differenced and standardized.

Parker and Sul's (2016) method relies on the estimation of the factor number. It is very difficult to identify the latent factors if the selected factor number is not stable over time or across subsamples. Hence it is important to investigate the stability of the estimated factor number over different subsamples. Figure 5.3 reports the selected factor numbers with recursive samples. The first sample contains the full sample from 1999.M1 to 2015.M12. The next sample contains the subsample from 1999.M2 to 2015.M12, and so on. The two panel data sets are examined: the standardized Δs_{it}^{nz} and the standardized $\Delta \tilde{s}_{it}^{nz}$, where $\Delta \tilde{s}_{it}^{nz} = \Delta s_{it}^{nz} - n^{-1}\sum_{i=1}^{n} s_{it}^{nz}$. Except for the period of the subprime mortgage crisis, the selected factor number with Δs_{it}^{nz} becomes three. As the beginning of the sample starts from the subprime mortgage crisis, the selected factor number seems to be more unstable. However, the selected factor number with $\Delta \tilde{s}_{it}^{nz}$ is very stable

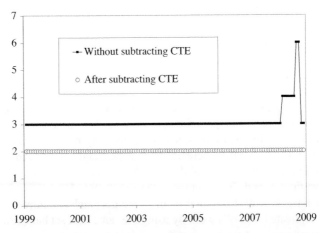

FIGURE 5.3 The number of common factors with 27 bilateral exchange rates with NZ dollar numeraire from 1999 to 2015

TABLE 5.2 Identifying common factors with 27 spot rates

First Regressor	Second Regressor		
	$s_{us,t}$	$s_{eu,t}$	$s^{us}_{swe,t}$
$\hat{F}_{1t}$	1	0	1
$\hat{F}_{2t}$	0	1	0
$s_{eu,t}$	0		
$s^{us}_{swe,t}$	1	1	

regardless of the starting year. This implies that the use of $\Delta\tilde{s}^{nz}_{it}$ leads to a robust result, even for the identification of the common factors. Of course, in this example, the selected factor number with Δs^{nz}_{it} is widely stable though.

To demonstrate the factor identification procedure, three potential factors are selected: $s_{us,t}$, $s_{eu,t}$ and $s^{us}_{swe,t}$. Table 5.2 shows the estimated factor number with the residuals from the regression of the New Zealand Dollar depreciation rates on the selected first and second regressors. The table reports the results with the non-standardized residuals only because the results with the standardized residuals are exactly same. Interestingly, $s^{us}_{swe,t}$ is selected as a potential factor since the estimated factor number becomes zero when the regressors become $\hat{F}_{2t}$ and $s^{us}_{swe,t}$. Next, to confirm whether $s^{us}_{swe,t}$ is a true factor, the first regressor is replaced by $s_{eu,t}$. Evidently, the factor number for the regression residuals only with $s_{us,t}$ and $s_{eu,t}$ becomes zero. When $s^{us}_{swe,t}$ becomes one of the regressors, the IC_2 always selects the non-zero factor number. It is worth noting that the results with various subsamples are identical.

5.5 Practice: identifying common factors

We study MATLAB codes first in this chapter. Practices with GAUSS and STATA come next.

5.5.1 MATLAB practice I: leadership model

When we estimated the PC factors and factor loadings, we did not prewhiten a panel data of interest, but standardized the data. Meanwhile, when we estimate the number of common factors, we need to prewhiten and standardize the data. To identify the latent factors, we have to rely on the estimation of the factor number so that we should prewhiten and standardize the data. Here the MATLAB codes for the leadership model are presented. The MATLAB program includes three parts. The first part is the estimation of the factor numbers by using IC_2 criterion, which we studied in Chapter 3. The second part is the procedure for the leadership model. The last part is for a robust check by using 10 recursive subsamples.

MATLAB EX 5-1

```
% Part I: Factor Number Estimation ====
clear;
load MATn46_t39.csv; p = MATn46_t39;
              ⋮
dp = (p1(2:T,:) - p1(1:T-1,:))./p1(1:T-1,:);
d2p = dp(2:T-1,:) - dp(1:T-2,:);
d2ps = d2p./(ones(T-2,1)*(sqrt(var(d2p))));
BN(d2ps,8)

% Part II: Price Leadership Model ====
res = [];
for i=1:n;
   if i == 1; xx = d2ps(:,2:n); end;
   if i > 1 && i == n; xx = [d2ps(:,1:i-1) d2ps(:,i+1:n)];
      end;
   if i == n; xx = d2ps(:,1:n-1); end;
   x1 = [ones(T-2,1) d2ps(:,i)];
   prx = xx - x1*inv(x1'*x1)*x1'*xx;
   res = [res; i BN(prx,8)];
end;
[res]
```

Here we are examining whether one price item can be a latent factor to all 46 inflations rates. That is,

$$\Delta\pi_{it} = a_i + \lambda_i\Delta\pi_{jt} + \Delta\pi_{it}^o \text{ for } i \neq j.$$

Since $\Delta\pi_{it}$ should not include $\Delta\pi_{jt}$, the first and third lines after the statement exclude $\Delta\pi_{1t}$ and $\Delta\pi_{nt}$, respectively. The second line after the statement excludes π_{jt} for $1 < j < n$ res accumulates selected IC$_2$. And the last line prints the following result.

```
1 1
2 1
3 1
4 0
5 0
6 1
7 1
  ⋮
```

Surprisingly, the aforementioned results show that only fourth (clothing) and fifth (footwear) inflations become the latent factor to 46 inflation rates. Before we make any further stories based on these results, we need to check the robustness of this finding.

```
%Part III: Robust Check
for i=1:46;
   if i == 1; xx = d2ps(:,2:n); end;
   if i > 1 && i == n; xx =[d2ps(:,1:i-1) d2ps(:,i+1:n)];
      end;
   if i == n; xx = d2ps(:,1:n-1); end;

res =[] ;
   for j=1:10;
   xxp = xx(j:T-2,:);
   xp = d2ps(j:T-2,i);
   x1 =[ones(T-2-j+1,1) xp] ;
   prx = xxp - x1*inv(x1'*x1)*x1'*xxp;
   res =[res; i j BN(prx,8)] ;
   end;
[res]
end;
```

Inside the first do loop, another do loop is included. The second statement generates 10 recursive subsamples and re-estimates IC$_2$. The results are as follows:

```
4 1 0
4 2 0
4 3 0
4 4 1
4 5 1
4 6 1
4 7 1

    ⋮

5 1 0
5 2 0
5 3 1
5 4 1
5 5 1
5 6 1

    ⋮
```

With 'clothing' as the potential factor, IC$_2$ selects zero factor in the first three recursive subsamples. Meanwhile, for the rest of the subsamples, there is no evidence that 'clothing' is the true factor. For 'footwear,' IC$_2$ selects zero factor only in the first two recursive subsamples. Hence both results are not robust at all so that the leadership model does not work with 46 PCE inflation rates. In other words, any single PCE inflation rate cannot be representative of all 46 PCE inflation rates.

5.5.2   MATLAB practice II: multiple variables as single factor

Next, we will study how to use external variables to identify the common factor. For a single variable, we can just run the following regression, obtain the residuals, and check whether the residuals have any factor.

$$\Delta\pi_{it} = a_i + \lambda_i \Delta x_{jt} + \Delta\pi_{it}^o \text{ for } i = 1, ..., n.$$

For multiple variables (for example, we have x_{1t} and x_{2t}), we need to run the following regression first,

$$\Delta\hat{F}_t = a + \beta_1 \Delta x_{1t} + \beta_2 \Delta x_{2t} + u_t,$$

and get the fitted value of $\Delta\hat{F}_t$. Define $\Delta\tilde{F}_t = \hat{a} + \hat{\beta}_1 \Delta x_{1t} + \hat{\beta}_2 \Delta x_{2t}$. Next, we run the following regression.

$$\Delta\pi_{it} = a_i + \lambda_i \Delta\tilde{F}_t + \varepsilon_{it}$$

and examine whether $\hat{\varepsilon}_{it}$ has any factor.

'MATn3_t39.csv' contains three sub-PCE prices: Durable, nondurable, and service PCE price indexes. Note that the PCE inflation rate, π_t, is the weighted average of 46 for each t.

$$\pi_t = \frac{\sum_{i=1}^{n} \omega_{it}\pi_{it}}{\sum_{i=1}^{n} \omega_{it}},$$

where ω_{it} is a weight for the ith item at time t. Usually, the weight is calculated by the real PCE. Similarly, the PCE inflation can be rewritten as

$$\pi_t = \beta_{1t}\pi_t^d + \beta_{2t}\pi_t^n + \beta_{3t}\pi_t^s,$$

where β_{jt} is the j-th time-varying weight. Interestingly, this PCE inflation or headline inflation is very similar to the sample cross-sectional average, which can be defined as

$$\bar{\pi}_t = \frac{1}{n}\sum_{i=1}^{n} \pi_{it}. \tag{5.21}$$

As we studied early, the sample CSA is a good proxy for the common factor. Then we can replace π_t by $\bar{\pi}_t$. If β_{jt} is rather a stable function over time, then we may rewrite

$$\bar{\pi}_t = \beta_1\pi_t^d + \beta_2\pi_t^n + \beta_3\pi_t^s + u_t. \tag{5.22}$$

If u_t were small enough to ignore, then the residuals from the following regression, $\hat{\varepsilon}_{it}$, does not have any factor.

$$\pi_{it} = a_i + \delta_i \hat{\pi}_t + \epsilon_{it}, \tag{5.23}$$

where $\hat{\pi}_t = \hat{\beta}_1 \pi_t^d + \hat{\beta}_2 \pi_t^n + \hat{\beta}_3 \pi_t^s$. Otherwise, we can say that the weights must be time varying.

See the MATLAB codes.

MATLAB EX 5-2
```
load MATn3_t39.csv;
dp3 = (p3(2:T,2:4) - p3(1:T-1,2:4))./p3(1:T-1,2:4);
d2p3 = dp3(2:T-1,:) - dp3(1:T-2,:);
```

Load three prices from MATn3_t39.csv. Make $\Delta\pi_{jt}$ for j = durable, nondurable, and service. Next, we examine whether a linear combination among three inflation rates can be a common factor to 46 inflation rates over 10 recursive subsamples.

```
% Multiple Variables
mdp2 = (mean(d2p'))'; % sample CSA in (5.21)
for j=1:10;
    x4 = [ones(T-2-j+1,1) d2p3(j:T-2,:)];
    hx4 = x4*inv(x4'*x4)*x4'*mdp2(j:T-2,:); % hx4 is \hat
pi_t in (5.22)
    x4 = [ones(T-2-j+1,1) hx4] ; %
    xx4 = d2ps(j:T-2,:) - x4*inv(x4'*x4)*x4'*d2ps(j:T-
2,:); % Panel of ê_it in (5.23)
    [j BN(xx4,8)]
end;
```

The result shows that IC_2 equals to unity for all subsamples. This results imply that the weights, β_{jt}, are time varying.

5.5.3 Practice with GAUSS

In the following, GAUSS version codes for MATLAB EX 5-1 and MATLAB EX 5-2 are presented.

GAUSS EX 5-1
```
clear; t=39; n=46;
load p[t,n+1] = n46_t39.csv;
dp = (p[2:t,2:n+1] - p1[1:t-1,2:n+1])./p1[1:t-1,2:n+1] ;
        ⋮
// Part II: Price Leadership Model ====
```

```
for i(1,n,1);
   if i == 1; xx = d2ps[.,2:n] ; endif;
   if i > 1 and i == n; xx = d2ps[.,1:i-1 i+1:n] ; endif;
   if i == n; xx = d2ps[.,2:n-1] ; endif;
   x1 = ones(rows(d2ps),1)~d2ps[.,i] ;
   prx = xx - x1*invpd(x1' x1)*x1' xx;
i~bn(prx,8);
endfor;
//Part III: Robust Check
for i(1,n,1);
   if i == 1; xx = d2ps[.,2:n] ; endif;
   if i > 1 and i == n; xx = d2ps[.,1:i-1 i+1:n] ; endif;
   if i == n; xx = d2ps[.,2:n-1] ; endif;
     for j(1,10,1);
       xxp = xx[j:rows(xx),.] ;
         xp = d2ps[j:rows(d2ps),i] ;
         x1 = ones(rows(xp),1)~xp;
       prx = xxp - x1*invpd(x1' x1)*x1' xxp;
         i~j~bn(prx,8);
     endfor;
endfor;
```

GAUSS EX 5-2

```
// the below lines must be added after Part III.
load p3[t,4] = n3_t39.csv;
dp3 = (p3[2:t,2:4] - p3[1:t-1,2:4] )./p3[1:t-1,2:4] ;
d2p3 = dp3[2:rows(dp3),.] - dp3[1:rows(dp3)-1,.] ;
mdp2 = meanc(d2p' );
for j(1,10,1);
   x4 = ones(T-2-j+1,1)~d2p3[j:rows(d2p3),.] ;
   hx4 = x4*invpd(x4' x4)*mdp2[j:T-2,.] ;
   x4 = ones(T-2-j+1,1)~hx4;
   xx4 = d2ps[j:rows(d2ps),.] - x4*inv(x4' x4)*x4'*d2ps[j:
   rows(d2ps),.] ;
   j~bn(xx4,8)
endfor;
```

5.5.4 Practice with STATA

Programming a do loop in STATA is not hard but inconvenient. Here the leadership model is given next. The potential leader was assumed to be $\Delta\pi_{46,\ t}$. Note that 'BNT.ado' is the program file for IC_2 criterion with the transposed panel data. In the following, I generate a $T \times N$ matrix (see reshape statement) so that we need to use BNT.ado.

STATA EX 5-1

```
clear
insheet using pce.csv, comma
xtset id year
gen p = pce
gen dp = (p - L.p) / L.p
egen sd_dp = sd(dp), by(id)
gen dps = dp / sd_dp
gen dp2 = dp - L.dp
egen sd_dp2 = sd(dp2), by(id)
gen dp2s = dp2 / sd_dp2
drop if year < 1980
//leadership model
keep dp2s id year
reshape wide dp2s, i(year) j(id)
forvalue i=1/45 {
  qui reg dp2s`i' dp2s46
  qui predict resid`i'
  }
BNT resid1-resid45, kmax(8)
```

Consider the case where the potential leader becomes $\Delta \pi_{jt}$ for $1 < j < n$. For example, let $j = 2$, then you need to include the following three lines before `forvalue`.

```
gen tempv = dp2s2
replace dp2s2 = dp2s46
replace dp2s46 = tempv
forvalue i=1/45 {
```

If $j = 3$, then you need to replace $dp2s2$ by $dp2s3$, and so on. When $j = 1$, then you do not need to add three lines but change the starting value of `forvalue`. That is,

```
reshape wide dp2s, i(year) j(id)
forvalue i=2/46 {
  qui reg dp2s`i' dp2s1
  qui predict resid`i'
  }
BN resid2-resid46, kmax(8)
```

Obviously, one can construct another `forvalue` statement to include all three cases. I will leave this task for your exercise. Next, use 'PCE1.csv', which includes three more price indexes: Durable, nondurable, and service. The MATLAB EX 5-2 can be translated as follows.

STATA EX 5-2

```
keep dp2s id year
egen mp2 = mean(dp2s), by(year)
reshape wide dp2s mp2, i(year) j(id)
qui reg mp21 dp2s47 dp2s48 dp2s49
qui predict fitted
gen hmp2 = fitted
forvalue i=1/46{
   qui reg dp2s`i' hmp2
   qui predict resid`i'
   }
BN resid1-resid46, kmax(8)
```

Here we are using the full sample. If you want to start the beginning sample from 1981, then replace 1980 by 1981 in the following line.

```
drop if year < 1981
```

Notes

1   See Bai and Ng (2013) for more required identification conditions.
2   Note that Chudik and Pesaran (2013) use a similar notion of weak factor, where $\lambda_i' F_t = O_p(n^{-1/2})$, but $F_t = O_p(1)$. That is, the common factors are random variables, but the common components are vanished away as $n \to \infty$.

6

STATIC AND DYNAMIC RELATIONSHIPS

Consider two panel data y_{it} and x_{it} for notational simplicity. We rewrite (6.1) as

$$y_{it} = \mu_{y,i} + y_{it}^*, \quad x_{it} = \mu_{x,i} + x_{it}^*, \tag{6.1}$$

where $\mu_{y,i}$ and $\mu_{x,i}$ are the long-run values of $\{y\}$ and $\{x\}$, and y_{it}^* and x_{it}^* are the time-varying components with zero means and finite variances.

The long-run or static relationship between $\{y\}$ and $\{x\}$ is given by

$$\mu_{y,i} = \alpha + \beta \mu_{x,i} + v_i. \tag{6.2}$$

Meanwhile, the time-varying variables can be further decomposed into common and idiosyncratic (or individual specific) components.

$$y_{it}^* = h_{it}^y + y_{it}^o, \quad x_{it}^* = h_{it}^x + x_{it}^o, \tag{6.3}$$

and the relationships between the common components and between the idiosyncratic components will be called '*common and idiosyncratic dynamic relationship,*' respectively.

$$h_{it}^y = \alpha_h + \phi h_{it}^x + e_{it}, \quad y_{it}^o = \alpha_o + \gamma x_{it}^o + m_{it}. \tag{6.4}$$

There is a possibility that the static relationship (β) may not be equal to the dynamic relationship (ϕ or γ).

The econometric modeling in (6.2) and (6.3) delivers intuitive explanations for the reason the cross-sectional and pooled OLS (or random effects) estimators are so different from the time series and fixed effects estimators in general. The static relationship is the relationship between time invariant random variables, so this relationship can be thought of as the relationship between the two random variables of y_{it} and x_{it} in the long run. In other words, the static relationship

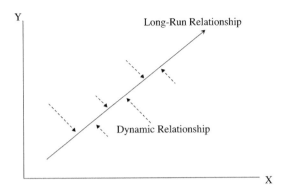

FIGURE 6.1   An example of static and dynamic relationships

can be interpreted as the long-run relationship if the long-run value of each variable is well defined. The long-run value of a random variable $\{x\}$ exists if and only if $\text{plim}_{T \to \infty} T^{-1} \sum_{t=1}^{T} x_{it} = \mu_{x,i}$.

For the time being, assume that either the factor loading is homogeneous or common components are small enough to ignore. Under this restriction, the representative dynamic relationship becomes γ. Figure 6.1 shows the difference between the static and dynamic relationships: The static relationship is positive; meanwhile, the dynamic relationship is negative. If a positive or negative shock enters into the system, over time the shock is neutralized, and then the dynamic relationship becomes possibly negative as shown in Figure 6.1. The static relationship can be identified either when the independent variables are time invariant $\left(x_{it}^* = 0 \text{ for all } i \text{ and } t \right)$ or when the time-varying component, x_{it}^*, is small enough to ignore. In this case, the cross-sectional regression of y_{it} on a constant and x_{it} will estimate the static slope coefficient β consistently for any t. Otherwise, the cross-sectional regression becomes inconsistent and fails to estimate the static relationship.

Since the static relationship is different from the common or idio-dynamic relationship in general, it is very important to know which relationship becomes of interest in the first place. We will study first the economic meaning of each relationship and then discuss how to identify and estimate each relationship consistently. Just running fixed effects panel regression with time dummies leads to, sometimes, spurious regression results.

6.1   Static and dynamic relationship under cross-sectional independence

In order to demonstrate the central issue, we exclude the common components on purpose in this section. Of course, in reality, it is hard to find random variables that don't have any cross-sectional dependence. For the time being, we will ignore the dependent term. That is, we set $\phi = 0$ but $\gamma \neq \beta$. After imposing these restrictions, we rewrite (6.1) as

$$y_{it} = \mu_{y,i} + y_{it}^o, \quad x_{it} = \mu_{x,i} + x_{it}^o. \tag{6.5}$$
$$\mu_{y,i} = a + \beta\mu_{x,i} + v_i,$$
$$y_{it}^o = \alpha + \gamma x_{it}^o + m_{it}.$$

Here we consider only the case of a single regressor simply because of notational simplicity and intuitive explanations. The generalization for multiple regressors is straightforward. See the appendix for more detailed derivations.

When the static relationship is different from the dynamic relationship ($\beta \neq \gamma$), it is difficult to define the unique relationship between y_{it} and x_{it}. From the direct calculation, we can show that the true data generating process (not a regression) is given by

$$y_{it} = \begin{cases} a_o + \beta x_{it} + u_{it} & \text{with } u_{it} = v_i + (\gamma - \beta)x_{it}^o + m_{it}, \\ \\ a_o + \gamma x_{it} + e_{it} & \text{with } e_{it} = v_i + (\beta - \gamma)\mu_{x,i} + m_{it}, \end{cases} \tag{6.6}$$

where $a_o = a + \alpha$. Only when $\beta = \gamma$, the slope coefficient becomes well defined, and the regressor is not correlated with the regression error. Otherwise, a cross-sectional regression result becomes very different from a time series regression result. We consider the cross-sectional regression first.

6.1.1   Spurious cross-sectional regression

Consider the following T cross-sectional regressions for each t.

$$y_{i1} = a_1 + b_1 x_{i1} + \varepsilon_{i1},$$
$$\vdots$$
$$y_{it} = a_t + b_t x_{it} + \varepsilon_{it}, \tag{6.7}$$
$$\vdots$$
$$y_{iT} = a_T + b_T x_{iT} + \varepsilon_{iT}.$$

Note that if you run a cross-sectional regression for a particular t, then both the slope coefficients and the least-squares estimates are different for each t. It is easy to show that the expected value of the cross-sectional estimator, $\hat{b}_{\text{cross},t}$, becomes

$$\mathbb{E}\hat{b}_{\text{cross},t} = \omega_t\beta + (1 - \omega_t)\gamma, \tag{6.8}$$

where

$$\omega_t = \frac{\sigma_{x,\mu}^2}{\sigma_{x,\mu}^2 + \sigma_{xo,t}^2},$$

and

$$\sigma_{x,\mu}^2 = \mathbb{E}\frac{1}{n}\sum_{i=1}^{n}\left(\mu_{x,i} - \frac{1}{n}\sum_{i=1}^{n}\mu_{x,i}\right)^2, \quad \sigma_{xo,t}^2 = \mathbb{E}\frac{1}{n}\sum_{i=1}^{n}\left(x_{it}^o - \frac{1}{n}\sum_{i=1}^{n}x_{it}^o\right)^2.$$

Note that ω_t measures the relative variance ratio, which lies between 0 and 1. If x_{it} is not time varying (or $x_{it}^o = 0$ for all i, so that $\sigma_{x,t}^2 = 0$), then ω_t becomes unity. If $x_{it} = x_{it}^o$ for all i, then ω_t becomes zero. Unless $\omega_t = 1$, the least-squares estimators from the cross-sectional regression do not converge either the static relationship or the dynamic relationship. In other words, if the independent variable in a cross-sectional regression is time dependent, then the cross-sectional regression estimators become spurious. Here is an interesting example.

Example 6.1: SAT scores and parents' income

Every year, College Board reports the relationship between SAT scores and parents' income.[1] The cross-sectional regression result in 2013 is shown next.

$$\widehat{SAT}_i = -116.5 + 143.8 \times \ln(Income_i), \tag{6.9}$$
$$\phantom{\widehat{SAT}_i = } (49.44) \quad (4.36)$$

where SAT_i stands for an individual average SAT score (total score is 2,400), $Income_i$ is the parents' income of the ith student. The standard errors are reported in parentheses. Since the log income is definitely changing over time, the cross-sectional result in (6.9) becomes spurious.

In the case of multiple regressors, the cross-sectional regression becomes spurious if any independent variable becomes time varying. A dependent variable can be time varying – the time-varying term can be treated as the regression error, but the independent variables should not be time varying.

It is important to address the fact that the economic interpretations on the static and dynamic relationships are very different. Let $\beta = 1$ and $\gamma = -1$. Then equation (6.1) can be rewritten as

$$\mu_{yi} = \mu_{xi} + v_i, \quad y_{it}^o = -x_{it}^o + m_{it}.$$

Further assume that both time-varying components are small enough so that they can be ignored.

$$y_{it} = \mu_{yi} + y_{it}^o \simeq \mu_{yi}, \quad x_{it} = \mu_{xi} + x_{it}^o \simeq \mu_{xi}.$$

One runs the following cross-sectional regression at $t = 0$ and obtains the point estimate of 0.95. Then the predicted value of y_{i0} becomes

$$\hat{y}_{i0} = 0.95 \times x_{i0}.$$

Typically, this estimation result is interpreted as follows: If x_{i0} increases by one, y_{i0} will increase 0.95. This interpretation is, however, problematic. As we assumed before, the dynamic relationship between $\{y\}$ and $\{x\}$ is negative. Hence as $\{x\}$ increases by one, $\{y\}$ should decrease by one since $\gamma = -1$. The static or long-run value of $\{x\}$ cannot change over time. This confusion arises especially when $\{x\}$ variables have time-varying components. However, when the regressors are not time varying, the cross-sectional estimates are well-defined. Consider drug experiments as an example. Let x_i be the amount of a drug dosage for the ith subject and y_i the health outcome. Then the marginal effect, $\Delta y / \Delta x$, can be captured by running y_i on x_i and a constant. In this case, the static relationship β can be interpreted that as the drug dosage is increased by one, the health outcome increases by β, which is the typical interpretation.

Example 6.1 continued: SAT scores and parents' income

Figure 6.2 plots the nonlinear relationship between the level of parents' income and SAT scores. Suppose that the time-varying components are small enough to be ignored. Then we can interpret this result as follows: If ln(income) increases by 1, then are the children's SAT scores increased by 144 in average? Alternatively, if one makes more income, then will his (her) children get better SAT scores? The answer is no. If parents' income data are not time varying as we assumed, then the parents' income cannot either increase or decrease. Hence this result should be interpreted as the

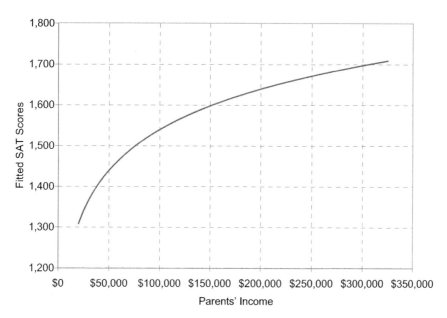

FIGURE 6.2 Fitted SAT scores and parents' income, 2013

SAT scores of children with richer parents are higher than those of children with less rich parents. Here the income variable may capture or provide condensed information about the quality of a school zone, peer group effects, parents' education level, etc. Suppose that the true determinant was the quality of a school zone, then parents who want to increase their children's SAT scores should not try to make more money but try to move to a better school zone. In fact, as parents work more to make more money, their children's SAT scores could decrease more likely because parents may pay less attention to their children's education. If so, the cross-sectional regression result in (6.9) is underestimating the static relationship, and the true static relationship must be much higher than $\hat{b}_{\text{cross}}$.

6.1.2 Spurious pooled OLS estimator

After imposing the homogeneity restriction on a_t in (6.7), we can consider the following pooled OLS regression.

$$y_{it} = a + bx_{it} + \varepsilon_{it}.$$

Denote ω as

$$\omega = \sigma_{x,\mu}^2 / \left(\sigma_{x,\mu}^2 + \sigma_{x,o}^2 \right), \tag{6.10}$$

where

$$\sigma_{x,o}^2 = \mathbb{E} \frac{1}{nT} \sum_{t=1}^{T} \sum_{i=1}^{n} \left(x_{it}^o - \frac{1}{nT} \sum_{t=1}^{T} \sum_{i=1}^{n} x_{it}^o \right)^2.$$

Then the expected value of the pooled OLS (POLS) estimator becomes

$$\mathbb{E}\hat{b}_{\text{pols}} = \omega\beta + (1 - \omega)\gamma. \tag{6.11}$$

Obviously, when $\beta \neq \gamma$, the POLS estimator does not estimate either the static or dynamic relationship since the regressor, x_{it}, is correlated with the regression error.

Next, we consider what an individual time series regression estimates.

6.1.3 Time series and panel-fixed effect regressions

One can run total n time series regressions for each i.

$$y_{1t} = a_1 + b_1 x_{1t} + \varepsilon_{1t,}$$
$$\vdots$$
$$y_{it} = a_i + b_i x_{it} + \varepsilon_{it}, \tag{6.12}$$
$$\vdots$$
$$y_{nt} = a_n + b_n x_{nT} + \varepsilon_{nt}.$$

If the dynamic relationship is homogeneous across individuals, then it is easy to show that the probability limit of an individual time series estimates the dynamic relationship consistently as $T \to \infty$. Denote $\hat{b}_{time,i}$ as the least-squares estimator in the i–th time series regression in (6.12). Then,

$$\text{plim}_{T \to \infty} \hat{b}_{time,i} = \gamma. \qquad (6.13)$$

From (6.6), the true data generating process can be rewritten as

$$y_{it} = a_i + \gamma x_{it} + m_{it} \text{ with } a_i = a_o + v_i + (\beta - \gamma)\mu_{x,i}.$$

Hence including the heterogeneous constant, a_i, in the time series regression in (6.12) eliminates the potential source of the inconsistency so that the time series regression can estimate the dynamic relationship if and only if there is no cross-sectional dependence.

It is widely known that the panel fixed-effect (or within group) estimator is a weighted average of the individual time series estimators. The weight function is the variance of the regressor. That is,

$$\hat{b}_{wg} = \frac{\sum_{i=1}^{n} W_i \hat{b}_{time,i}}{\sum_{i=1}^{n} W_i} \text{ with } W_i = \frac{1}{T-1} \sum_{t=1}^{T} \left(x_{it} - \frac{1}{T} \sum_{t=1}^{T} x_{it} \right)^2. \qquad (6.14)$$

Naturally, the dynamic relationship can be identified and estimated consistently by running the panel fixed-effect regression as long as (6.6) holds. Also, the following simple mean group (MG) estimator can be used for the consistent estimation of the dynamic relationship.

$$\hat{b}_{mg} = \frac{1}{n} \sum_{i=1}^{n} \hat{b}_{time,i}$$

Note that the fixed-effect estimators do not always identify the dynamic relationship. Here is one example.

Counter example (pseudo fixed effects: twin studies)

Twin data are often used in health economics to control for unobserved characteristics of mothers or families. Among many examples, see Almond, Chay, and Lee (2005) and Royer (2009) for the relationship between low birth weight and infant mortality rates, and Behrman and Rosenzweig (2002), and Black, Devereus, and Slavanes (2007) for the relationship between low birth weight and schooling outcomes. The typical data-generating process or true model is assumed to be

$$y_{ij} = a + bx_{ij} + \mathbf{z}_j\boldsymbol{\delta} + v_{ij},$$

where j stands for the jth mother in the sample, and $\mathbf{z}_j$ is the vector of the unobserved mother's characteristics, which are generally correlated with the observed variable x_{ij}. Running the pooled OLS regression without including $\mathbf{z}_j$ leads to an inconsistent estimator of b due to the missing variables. The twin data are used for controlling out the unobserved variable $\mathbf{z}_j$. To be specific, researchers have usually used the difference in the twin variables to isolate the characteristic of mothers. Let the subscript (i, i') denote a set of twins. Then by taking the difference between the twins, one can eliminate $\mathbf{z}_j$ variables from the regression. That is,

$$y_{ij} - y_{i'j} = b\left(x_{ij} - x_{i'j}\right) + \left(v_{ij} - v_{i'j}\right).$$

This fixed effects estimator is not related to the dynamic relationship.

Nonetheless, even when there is no cross-sectional dependence, none of the conventional estimators are identifying or estimating the static relationship correctly. However, if the number of times series observations is large, then there exists one estimator that identifies and estimates the static relationship consistently.

6.1.4 Between-group estimator

The between-group estimation is one of the most popular methods used by macroeconomists, but this estimation is called 'cross-country growth regression' or 'augmented Solow regression' rather than the between-group estimation. Denote $\bar{y}_{iT}$ and $\bar{x}_{iT}$ as time series averages of y_{it} and x_{it}. From (6.5), we have

$$\bar{y}_{iT} \; = \; T^{-1}\sum\nolimits_{t=1}^{T} y_{it} = \mu_{y,i} + T^{-1}\sum\nolimits_{t=1}^{T} y_{it}^o \simeq \mu_{y,i}, \qquad (6.15)$$

$$\bar{x}_{iT} \; = \; T^{-1}\sum\nolimits_{t=1}^{T} x_{it} = \mu_{x,i} + T^{-1}\sum\nolimits_{t=1}^{T} x_{it}^o \simeq \mu_{x,i}. \qquad (6.16)$$

Hence the following between-group regression can identify the long-run or static relationship with a large T.

$$y_{iT} = a + bx_{iT} + u_i$$

As we studied in Chapter 1, when y_{it} and x_{it} have trending components, the first differenced series should be used. To be specific, instead of (6.5), let

$$y_{it} = a_{y,i} + b_{y,i}t + y_{it}^*, \quad x_{it} = a_{x,i} + b_{x,i}t + x_{it}^*. \qquad (6.17)$$

In this case, the long-run relationship should be defined as

$$b_{y,i} = a + \beta b_{x,i} + v_i. \qquad (6.18)$$

From (6.17) and (1.11), the time series average of the first difference becomes

$$\frac{1}{T-1}\sum_{t=2}^{T}\Delta y_{it} = \frac{y_{iT}-y_{i1}}{T-1} \simeq b_{y,i}.$$

Hence the following between-group regression can identify the long-run relationship.

$$\frac{y_{iT}-y_{i1}}{T-1} = a + b\frac{x_{iT}-x_{i1}}{T-1} + \frac{u_{iT}-u_{i1}}{T-1}$$

Instead of the initial error of u_{i1}, Barro and Sala-i-Martin (1992) suggest we use the initial income, y_{i1}. Then we have

$$\frac{y_{iT}-y_{i1}}{T-1} = a + \delta y_{i1} + b\frac{x_{iT}-x_{i1}}{T-1} + \frac{u_{iT}}{T-1}.$$

This modified between-group regression is called 'augmented Solow regression' or 'cross-country growth regression.'

Note that only with a large T, the between-group regression estimates the long-run or static relationship consistently. If T is small, then the between-group estimator becomes biased. The source of the bias comes from the fact that the time series average is not exactly the same as the time invariant term. To see this, let's consider the expected value of the covariance between $\bar{y}_{iT}$ and $\bar{x}_{iT}$ given in (6.15) and (6.16).

$$\mathbb{E}\frac{1}{n}\sum_{i=1}^{n}\left(\bar{y}_{iT}-\frac{1}{n}\sum_{i=1}^{n}\bar{y}_{iT}\right)\left(\bar{x}_{iT}-\frac{1}{n}\sum_{i=1}^{n}\bar{x}_{iT}\right)$$

$$= \mathbb{E}\frac{1}{n}\sum_{i=1}^{n}\left(\mu_{y,i}-\frac{1}{n}\sum_{i=1}^{n}\mu_{y,i}\right)\left(\mu_{x,i}-\frac{1}{n}\sum_{i=1}^{n}\mu_{x,i}\right)+\Omega_{xyo}/T,$$

where Ω_{xyo} is the covariance between the idiosyncratic terms. See Appendix A for more detailed derivations. Nonetheless, when T is small, the covariance between $\bar{y}_{iT}$ and $\bar{x}_{iT}$ is not exactly same as that between $\mu_{y,i}$ and $\mu_{x,i}$. This discrepancy leads to the small sample bias of the between group estimator. See Appendix B for a modified between-group estimator, which attenuates the bias.

Nonetheless, in general, we can expect the following simple rule under the cross-sectional independence.

$$\begin{aligned}\text{plim}_{n\to\infty}\hat{b}_{cross,t} \leq \text{plim}_{n\to\infty}\hat{b}_{bw} \leq \text{plim}_{T\to\infty}\hat{b}_{time,i} \quad &\text{if} \quad \beta \leq \gamma, \\ \text{plim}_{n\to\infty}\hat{b}_{cross,t} > \text{plim}_{n\to\infty}\hat{b}_{bw} > \text{plim}_{T\to\infty}\hat{b}_{time,i} \quad &\text{if} \quad \beta > \gamma.\end{aligned} \quad (6.19)$$

6.2   Static and dynamic relationship under cross-sectional dependence

In the previous section, the dynamic relationship between common components is not considered. This section studies how the existence of the common factors influences the cross-sectional and panel regressions. By adding the time invariant mean, y_{it} can be rewritten as

$$y_{it} = \mu_{yi} + h_{it}^y + y_{it}^o, \quad \text{for } h_{it}^y = \lambda_{yi}' F_{yt}, \tag{6.20}$$

and, similarly,

$$x_{it} = \mu_{xi} + h_{it}^x + x_{it}^o, \quad \text{for } h_{it}^x = \lambda_{xi}' F_{xt},$$

where λ_{yi} is a $(r \times 1)$ vector of the factor loadings, F_{yt} is a $(r \times 1)$ vector of the common factors, and y_{it}^o is the idiosyncratic component.

Naturally, we introduce three relationships between y_{it} and x_{it} as

Static Relationship:	$\mu_{yi} = \beta \mu_{xi} + v_i,$
Idio-Dynamic Relationship :	$y_{it}^o = \gamma x_{it}^o + m_{it},$
Common-Dynamic Relationship:	$h_{it}^y = \phi h_{it}^x + e_{it},$

$$\tag{6.21}$$

where h_{it}^y and h_{it}^x have both zero means. The common-dynamic relationship can be interpreted as the macro-relationship since this relationship can be revealed with cross-sectionally aggregated data.[2] Meanwhile, the idio-dynamic relationship is the micro-relationship, which is often of interest in treatment literatures. We can write up the linear relationships between y_{it} and x_{it} as follows:

$$y_{it} = v_i + \beta x_{it} + k_{it}, \quad k_{it} = (\phi - \beta) h_{it}^x + (\gamma - \beta) x_{it}^o + m_{it} + e_{it}, \tag{6.22}$$

$$= a_i + \gamma x_{it} + w_{it}, \quad a_i = (\beta - \gamma) \mu_{xi} + v_i, \quad w_{it} = (\phi - \gamma) h_{it}^x + m_{it} + e_{it}, \tag{6.23}$$

$$= a_i + \phi x_{it} + \varepsilon_{it}, \quad \varepsilon_{it} = (\gamma - \phi) x_{it}^o + m_{it} + e_{it}. \tag{6.24}$$

In the cross-sectional regression for each t, the parameters of interest become β. Hence equation (6.22) becomes the true DGP for the cross-sectional regression. Obviously, the regressors are correlated with the errors. In the panel regressions with fixed effects, the parameters of interest become γ, which is the idio-dynamic relationship. However, in equation (6.23), the regressors are correlated with the common factors. Pesaran (2006), Bai (2009), and Greenaway-McGrevy, Han, and Sul (2012a, GHS) consider exactly the same problem of (6.23) and propose similar estimators.

As we studied earlier, we investigate the probability limits of the conventional regressions and then consider how to identify and estimate three different relationships. For the intuitive explanation, we introduce the cross-sectional dependence via homogeneous factor loadings first. Later, we will consider heterogeneous loadings.

6.2.1 Homogeneous factor loadings

Here we assume $\lambda_i = \lambda$ for all i. In this case, the simple inclusion of the common time effects or year dummies can eliminate the cross-sectional dependence completely. Consider the following regressions with and without fixed effects.

Cross-Sectional:	$y_{it} = a_t + x_{it} b_t + \varepsilon_{it}$, for $t = 1, ..., T$.
POLS:	$y_{it} = a + x_{it} b_1 + e_{it}$,
State-Fixed Effects	$y_{it} = a_i + x_{it} b_2 + u_{it}$,
State- and Year-Fixed Effects:	$y_{it} = a_i + \theta_t + x_{it} b_3 + \epsilon_{it}$,
Aggregated Time Series:	$\bar{y}_t = a + \bar{x}_t b_4 + \bar{e}_t$,

where $e_{it} = (\alpha_i - \alpha) + \theta_t + \epsilon_{it}$ and $\varepsilon_{it} = \theta_t + \epsilon_{it}$. We assume that the regressand and regressors have a single common factor and that their factor loadings are identical across states. Also, we assume that the regression errors are stationary. Under these assumptions, the probability limit of each estimator is given by

$$\text{plim}_{n,T\to\infty} \hat{b}_{\text{cross},t} = \omega\beta + (1 - \omega)\gamma,$$
$$\text{plim}_{n,T\to\infty} \hat{b}_1 = \varpi\beta + (1 - \varpi)[\bar{\varrho}\gamma + (1 - \bar{\varrho})\phi],$$
$$\text{plim}_{n,T\to\infty} \hat{b}_2 = \bar{\varrho}\gamma + (1 - \bar{\varrho})\phi, \qquad (6.25)$$
$$\text{plim}_{n,T\to\infty} \hat{b}_3 = \gamma,$$
$$\text{plim}_{n,T\to\infty} \hat{b}_4 = \phi,$$

where ω was defined in (6.10), and

$$\varpi = \frac{\sigma_{\mu x}^2}{\sigma_{\mu x}^2 + \sigma_{xo}^2 + \sigma_h^2}, \quad \bar{\varrho} = \frac{\sigma_{xo}^2}{\sigma_{xo}^2 + \sigma_h^2},$$

with

$$\sigma_h^2 = \mathbb{E}\frac{1}{nT}\sum_{t=1}^{T}\sum_{i=1}^{n}\left(h_t^x - \frac{1}{nT}\sum_{t=1}^{T}\sum_{i=1}^{n}h_t^x\right)^2.$$

Interestingly, the probability limit of the cross-sectional regression does not change under the presence of the homogeneous common factor. The underlying reason is rather obvious: The constant term in the cross-sectional regression changes for each time so that this time-varying constant term works exactly as the time dummy or time-fixed effect.

Example: determination of crime

In the empirical studies of the economics on crime, the most important task is the explanation of the sudden decline of national crime after the 1990s.[3] Figure 6.3 shows the national average of the log per capita property crimes and sworn police officers across 50 states from 1970 to 2005.[4] Evidently, property crime has declined since 1992; meanwhile, the number of sworn officers gradually increased. Nonetheless, all empirical studies in this literature have run the following panel regressions.

$$\Delta y_{it} = a_i + \theta_t + \mathbf{X}_{it-1}\mathbf{b} + u_{it},$$

where y_{it} is the number of crimes in the ith state (or city) at time t. The determinant variables include many social and economic variables. The parameters of interest become the common-dynamic relationships (ϕ) rather than the idio-dynamic relationships (γ). However, by excluding the common components, the most important information is eliminated from the empirical analysis. To see this, we take the first difference of the log police and crime, and run the following dynamic panel regressions. Note that we do not correct the Nickell bias since our purpose is to demonstrate the role at the time-fixed effects (excluding the common components). We also do not include other control variables. Table 6.1 shows the empirical results. When the time-fixed effects (year dummies) are not included in the regressions, the point estimates of lagged crime and lagged police are significantly different from zero. Interestingly, the POLS estimates are similar to the within group estimates without including time-fixed effects since the

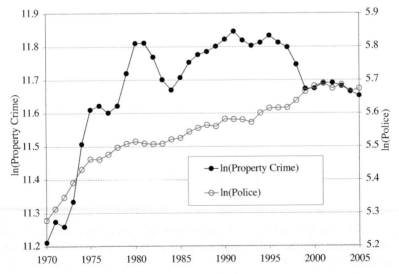

FIGURE 6.3 Trends in crime and police

TABLE 6.1 Relationships between police and crime

Independent	Dependent Variables				
	Δy_{it}			$\Delta \bar{y}_t$	$\Delta \bar{y}_i$
	$\hat{b}_1$	$\hat{b}_2$	$\hat{b}_3$	$\hat{b}_4$	
Δx_{it-1}	0.292*	0.269*	−0.001		
Δy_{it-1}	0.244*	0.246*	−0.009		
$\Delta \bar{x}_{t-1}$				0.374*	
$\Delta \bar{y}_{t-1}$				1.295*	
$\Delta \bar{x}_i$					0.715*
fixed effects	No	Yes	Yes	n.a	n.a
time effects	No	No	Yes	n.a	n.a

Note that '*' stands for the significance at the 5% level.

heterogeneity of individual fixed effects is very limited at state-level aggregated data. As Figure 6.3 showed, the relationship between the two are in general positive. However, as the year effects were included, the relationship changed from the significantly positive to insignificantly negative. Hence the idio-dynamic relationship is close to zero. In other words, a pure idiosyncratic increase in sworn officers does not result in a decrease in crime. Next, we take the cross-sectional averages of the crime and police, and run the time series regression. Since the two series are highly correlated, as shown in Figure 6.3, the relationship becomes strongly positive. Lastly, we run the cross-sectional regression with the time series averages of Δy_{it} and Δx_{it}, and find that the static relationship is positive. In other words, the states with more sworn officers have more property crimes. Again, the results in Table 6.1 should not be considered seriously since other control variables are not included. More importantly, the two variables might be cointegrated with each other. A more careful empirical investigation is required.

Next, we consider the case where the factor loadings are heterogeneous.

6.2.2 Heterogeneous factor loadings: factor-augmented panel regression

To eliminate the common-dynamic relationship, the factor-augmented regressions should be used. It is very important to note that the individual de-factored series should not be used for the estimation of the idio-dynamic relationship. To be specific, one eliminates the common components by running the following regressions.

$$x_{it} = a_i^x + \lambda'_x \hat{F}_{x,t} + x_{it}^o,$$
$$y_{it} = a_i^y + \lambda'_{y,i} \hat{F}_{y,t} + y_{it}^o,$$

(6.26)

where $\hat{\mathbf{F}}_{x,t}$ and $\hat{\mathbf{F}}_{y,t}$ are the estimates of the common components. Let $\hat{x}_{it}^o$ and $\hat{y}_{it}^o$ be the regression residuals from (6.26), respectively. Running $\hat{y}_{it}^o$ on $\hat{x}_{it}^o$, however, leads to the biased estimation of the idio-dynamic relationship. The underlying reason goes like that. The residuals contain the factor estimation error so that they are not free from the common-dynamic relationship. To eliminate the common-dynamic relationship completely, one should include both common factors from x_{it} and y_{it}. That is, the residuals from the following regressions do not include the common-dynamic relationship asymptotically.

$$
\begin{aligned}
x_{it} &= a_i^x + \lambda'_{x,i}\hat{\mathbf{F}}_{x,t} + \lambda'_{y,i}\hat{\mathbf{F}}_{y,t} + x_{it}^o, \\
y_{it} &= a_i^y + \delta'_{x,i}\hat{\mathbf{F}}_{x,t} + \delta'_{y,i}\hat{\mathbf{F}}_{y,t} + y_{it}^o.
\end{aligned}
\tag{6.27}
$$

Equivalently, the following factor-augmented regression can be used for the estimation of the idio-dynamic relationship.

$$
y_{it} = a_i + \gamma x_{it} + \lambda'_{1,i}\hat{\mathbf{F}}_{x,t} + \lambda'_{2,i}\hat{\mathbf{F}}_{y,t} + \varepsilon_{it}.
$$

Depending on the choice of the estimation for the common factors, several factor-augmented estimators are available. Pesaran (2006) suggested to use the sample cross-sectional averages to approximate the common factors to the regressors. This estimator is called the 'commonly correlated estimator' (CCE). Bai (2009) proposed to use the PC factors of the regression residuals from the regression of y_{it} on fixed effects and regressors. Since the within group (or least-squares dummy variable) estimator is minimizing the sum of the square errors literally, the PC estimator of the common factors to the regression errors consistently estimates the common factors of $\mathbf{F}_{x,t}$ and $\mathbf{F}_{y,t}$. Since the initial within group estimator is inconsistent, Bai (2009) suggested the use of the iterative method. Bai called this estimation 'iterative interactive fixed effects model' (IIFE). Meanwhile, Greenaway-McGrevy et al. (2012a) suggested the use of the PC estimates of $\mathbf{F}_{x,t}$ and $\mathbf{F}_{y,t}$ directly from y_{it} and x_{it}. They call this method the 'factor-augmented estimator.' However, even though all three estimators share almost the same asymptotic properties, surprisingly, all estimators are somewhat different from each other. The finite sample performance of the CCE is not good if the variances of factor loadings are large. In this case, the sample cross-sectional averages of y_{it} and x_{it} are less accurate due to large variances of the factor loadings. Meanwhile, IIFE or factor-augmented estimator are very efficient in this case since the large variances of factor loadings imply a strong signal for cross-sectional dependence so that the PC estimates for common factors become more accurate. Also note that the IIFE is more efficient than the factor-augmented estimator if the common-dynamic relationship is identical to the idio-dynamic relationship. In fact, in this case, the within group regression estimates both the common and idio-dynamic relationship so that the factor-augmented regression is not needed. To compensate these differences, one can utilize the asymptotic finding by Moon and Weidner (2015): The factor-augmented estimators in (6.27) are consistent as long as enough common factors are included in the regression. Hence one can include both CCE factors – sample cross-sectional averages – and PC factors as well.

6.2.3 Cross-sectional regressions with nonstationary common factors

When the time-varying components are integrated (or follow random walks), the long-run values do not exist since the time series averages are not converging to fixed constants, even when the number of time series observations goes to infinity. Since the long-run averages cannot be defined, naturally, the static relationship does not exist. In this case, the long-run relationship can be defined as the cointegrating relationship between time-varying components. In fact, it is unknown what the cross-sectional regressions with nonstationary components estimate. In this subsection, this issue is discussed based on the level of aggregation. To be specific, we consider two different cross-sectional regressions: Micro-survey (individual-level) data and city-, state-, or national-level aggregated data.

Micro-survey data

As we discussed before, the household-level data may not be cross-sectionally dependent. Moreover, it is not realistic to say that the household income is non-stationary simply because the life span of an individual is finite. As a person's age approaches the retirement age, it is hard to say that his (her) income will follow a random walk process. Meanwhile, city- or state-level aggregate income data are distinctly nonstationary. City- and state-level aggregate data are simple cross-sectional averages across individuals.[5] As we studied earlier, small nonstationary common factors at the individual level become more distinct as the level of aggregation becomes higher. Rewrite (6.20) as

$$y_{it} = \mu_{yi} + \lambda_{yi} F_{yt} + y_{it}^o,$$

where for simplicity we assume just single-factor structure, but the factor, F_{yt}, is nonstationary or follows a random walk. Here we treat the common factor F_{yt} as an exogenous macro factor, the influence of which on each individual is very limited. In fact, new young individuals enter the set of $\{y\}$, and in the same year, some individuals leave the set. The common factor F_{yt} may not be influenced much by these new entries and exits for every t.[6] Then modeling the stochastic process of y_{it} at the individual level – heterogeneous economic agents – should be focused on μ_{yi} and y_{it}^o. Meanwhile, the average individuals or aggregated data become purely dependent on the common factor F_{yt}. Hence modeling a representative economic agent's behavior should be very different from modeling heterogeneous economic agents' behaviors. There is no direct empirical evidence of whether the idiosyncratic components are stationary simply because of the lack of time dimension and data. However, indirectly, we can conjecture this by using state-level aggregation data. For example, Evans and Karras (1996) examine carefully whether per capita real state incomes share the same nonstationary common factor. After controlling the common time-fixed effects, Evans and Karras (1996) show that the idiosyncratic components at the state level are stationary. Also, Phillips and Sul (2009) show that the per capita real incomes are relatively converging across states. Hence it is not reasonable to assume that the micro-survey data contain a very tiny amount of a nonstationary common factor.

Cross-sectionally aggregate data

Once individual data are cross-sectionally aggregated, the fraction of the common factors is no longer ignorable. As Andrews (2005) points out, for a given t, the probability limit of the cross-sectional estimators can be either a constant or random, even when the number of cross-sectional units becomes infinity. However, if the common factors are nonstationary, then as t goes to infinity, the fraction of the common components becomes larger since $\mathrm{E}\left(F_{yt}^2\right)$ goes to infinity. Let J be the number of cross-sectional units of the cross-sectionally aggregated data y_{jt}. Let

$$
\varpi_t = \frac{\sigma_{\mu x}^2}{\sigma_{\mu x}^2 + \sigma_{xo,t}^2 + \sigma_{h,t}^2}, \quad \bar{\varrho}_t = \frac{\sigma_{xo,t}^2}{\sigma_{xo,t}^2 + \sigma_{h,t}^2},
$$

where

$$
\sigma_{h,t}^2 = \mathrm{E}\frac{1}{n}\sum_{i=1}^n \left(h_{it}^x - \frac{1}{n}\sum_{i=1}^n h_{it}^x\right)^2.
$$

Then the cross-sectional estimators have the following properties.

$$
\lim_{t\to\infty}\operatorname{plim}_{n\to\infty}\hat{b}_{\mathrm{cross},t} = \begin{cases} \phi & \text{if } y_{jt}^o \sim I(0) \\ \bar{\varrho}_t\gamma + (1 - \bar{\varrho}_t)\phi & \text{if } y_{jt}^o \sim I(1) \end{cases}. \tag{6.28}
$$

The proof for (6.28) becomes obvious, so it is omitted. From (6.25), the cross-sectional estimators are dependent on the weight matrices ϖ and $\bar{\varrho}$. When the idiosyncratic terms are stationary, the cross-sectional estimators become heavily dependent on the variance of the common component, σ_{ht}^2, which becomes dominant as t increases. Naturally, as $t \to \infty$, $\varpi_t \to 0$ and $\bar{\varrho}_t \to 0$ as well. However, when the idiosyncratic terms are nonstationary, the cross-sectional estimators become dependent on the variance ratio between the common and idiosyncratic components.

Now we are ready to examine the following famous puzzles.

Solving consumption puzzle

The famous consumption or Kuznets' puzzle (1946) is based on the following two simple regressions.

$$\ln C_{it} = a_t + b_t \ln Y_{it} + u_{it}, \tag{6.29}$$

$$\ln \bar{C}_t = a + b \ln \bar{Y}_t + u_t, \tag{6.30}$$

where C_{it} is the expenditure, Y_{it} is the disposable income for the i-th household at time t; meanwhile, $\bar{C}_t$ and $\bar{Y}_t$ stand for the aggregated consumption and disposable income (per capita real consumption and disposable income), respectively. The cross-sectional estimates of b_t with a micro-survey data range from 0.4 to 0.5, and a_t is significantly positive; meanwhile, the aggregate time series estimates of b are more or less unity but a is close to zero. The cross-sectional household survey results had been interpreted as meaning that the wealthy households save more, but the poor households spend more than what they make. This interpretation, however, is problematic.

For an intuitive explanation, assume that $\ln Y_{it}$ and $\ln C_{it}$ have single factors of θ_{yt} and θ_{ct}, respectively. Then without the loss of generality, the individual logs disposable income and consumption at year t, $\ln Y_{it}$ and $\ln C_{it}$, can be rewritten as

$$\ln Y_{it} = a_i^y + \lambda_{yi}\theta_{yt} + y_{it}^o, \quad \ln C_{it} = a_i^c + \lambda_{ci}\theta_{ct} + c_{it}^o, \tag{6.31}$$

where the common factors θ_{yt} and θ_{ct} include stochastic trends. It is important to note that the stochastic common factor to $\ln Y_{it}$ is not the permanent income for the ith household. The permanent income can be decomposed into the common and the idiosyncratic income. Hence the common factor model in (6.31) does not represent the labor income process, but simply factor decomposition. The time invariant term a_i^c may include the information about personal characteristics such as time preference and risk aversion.

We re-examine this famous consumption puzzle by using two different data sets: Household survey data and 70 countries from World Development Indicators. For both data sets, we will run the cross-sectional, aggregated time series and panel factor-augmented regressions.

Consumption puzzle with KLIPS

First we examine the consumption puzzle with KLIPS data. KLIPS (Korean Labor Income Panel Study) provides 17 years of a balance panel data for 1,875 households (for annual wage and expenditure). Since the number of time series observations is not big enough, it is not easy to estimate the common components accurately. Table 6.2 reports 'rough' estimation of the variance decomposition. The common factors are estimated in two ways: PC estimation (after taking the first difference, standardizing the samples, estimating the PC factor, and then cumulating the PC factor) and the sample cross-sectional

TABLE 6.2 Variance decomposition of KLIPS data

Estimation	Variables	Fixed Effects	Common Components	Idiosyncratic Components
PC Estimate (%)	Log Wage	0.3980	0.0206	0.1596
		(0.6883)	(0.0356)	(0.2760)
	Log Consumption	0.5858	0.0261	0.3268
		(0.6241)	(0.0278)	(0.3481)
Sample Mean (%)	Log Wage	0.3697	0.0504	0.0928
		(0.7208)	(0.0983)	(0.1809)
	Log Consumption	0.5779	0.0784	0.2504
		(0.6374)	(0.0865)	(0.2762)

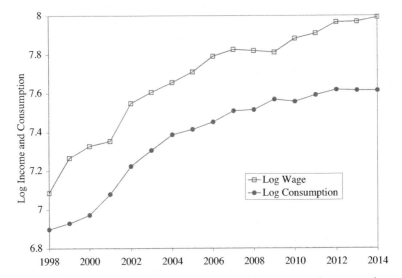

FIGURE 6.4 The sample cross-sectional averages of log wage and consumption

average. For PC estimation, the first observation is lost due to the first differencing. The factor loadings are estimated by running (6.31) with the estimated common factors. Interestingly, the variances of fixed effects are not much different across the estimation methods. Meanwhile, the variances of the idiosyncratic and common components are very sensitive to the choice of the estimation. It is rather natural since the number of time series samples is limited. However roughly, the variances of the fixed effects are almost twice as large as those of the idiosyncratic components. And then the variances of the common components are two to ten times smaller than those of the idiosyncratic components.

Figure 6.4 plots the sample cross-sectional averages of the log wage and consumption between 1998 and 2014. Evidently, both estimates for the common

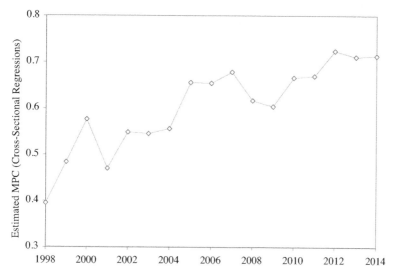

FIGURE 6.5   Spurious cross-sectional estimates of MPC

factors are increasing over time. Also, as it is well known, the common factor of the log consumption is much smoother than that of the log wage. Of course, taking cross-sectional averages for all households leads to national-level consumption, so the estimated common factors in Figure 6.4 can be thought of as proxies of the national level of log wage and personal consumption.

Figure 6.5 shows the point estimates of MPC from the cross-sectional regression of the log consumption on a constant and the log wage. As we discussed before, the cross sectional estimates of MPC – slope coefficient of b_t in (6.29) – are time varying. Since the common factor is increasing over time as shown in Figure 6.4, the cross-sectional estimates of MPC approaches to the time series estimate of MPC as t increases. Of course, the increasing pattern of the cross-sectional estimates of MPC can be shown here because the balanced panel data are used in the regression. If pure cross-sectional survey data are used – households in the survey at each year are different possibly – then such increasing patterns may not be observable.

The idio-dynamic relationship is estimated from the following factor-augmented regressions.

$$\ln C_{it} = a_i + \beta \ln Y_{it} + \lambda_{1i}\hat{\theta}_{1t} + \lambda_{2i}\hat{\theta}_{2t} + \varepsilon_{it},$$

Various estimated factors are used: Cross-sectional averages, PC estimates, and time dummies. When the cross-sectional averages are used, $\hat{\theta}_{1t} = \ln \bar{Y}_t$ and $\hat{\theta}_{2t} = \ln \bar{C}_t$. When the PC estimates are used, $\hat{\theta}_{1t} = \hat{F}_{yt}$, and $\hat{\theta}_{2t} = \hat{F}_{ct}$, where $\hat{F}_{yt}$ is the estimated PC common factor with the log wages and $\hat{F}_{ct}$ is

TABLE 6.3 Re-examination of consumption puzzle

Data Set	CSR Ave. $T^{-1} \sum \hat{b}_t$	Time FE $\hat{b}_3$	PC $\hat{b}_4$	CCE $\hat{b}_5$	PC and CCE $\hat{b}_6$	Time Agg. $\hat{b}_7$
KLIPS	0.604	0.312	0.430	0.226	0.240	0.915
WDI	0.916	0.887	0.853	0.896	0.905	0.872

the estimated PC common factor with the log consumption. When the time dummy is used, the factor loadings are assumed identical, and $\hat{\theta}_{1t} = \hat{\theta}_{2t}$ as well.

Table 6.3 reports the estimation results of the following regressions.

CSR Ave.	$y_{it} = \theta_t + b_t x_{it} + \varepsilon_{it}$,
Time FE	$y_{it} = a_i + b_3 x_{it} + \theta_t + \epsilon_{it}$,
PC	$y_{it} = a_i + b_4 x_{it} + \lambda_{1i}\hat{\theta}_{1t} + \lambda_{2i}\hat{\theta}_{2t} + \epsilon_{it}^+$,
CCE	$y_{it} = a_i + b_5 x_{it} + \delta_{1i}\bar{y}_t + \delta_{2i}\bar{x}_t + \epsilon_{it}^*$,
PC and CCE	$y_{it} = a_i + b_6 x_{it} + \lambda_{1i}\hat{\theta}_{1t} + \lambda_{2i}\hat{\theta}_{2t} + \delta_{1i}\bar{y}_t + \delta_{2i}\bar{x}_t + \epsilon_{it}^\dagger$,
Time Agg.	$\bar{y}_t = a + b_7 \bar{x}_t + u_t$.

The average MPC of 17 cross-sectional regression estimators is expressed as 'CSR Ave.,' which is around 0.6. This estimate is not reliable since it does not estimate either static or dynamic relationship. The conventional time and individual fixed effect estimate is around 0.31, but this estimate becomes invalid if the factor loadings are heterogeneous. The factor-augmented estimates are slightly different but the joint PC and CCE estimate becomes around 0.24. This estimate must be a good proxy for the idiosyncratic relationship. Lastly, the least-squares estimate from the time series regression with the cross-sectional averages is around 0.9, which is reasonably large.

Consumption puzzle with WDI

Lastly, we construct a panel data of 70 countries from World Development Indicator (WDI) based on the data availability from 1970 to 2000. Real private household consumption per capita and real GDP per capita data are used. Table 6.3 reports the estimation results. The results with WDI are very different from the household survey data. The average MPC estimate over 31 cross-sectional regressions is around 0.9. Note that the MPC estimates from the cross-sectional regressions are slightly increasing over time, but the minimum value – which is around 0.903 – is not much different from the maximum value of 0.925, which is estimated in 1988. The panel factor-augmented estimators are also similar each other. The least-squares estimator from the time series regression with the cross-sectional averages is also around 0.9 as well. The underlying reason is rather straightforward: Taking the cross-sectional averages yields a consistent estimate of the common factor. Since the consumption and income share the same common stochastic trend, running the cross-sectional regressions with cross-sectionally aggregated data yields the dynamic relationship among the common components. In other words, the dynamic relationships among common and idiosyncratic components are almost identical with WDI data, hence all estimators are similar to each other.

6.3   Practice: factor-augmented and aggregation regressions

In this section, we will study how to run factor-augmented regressions with actual data: Purchasing power parity with 25 bilateral exchange rates and relative inflation rates. I exclude Israel and Turkey on purpose. In the next edition of this book, I will include the pitfall of the within group estimator and discuss this issue again. Denote s_{it} as the i-th country's log spot exchange rate against US dollar. If this value increases, the value of the US dollar becomes relatively increased so that the ith currency depreciates. p_{it} is the log CPI. Define the relative price index as

$$\tilde{p}_{it} = p_{it} - p_t^*,$$

where p_t^* is the price index in USA. Next, we assume that

$$\Delta s_{it} = \lambda_i' F_t + \Delta s_{it}^o, \quad \Delta \tilde{p}_{it} = \delta_i' G_t + \Delta \tilde{p}_{it}^o.$$

We are interested in the idio-dynamic relationship between Δs_{it}^o and $\Delta \tilde{p}_{it}^o$, and the common-dynamic relationship between F_t and G_t.

We will study GAUSS codes first.

6.3.1   Practice with GAUSS I: common-dynamic relationship

As long as the factor loadings are not time varying, the common-dynamic relationship can be approximated by the relationship between two cross-sectional averages of dependent and independent variables. However, as we studied in Chapter 5, the common factors to the exchange rates are the USD and Euro, and the USD value can be approximated by taking the cross-sectional average of Δs_{it} – since the numeraire of s_{it} is USD – due to the unique feature of the bilateral exchange rate. Meanwhile, the Euro value can be approximated by taking the cross-sectional average of $\Delta s_{it} - \Delta s_{eu,t}$. Let $\Delta \bar{s}_t$, $\Delta \bar{s}_{eu,t}$, and $\Delta \bar{p}_t$ be the cross-sectional averages of Δs_{it}, $\Delta s_{it} - \Delta s_{eu,t}$, and $\Delta \tilde{p}_{it}$, respectively. Then the common-dynamic relationship, ϕ_1, can be measured by running the following time series regression.

$$\Delta \bar{s}_t = a + \phi_1 \Delta \bar{p}_t + \phi_2 \Delta \bar{s}_{eu,t} + u_t,$$

where $\Delta \bar{s}_{eu,t}$ serves as a control variable.

GAUSS EX 6-1

```
new; cls;
t = 203; n = 27;
load spot[t,n+3] = spot99_MA.csv;
load pric[t,n+2] = cpi99.csv;
s = ln(spot[.,3:n+2]);
p = ln(pric[.,2:n+1]./pric[.,n+2]);
dp = p[2:t,.] - p[1:t-1,.]; // inflation
ds = s[2:t,.] - s[1:t-1,.];
su = ln(spot[.,3:n+3]);
seu = su[.,1:6 8:28] - su[.,7];
deu = seu[2:t,.] - seu[1:t-1,.];
//==== Estimation the common-dynamic relationship ====
mdus = meanc(ds'); mdeu = meanc(deu'); mdp = meanc(dp');
xx = ones(rows(mdus),1)~mdp;
b1 = invpd(xx'xx)*xx'mdus;
xx = ones(rows(mdus),1)~mdp~mdeu;
b2 = invpd(xx'xx)*xx'mdus;
```

Note that mdus ($=\Delta\bar{s}_t$), mdeu ($=\Delta\bar{s}_{eu,t}$), and mdp ($=\Delta\bar{p}_t$) are the sample cross-sectional averages. The first regression does not include $\Delta\bar{s}_{eu,t}$, but the second regression includes both $\Delta\bar{p}_t$ and $\Delta\bar{s}_{eu,t}$. The outputs for b1 and b2 are as follows:

b1: $\hat{a} = -0.002$, $\hat{\phi}_1 = 2.561$
b2: $\hat{a} = -0.002$, $\hat{\phi}_1 = 2.516$, $\hat{\phi}_2 = -0.201$.

To get the heteroskedasticity and autocorrelation consistent (HAC) standard error, you need to add the following five more lines right after the OLS estimation.

```
b1 = invpd(xx'xx)*xx'mdus;
re = mdus - xx*be; res = re.*xx;
sig = nwest(res,round(t^(1/3)));
xq = invpd(xx'xx)*sig*invpd(xx'xx)*rows(xx);
se = sqrt(diag(xq));
be~se~be./sqrt(se);
```

The HAC standard error of $\hat{\phi}_1$ is 0.620 so that its t-ratio becomes $t_{\hat{\phi}_1} = 2.516/0.620 = 4.132$. Nonetheless, the estimate of $\hat{\phi}_1$ is strongly positive. If you make a general procedure to get the HAC standard error, see the procedure name 'olshac(y,x)' in EX6_1.pgm as example. EX6_1.pgm can be downloaded from the book website. You can add $\bar{R}^2$ and other statistics you want.

6.3.2   Practice with GAUSS II: idio-dynamic relationship

The idio-dynamic relationship can be consistently estimated by running the following regression.

$$\Delta s_{it} = \alpha_i + \gamma \Delta \tilde{p}_{it} + \lambda_i' F_t + \epsilon_{it}$$

The number of the common factors should be estimated first. Since we already knew that the exchange rates have two factors, we need to investigate the relative inflation rate. See the following GAUSS codes (ex6_2.pgm).

GAUSS EX 6-2

```
new; cls;
t = 203; n = 27;
load spot[t,n+3] = spot99_MA.csv;
load pric[t,n+2] = cpi99.csv;
s = ln(spot[.,3:n+2] );
p = ln(pric[.,2:n+1] ./pric[.,n+2] );
dp = p[2:t,.] - p[1:t-1,.] ; // inflation
d2p=dp[2:rows(dp),.] -dp[1:rows(dp)-1,.] ; //prewhitening
i = 1; do while i <= 50;
sdp = dp[i:rows(dp),.] ./sqrt(diag(vcx(dp[i:
   rows(dp),.] ))' );
sd2p = d2p[i:rows(d2p),.] ./sqrt(diag(vcx(d2p[i:
   rows(d2p),.] ))' );
i~bn(sd2p,8)~bn(sdp,8);
i = i + 1; endo;
```

Note that sdp and sd2p are standardized inflation rates (dp) and the standardization of the first differenced in inflation rates (d2p). Since the inflation rates are persistent, the first differenced series are needed. We check the robustness by using 50 recursive subsamples. The output shows that after prewhitening (or first differenced), the inflation rates have a single factor for all subsamples. Next, we will run the following CCE regression.

$$\Delta s_{it} = \alpha_i + \gamma \Delta \tilde{p}_{it} + \delta_{1i} \Delta \bar{s}_t + \delta_{2i} \Delta \bar{p}_t + \epsilon_{it}$$

Note that the coefficients on the common factors are heterogeneous. We first project the common factors. Let the projection matrix be M_c, which can be defined as

$$M_c = I - \hat{F}^{c\prime}(\hat{F}^{c\prime}\hat{F}^c)\hat{F}^c,$$

where $\hat{F}^c = [i, \Delta\bar{s}, \Delta\bar{p}_t]$ with $i = [1, ..., 1]$, $\Delta\bar{s} = [\Delta\bar{s}_1, ..., \Delta\bar{s}_T]'$ and $\Delta\bar{p} = [\Delta\bar{p}_1, ..., \Delta\bar{p}_T]'$. Then we run

$$\Delta s_{it} = a_{1i} + b_{11,i}\Delta\bar{s}_t + b_{12,i}\Delta\bar{p}_t + \Delta s_{it}^+,$$
$$\Delta\tilde{p}_{it} = a_{2i} + b_{21,i}\Delta\bar{s}_t + b_{22,i}\Delta\bar{p}_t + \Delta\tilde{p}_{it}^+.$$

The first estimate of the coefficient vector, $\hat{b}_{1i}$, can be written as

$$\hat{b}_{1i} = (\hat{F}^{c\prime}\hat{F}^c)^{-1}\hat{F}^{c\prime}\Delta s_i.$$

Then Δs_{it}^+ – which is the term after projecting out $\Delta\bar{s}_t$ and $\Delta\bar{p}_t$ – is written as

$$\Delta\hat{s}_{it}^+ = \Delta s_{it} - \hat{F}_t^c\hat{b},$$

where $\hat{b}_1 = [\hat{b}_{11}, ..., \hat{b}_{1n}]$. Or in GAUSS codes, we can express it as follows.

CCE with two factors

```
xx1 = ones (rows (mdp) ,1) ~mdp~mdus;
dsc = ds - xx1* invpd (xx1' xx1)* xx1' ds;
dpc = dp - xx1* invpd (xx1' xx1)* xx1' dp;
bcce = sumc (sumc (dsc.* dpc)) /sumc (sumc (dpc.* dpc)) ;
bcce;
```

where $\text{xx1} = F^c$, $\text{dsc} = \Delta\hat{s}_{it}^+$, $\text{dpc} = \Delta\hat{p}_{it}^+$, which is the fitted value of $\Delta\tilde{p}_{it}^+$. If you run this, you will get $\text{bcce} = 0.704$. Note that this value, however, is not consistent since only two factors are included in the regression. The total unknown factors are three. Since we know that the exchange rates have another factor of $\Delta\bar{s}_{eu,t}$, we include it in the following regression. Note that since the number of regressors is single, we use a simple summation to get the LS estimate. If the number of regressors is more than one, then you need to run like this. Suppose that you have two regressors dp1 and dp2. Then instead of the aforementioned codes, you need to run the following codes.

```
dpc1 = dp1 - xx1* invpd (xx1' xx1)* xx1' dp1;
dpc2 = dp2 - xx1* invpd (xx1' xx1)* xx1' dp2;
xx = vec (dpc1) ~vec (dpc2) ;
bcce = invpd (xx' xx)* xx' vec (dsc) ;
bcce;
```

CCE with three factors

```
xx1 = ones (rows (mdp) ,1) ~mdp~mdus~mdeu;
dsc = ds - xx1* invpd (xx1' xx1)* xx1' ds;
dpc = dp - xx1* invpd (xx1' xx1)* xx1' dp;
bcce = sumc (sumc (dsc.* dpc)) /sumc (sumc (dpc.* dpc)) ;
bcce;
```

Now you will get `bcce = 0.666`, which is slightly lower than 0.704.

Next, we will consider GHS's method. First, we estimate the PC common factors after standardization and then replace them with the cross-sectional averages.

GHS estimation with three factors

```
sds = ds./sqrt(diag(vcx(ds))');
sdp = dp./sqrt(diag(vcx(dp))');
  {fs,ls,es,vs} = pc(sds,2);
  {fp,lp,ep,vp} = pc(sdp,1);
  ff = ones(rows(ds),1)~fs~fp;
  y3 = ds - ff*invpd(ff' ff)*ff' ds;
  x3 = dp - ff*invpd(ff' ff)*ff' dp;
  be1 = sumc(sumc(x3.*y3))./sumc(sumc(x3.*x3));
```

You will get `be1=0.674`, which is very similar to the previous CCE estimator with three factors. Next, we include both cross-sectional averages and PC estimates together.

```
  ff = ones(rows(ds),1)~fs~fp~mdp~mdus~mdeu;
  y3 = ds - ff*invpd(ff' ff)*ff' ds;
  x3 = dp - ff*invpd(ff' ff)*ff' dp;
  be3 = sumc(sumc(x3.*y3))./sumc(sumc(x3.*x3));
```

You will get `be3=0.519`, which is much lower than 0.704. Next, we will study how to construct panel robust covariance matrix and its associate *t*-ratio.

Panel robust *t*-ratio

```
  re = y3 - x3*be3;
  re = re.*x3;
  xq = sumc(re); xq = xq' xq; invxx =
    1./sumc(sumc(x3.*x3));
  xq = invxx*xq*invxx;
  xq = sqrt(diag(xq));
  tratio=be3/xq;
```

You will get `tratio= 4.358`. Lastly, we will study how to program Bai's iterative fixed effect estimation.

Iterative PC: Bai's estimator

```
  // Construct two-way fixed effect dep and indep variables...
  dp1 = dp - meanc(dp)'; dp1 = dp1 - meanc(dp1');
  ds1 = ds - meanc(ds)'; ds1 = ds1 - meanc(ds1');
  // run and get the residuals
  bb = sumc(sumc(ds1.*dp1))/sumc(sumc(dp1.*dp1));
```

```
here1:
  rs = ds - dp.*bb;
  rs = rs./sqrt(diag(vcx(rs))');
  k3 = bn(rs,8);
  {fr,lr,er,vr} = pc(rs,8);
// ff = ones(rows(ds),1)~fr~mdp~mdus~mdeu;
  ff = ones(rows(fr),1)~fr;
  x4 = dp - ff*invpd(ff' ff)*ff' dp;
  y4 = ds - ff*invpd(ff' ff)*ff' ds;
  be4 = sumc(sumc(x4.*y4))./sumc(sumc(x4.*x4));
  if abs(be4-bb) > 0.000000001; bb = be4; goto here1;
    endif;
```

Note that here 1: is the label. If $|be4 - bb| > 0.1 \times 10^{-6}$, then iteration continues. The initial estimator is a two-way fixed effect estimator. However, it does not matter which estimate is used. Bai's estimator usually converges the same value regardless of the initial value. You will get be4=0.741. The type of factors included in the factor-augmented regression matters, though. See '//' line in the earlier example, which include three more cross-sectional averages. If you activate this line (and deactivate the next line by adding '//'), then you will get a different estimate. You will get be4=0.709.

At this moment, readers wonder, then, which estimator they have to use. As I recommended, you need to use the combined (PC + CCE) estimator, which equals 0.519. To get the panel robust t-ratio, what you have to do is copy the previous codes and change x3 to x4, y3 to y4, and be3 to be4. In the next edition, I will explain more, but the idio-dynamic relationship becomes zero once a few outliers are excluded from the panel.

6.3.3 Practice with MATLAB

Here is MATLAB version of GAUSS EX6-1. See the previous subsection for detailed discussions. Note that MATLAB EX6-2 is available under the name of ex6_2.m from the website for this chapter.

MATLAB EX6-1
```
clear;clc;
load cpi99.csv; p = cpi99;
load spot99_MA.csv; spot = spot99_MA;
[T,n] = size(p);
s = log(spot(:,3:n));
ds = s(2:T,:) - s(1:T-1,:);
p = log(p(:,2:n-1)./(p(:,n)*ones(1,27)));
dp = p(2:T,:)-p(1:T-1,:);
su = log(spot(:,3:n+1));
```

```
seu = [su(:,1:6) su(:,8:28)];
seu = seu - su(:,7)*ones(1,27);
deu = seu(2:T,:) - seu(1:T-1,:);
% - - - Estimation the common-dynamic relationship - -
mdus = mean(ds,2);
mdeu = mean(deu,2);
mdp = mean(dp,2);
xx = [ones(T-1,1) mdp];
be = inv(xx'*xx)*xx'*mdus;
re = mdus - xx*be; res = [re.*xx(:,1) re.*xx(:,2)];
k1 = round(T^(1/3));
sig = nwest(res,k1);
xq = inv(xx'*xx)*sig*inv(xx'*xx)*T;
se = sqrt(diag(xq));
[be se be./se]
```

6.3.4   Practice with STATA

Various STATA codes are available. Eberhardt provides various links to STATA codes for CCE estimation. Furthermore, the STATA code for Bai's iterative PC estimation is available online. You can find more information and detailed links at the website for this chapter.

6.4   Appendix: modified between group estimators and an econometric application

6.4.1   Appendix A: relationships between the five estimators

Consider the following T cross-sectional regressions, n time series regressions, two-panel regressions and one between group regression.

Cross-Section: $\quad y_{it} = a_t + \mathbf{x}_{it}\mathbf{b}_t + u_{it} \quad$ for each $t = 1, ..., T$

Time Series: $\quad y_{it} = a_i + \mathbf{x}_{it}\mathbf{b}_i + e_{it} \quad$ for each $i = 1, ..., n$

Pooled OLS: $\quad y_{it} = a + \mathbf{x}_{it}\mathbf{b}_1 + \varepsilon_{it}$

Fixed Effects: $\quad y_{it} = a_i + \mathbf{x}_{it}\mathbf{b}_2 + \epsilon_{it}$

Between Group: $\quad \bar{y}_i = a + \bar{\mathbf{x}}_i\mathbf{b}_3 + \bar{\varepsilon}_i \quad \bar{y}_i = T^{-1}\sum_{t=1}^{T} y_{it}, \ \bar{\mathbf{x}}_i = T^{-1}\sum_{t=1}^{T} \mathbf{x}_{it},$

$$(6.32)$$

where $\mathbf{x}_{it}$ is a $1 \times k$ vector of explanatory variables, and the vector of slope coefficients, $\mathbf{b}$, is a $(k \times 1)$ vector. The true relationships are given by

$$\mu_{yi} = \mu_{xi}\beta + v_i, \quad y_{it}^o = \mathbf{x}_{it}^o\gamma + m_{it}. \qquad (6.33)$$

Here $\mathbf{x}_{it}^o$ and $\boldsymbol{\mu}_{xi}$ are assumed to be strictly exogenous and stationary. These assumptions are very strong, but they effectively deliver the core concept of this chapter.

The relationship between $\boldsymbol{\mu}_{yi}$ and $\boldsymbol{\mu}_{xi}$ can be interpreted as static or steady-state relationship in the sense that this relationship can be revealed when there are no time-varying shocks, y_{it}^o and x_{it}^o. It is important to note that the static relationship implies a 'long-run' relationship rather than a 'short-run' relationship. To see this, taking time series mean yields

$$\frac{1}{T}\sum_{t=1}^{T} y_{it} = \mu_{yi} + O_p\left(T^{-1/2}\right) = \mu_{xi}\beta + v_i + O_p\left(T^{-1/2}\right),$$

as long as y_{it}^o and x_{it}^o have zero means and finite variances. In other words, when both $T^{-1}\sum_{t=1}^{T} y_{it}^o$ and $T^{-1}\sum_{t=1}^{T} x_{it}^o$ converge to zero in probability, the static or steady-state relationship can be well defined as $T \rightarrow \infty$. Naturally, the between group estimator estimates the static relationship consistently as $T \rightarrow \infty$ since the regressors and regressand are time series averages.

Given (6.33) the true DGP can be expressed as

$$y_{it} = a_i + \mathbf{x}_{it}\gamma + m_{it} \tag{6.34}$$

$$= v_i + \mathbf{x}_{it}\beta + k_{it}, \tag{6.35}$$

where

$$a_i = \mu_{xi}(\beta - \gamma) + v_i, \quad k_{it} = \mathbf{x}_{it}^o(\gamma - \beta) + m_{it}.$$

When $\beta = \gamma$, the relationship between $\{y_{it}\}$ and $\{\mathbf{x}_{it}\}$ becomes unique. Otherwise, it is hard to define the relationship between the two variables if $\beta \neq \gamma$. Note that when $\beta \neq \gamma$, there is a correlation between fixed effects and regressors (a_i and $\mathbf{x}_{it}$) in (6.34), and the correlation coefficient on $\mathbf{x}_{it}$ represents the 'dynamic relationship' between $\{y\}$ and $\{\mathbf{x}\}$. Meanwhile, in (6.35) there is no correlation between the fixed effects and regressors (v_i and $\mathbf{x}_{it}$), but the regressors are correlated with the regression errors.

Here we provide more formal explanations of the five estimators. Define

$$\tilde{\mathbf{x}}_{it} = \mathbf{x}_{it} - \frac{1}{T}\sum_{t=1}^{T} \mathbf{x}_{it}, \quad \tilde{\mathbf{x}}_{it}^+ = \mathbf{x}_{it} - \frac{1}{n}\sum_{i=1}^{n} \mathbf{x}_{it} \quad \bar{\mathbf{x}}_i = \frac{1}{T}\sum_{t=1}^{T} \mathbf{x}_{it}$$

$$\tilde{y}_{it} = y_{it} - \frac{1}{T}\sum_{t=1}^{T} y_{it}, \quad \tilde{y}_{it}^+ = y_{it} - \frac{1}{n}\sum_{i=1}^{n} y_{it} \quad \bar{y}_i = \frac{1}{T}\sum_{t=1}^{T} y_{it}$$

$$\bar{\mathbf{x}}_i^* = \bar{\mathbf{x}}_i - \frac{1}{n}\sum_{i=1}^{n} \bar{\mathbf{x}}_i \quad \tilde{\mathbf{x}}_{it}^* = \mathbf{x}_{it} - \frac{1}{nT}\sum_{t=1}^{T}\sum_{i=1}^{n} \mathbf{x}_{it}$$

$$\bar{y}_i^* = \bar{y}_i - \frac{1}{n}\sum_{i=1}^{n} \bar{y}_i \quad \tilde{y}_{it}^* = y_{it} - \frac{1}{nT}\sum_{t=1}^{T}\sum_{i=1}^{n} y_{it};$$

then we have

$$\tilde{\mathbf{x}}_{it} = \mathbf{x}_{it}^o - \frac{1}{T}\sum_{t=1}^T \mathbf{x}_{it}^o, \qquad \bar{\mathbf{x}}_i = \mu_{xi} + \frac{1}{T}\sum_{t=1}^T \mathbf{x}_{it}^o, \qquad \tilde{\mathbf{x}}_{it}^+ = \mu_{xi} - \bar{\mu}_x + \left(\mathbf{x}_{it}^o - \frac{1}{n}\sum_{i=1}^n \mathbf{x}_{it}^o\right)$$

$$\bar{\mathbf{x}}_i^* = \mu_{xi} - \bar{\mu}_x + \left(\frac{1}{T}\sum_{t=1}^T \mathbf{x}_{it}^o - \frac{1}{nT}\sum_{t=1}^T\sum_{i=1}^n \mathbf{x}_{it}^o\right), \qquad \tilde{\mathbf{x}}_{it}^* = \mu_{xi} - \bar{\mu}_x + \left(\mathbf{x}_{it}^o - \frac{1}{nT}\sum_{t=1}^T\sum_{i=1}^n \mathbf{x}_{it}^o\right).$$

Now, further define the five estimators: cross-sectional ("cross"), time series ("time"), pooled OLS ("POLS"), within group ("WG"), and between group ("BG") estimators as

$$\hat{\mathbf{b}}_{\text{cross},t} \quad : \quad = \hat{\mathbf{b}}_t = \left(\tilde{\mathbf{x}}_t^{+\prime}\tilde{\mathbf{x}}_t^+\right)^{-1}\tilde{\mathbf{x}}_t^{+\prime}\tilde{\mathbf{y}}_t^+,$$

$$\hat{\mathbf{b}}_{\text{time},i} \quad : \quad = \hat{\mathbf{b}}_i = \left(\tilde{\mathbf{x}}_i'\tilde{\mathbf{x}}_i\right)^{-1}\tilde{\mathbf{x}}_i'\tilde{\mathbf{y}}_i,$$

$$\hat{\mathbf{b}}_{\text{pols}} \quad : \quad = \hat{\mathbf{b}}_1 = \left(\tilde{\mathbf{x}}^{*\prime}\tilde{\mathbf{x}}^*\right)^{-1}\tilde{\mathbf{x}}^{*\prime}\tilde{\mathbf{y}}^*,$$

$$\hat{\mathbf{b}}_{\text{wg}} \quad : \quad = \hat{\mathbf{b}}_2 = \left(\tilde{\mathbf{x}}'\tilde{\mathbf{x}}\right)^{-1}\tilde{\mathbf{x}}'\tilde{\mathbf{y}},$$

$$\hat{\mathbf{b}}_{\text{bw}} \quad : \quad = \hat{\mathbf{b}}_3 = \left(\bar{\mathbf{x}}^{*\prime}\bar{\mathbf{x}}^*\right)^{-1}\bar{\mathbf{x}}^{*\prime}\bar{\mathbf{y}}^*,$$

where $\tilde{\mathbf{x}}_t^+ = \left(\tilde{\mathbf{x}}_{1t}^{+\prime}, ..., \tilde{\mathbf{x}}_{Nt}^{+\prime}\right)'$, $\tilde{\mathbf{x}}_i = \left(\tilde{\mathbf{x}}_{i1}', ..., \tilde{\mathbf{x}}_{iT}'\right)'$, $\tilde{\mathbf{x}}^* = \left(\tilde{\mathbf{x}}_{11}^{*\prime}, ..., \tilde{\mathbf{x}}_{1T}^{*\prime}, \tilde{\mathbf{x}}_{21}^{*\prime}, ..., \tilde{\mathbf{x}}_{NT}^{*\prime}\right)'$, $\tilde{\mathbf{x}} = \left(\tilde{\mathbf{x}}_{11}', ..., \tilde{\mathbf{x}}_{1T}', \tilde{\mathbf{x}}_{21}', ..., \tilde{\mathbf{x}}_{NT}'\right)'$, $\bar{\mathbf{x}}^* = \left(\bar{\mathbf{x}}_1^{*\prime}, ..., \bar{\mathbf{x}}_N^{*\prime}\right)'$, and $\{y\}$ is also defined in the same way. Next, $\mathbf{x}_i^o = \left(\mathbf{x}_{i1}^{o\prime}, ..., \mathbf{x}_{iT}^{o\prime}\right)'$, $\mathbf{x}_t^o = \left(\mathbf{x}_{1t}^{o\prime}, ..., \mathbf{x}_{Nt}^{o\prime}\right)'$, $\mathbf{x}^o = \left(\mathbf{x}_{11}^{o\prime}, ..., \mathbf{x}_{NT}^{o\prime}\right)'$, $\bar{\mathbf{x}}^o = \left(\bar{\mathbf{x}}_1^{o\prime}, ..., \bar{\mathbf{x}}_N^{o\prime}\right)'$, $\bar{\mathbf{x}}_i^o = T^{-1}\sum_{t=1}^T \mathbf{x}_{it}^o$, and $\{y^o\}$ is also defined in the same way. Let

$$\mathbf{Q}_{xoi} = \lim_T \mathbb{E}\left(\frac{\mathbf{x}_i^{o\prime}\mathbf{x}_i^o}{T}\right) \qquad \mathbf{Q}_{xot} = \lim_n \mathbb{E}\left(\frac{\mathbf{x}_t^{o\prime}\mathbf{x}_t^o}{n}\right)$$

$$\mathbf{Q}_{xyoi} = \lim_T \mathbb{E}\left(\frac{\mathbf{x}_i^{o\prime}\mathbf{y}_i^o}{T}\right) \qquad \mathbf{Q}_{xyot} = \lim_n \mathbb{E}\left(\frac{\mathbf{x}_t^{o\prime}\mathbf{y}_t^o}{n}\right)$$

$$\mathbf{Q}_{xo} = \lim_n \mathbb{E}\left(\frac{\mathbf{x}^{o\prime}\mathbf{x}^o}{nT}\right) \qquad \Omega_{xo} = \lim_n \mathbb{E}\left(\frac{\bar{\mathbf{x}}^{o\prime}\bar{\mathbf{x}}^o}{n}\right)$$

$$\mathbf{Q}_{xyo} = \lim_n \mathbb{E}\left(\frac{\mathbf{x}^{o\prime}\mathbf{y}^o}{nT}\right) \qquad \Omega_{xyo} = \lim_n \mathbb{E}\left(\frac{\bar{\mathbf{x}}^{o\prime}\bar{\mathbf{y}}^o}{n}\right)$$

$$\mathbf{Q}_{\mu x} = \lim_n \mathbb{E}\frac{\left(\mu_x - \frac{1}{n}\sum_{i=1}^n \mu_{xi}\right)'\left(\mu_x - \frac{1}{n}\sum_{i=1}^n \mu_{xi}\right)}{n}$$

$$\mathbf{Q}_{\mu xy} = \lim_n \mathbb{E}\frac{\left(\mu_x - \frac{1}{n}\sum_{i=1}^n \mu_{xi}\right)'\left(\mu_y - \frac{1}{n}\sum_{i=1}^n \mu_{yi}\right)}{n}.$$

Then the probability limit for each estimator is given by

$$
\begin{align}
\text{(i)} \quad & \operatorname{plim}_{n\to\infty} \hat{\mathbf{b}}_{\text{cross},t} = \mathbf{W}_t\beta + (\mathbf{I} - \mathbf{W}_t)\gamma \neq \beta, \\
\text{(ii)} \quad & \operatorname{plim}_{n\to\infty} \hat{\mathbf{b}}_{\text{time},i} = \mathbf{Q}_{xoi}^{-1}\mathbf{Q}_{xyoi} = \gamma, \\
\text{(iii)} \quad & \operatorname{plim}_{n\to\infty} \hat{\mathbf{b}}_{\text{bw}} = (\mathbf{Q}_{\mu x} + T^{-1}\mathbf{\Omega}_{xo})^{-1}(\mathbf{Q}_{\mu xy} + T^{-1}\mathbf{\Omega}_{xyo}), \\
\text{(iv)} \quad & \operatorname{plim}_{n,T\to\infty} \hat{\mathbf{b}}_{\text{pols}} = \mathbf{W}\beta + (\mathbf{I} - \mathbf{W})\gamma \neq \beta, \\
\text{(v)} \quad & \operatorname{plim}_{n,T\to\infty} \hat{\mathbf{b}}_{\text{wg}} = \mathbf{Q}_{xo}^{-1}\mathbf{Q}_{xyo} = \gamma, \\
\text{(vi)} \quad & \operatorname{plim}_{n,T\to\infty} \hat{\mathbf{b}}_{\text{bw}} = \beta,
\end{align}
\tag{6.36}
$$

where $W_t = (\mathbf{Q}_{\mu x} + \mathbf{Q}_{xot})^{-1}\mathbf{Q}_{\mu x}$, and $W = (\mathbf{Q}_{\mu x} + \mathbf{Q}_{xo})^{-1}\mathbf{Q}_{\mu x}$. The proof of (6.36) is rather straightforward. Note that any non-singular matrix can be decomposed as

$$
\begin{align}
(\mathbf{A} + \mathbf{B})^{-1}(\mathbf{C} + \mathbf{D}) &= (\mathbf{A} + \mathbf{B})^{-1}\mathbf{C} + (\mathbf{A} + \mathbf{B})^{-1}\mathbf{D} \\
&= (\mathbf{A} + \mathbf{B})^{-1}\mathbf{A}\mathbf{A}^{-1}\mathbf{C} + (\mathbf{A} + \mathbf{B})^{-1}\mathbf{B}\mathbf{B}^{-1}\mathbf{D} \\
&= \alpha\mathbf{A}^{-1}\mathbf{C} + (\mathbf{I} - \alpha)\mathbf{B}^{-1}\mathbf{D}.
\end{align}
$$

By using this fact, we can prove (6.36).

When both regressors and regressand are cross-sectionally dependent, the asymptotic properties change. Let

$$
\mathbf{x}_{it} = \boldsymbol{\mu}_{xi} + \mathbf{h}_{it}^x + \mathbf{x}_{it}^o, \quad \text{for } \mathbf{h}_{it}^x = \boldsymbol{\lambda}_{xi}'\mathbf{F}_{xt},
$$

where $\boldsymbol{\lambda}_{yi}$ is a $(r \times 1)$ vector of the factor loadings, $\mathbf{F}_{yt}$ is a $(r \times 1)$ vector of the common factors, and $\mathbf{x}_{it}^o$ is the idiosyncratic component.

Rewrite (6.21) as

Static relationship: $\qquad\qquad \mu_{yi} = \boldsymbol{\mu}_{xi}\beta + v_i,$

Idio-dynamic relationship : $\qquad y_{it}^o = \mathbf{x}_{it}^o\gamma + m_{it},$ (6.37)

Common-dynamic relationship: $h_{it}^y = \mathbf{h}_{it}^x\phi + e_{it}.$

Then we have

$$
y_{it} = v_i + \mathbf{x}_{it}\beta + k_{it}, \quad k_{it} = \mathbf{h}_{it}^x(\phi - \beta) + \mathbf{x}_{it}^o(\gamma - \beta) + m_{it} + e_{it},
\tag{6.38}
$$

$$
= a_i + \mathbf{x}_{it}\gamma + w_{it}, \quad a_i = \boldsymbol{\mu}_{xi}(\beta - \gamma) + v_i, \quad w_{it} = \mathbf{h}_{it}^x(\phi - \gamma) + m_{it} + e_{it},
\tag{6.39}
$$

$$
= a_i + \mathbf{x}_{it}\phi + \varepsilon_{it}, \quad \varepsilon_{it} = \mathbf{x}_{it}^o(\gamma - \phi) + m_{it} + e_{it}.
\tag{6.40}
$$

The probability limits of the cross-sectional, POLS, and WG estimators with multiple regressors are given by

$$\text{plim}_{n\to\infty}\hat{\mathbf{b}}_{\text{cross},t} = \varpi_t\beta + (\mathbf{I} - \varpi_t)[\bar{\varrho}_t\gamma + (\mathbf{I} - \bar{\varrho}_t)\phi],$$

$$\text{plim}_{n,T\to\infty}\hat{\mathbf{b}}_{\text{pols}} = \varpi\beta + (\mathbf{I} - \varpi)[\bar{\varrho}\gamma + (\mathbf{I} - \bar{\varrho})\phi],$$

$$\text{plim}_{n,T\to\infty}\hat{\mathbf{b}}_{\text{wg}} = \bar{\varrho}\gamma + (\mathbf{I} - \bar{\varrho})\phi,$$

where

$$\mathbf{M}_t = [\mathbf{Q}_{\mu x,t} + (\mathbf{Q}_{xo,t} + \mathbf{Q}_{ht})]^{-1}\mathbf{Q}_{\mu x,t}, \quad \mathbf{C}_t = [\mathbf{Q}_{xot} + \mathbf{Q}_{ht}]^{-1}\mathbf{Q}_{xot},$$

$$\mathbf{M} = [\mathbf{Q}_{\mu x} + (\mathbf{Q}_{xo} + \mathbf{Q}_{h})]^{-1}\mathbf{Q}_{\mu x}, \quad \mathbf{C} = [\mathbf{Q}_{xo} + \mathbf{Q}_{h}]^{-1}\mathbf{Q}_{xo},$$

and

$$\mathbf{Q}_{hi} = \lim_T \mathbb{E}\left(\frac{\mathbf{h}'_i\mathbf{h}^o_i}{T}\right) \quad \mathbf{Q}_{ht} = \lim_n \mathbb{E}\left(\frac{\mathbf{h}'_t\mathbf{h}_t}{n}\right) \quad \mathbf{Q}_{ho} = \lim_{nT} \mathbb{E}\left(\frac{\mathbf{h}'\mathbf{h}}{nT}\right).$$

6.4.2 Appendix B: estimation of static relationships

As (6.36) states, with a large T, the between estimators $\hat{\mathbf{b}}_{\text{bw}}$ estimate the static relationships consistently. However, for a finite T dimension, the between estimators $\hat{\mathbf{b}}_{\text{bw}}$ become inconsistent. The order of inconsistency for large T can be expressed as follows

$$\text{plim}_{n\to\infty}\hat{\mathbf{b}}_{\text{bw}} = \beta + T^{-1}\left(\mathbf{Q}_{\mu x} + T^{-1}\Omega_{xo}\right)^{-1}\left(\Omega_{xyo} - \Omega_{xo}\beta\right) = \beta + O(T^{-1}). \quad (6.41)$$

To reduce the inconsistency up to a $O(T^{-2})$ term, we can consider the following modified between group estimators.

$$\hat{\mathbf{b}}_{\text{bw}}^+ = (\bar{\mathbf{x}}^{*\prime}\bar{\mathbf{x}}^* - \bar{\mathbf{x}}^{+\prime}\bar{\mathbf{x}}^+)^{-1}(\bar{\mathbf{x}}^{*\prime}\bar{\mathbf{y}}^* - \bar{\mathbf{x}}^{+\prime}\bar{\mathbf{y}}^+),$$

where

$$\tilde{\mathbf{x}}_{it}^+ = \mathbf{x}_{it} - \frac{2}{T}\sum_{t=1}^{T/2}\mathbf{x}_{it} = \mathbf{x}_{it}^o - \frac{2}{T}\sum_{t=1}^{T/2}\mathbf{x}_{it}^o,$$

and

$$\bar{\mathbf{x}}_i^+ = \frac{1}{T}\sum_{t=1}^{T}\tilde{\mathbf{x}}_{it}^+ = [-\mathbf{x}_{i1}^o - \dots - \mathbf{x}_{i,T/2}^o + \mathbf{x}_{i,T/2+1}^o + \dots + \mathbf{x}_{iT}^o]/T.$$

Then this modified estimators reduce the inconsistency to $O(T^{-2})$. Note that

$$\text{plim}_{n\to\infty} \frac{1}{n} \sum_{i=1}^{n} \left[(\bar{\mathbf{x}}_i - \bar{\mathbf{x}})'(\bar{\mathbf{x}}_i - \bar{\mathbf{x}}) - (\bar{\mathbf{x}}_i^{o+} - \bar{\mathbf{x}}^{o+})'(\bar{\mathbf{x}}_i^{o+} - \bar{\mathbf{x}}^{o+}) \right]$$

$$= \mathbf{Q}_{\mu x} + \frac{\Omega_{xo}}{T} - \frac{\Omega_{xo}^+}{T} = \mathbf{Q}_{\mu x} + O(T^{-2}).$$

Also we have

$$\frac{\Omega_{xo} - \Omega_{xo}^+}{T} = \mathbb{E} \frac{1}{n} \frac{1}{T^2} \sum_{i=1}^{n} \left(\sum_{t=1}^{T/2} \mathbf{x}_{it}^o \right)' \left(\sum_{t=T/2+1}^{T} \mathbf{x}_{it}^o \right) < \frac{4}{T^2} \sum_{s=1}^{T/2-1} s|\Gamma(s)|$$

$$< \frac{4}{T^2} \mathbf{M} = O(T^{-2}),$$

where $\Gamma(s) = \mathbb{E}\left(\mathbf{x}_{it}^{o\prime} \mathbf{x}_{it+s}^o\right)$. Hence the probability limit of $\hat{\mathbf{b}}_{bw}^+$ becomes

$$\text{plim}_{n\to\infty} \hat{\mathbf{b}}_{bw}^+ = \beta + O(T^{-2}).$$

Note that the adjusted term, $\bar{\mathbf{x}}^{+\prime}\bar{\mathbf{x}}^+$, eliminates the contemporaneous variance for the time-varying components completely and the covariance terms partially. Hence after the adjustment, the leftover term becomes sufficiently small and can be ignored. When the regressors are not serially correlated, there is no leftover term so that the biases do not exist at all. It is also important to note that the existence of the bias of the between group estimator causes a somewhat serious problem for statistical inference. The standard t-statistics of the between group estimators do not converge to the standard normal distribution unless $n/T^2 \to 0$ as $n, T \to \infty$. Meanwhile, the modified between group estimators require only $n/T^4 \to \infty$.

Get $\hat{\mathbf{b}}_{bw}^+$ and then construct the regression residuals

$$\hat{\mathbf{u}}^* = \bar{\mathbf{y}}^* - \bar{\mathbf{x}}^* \hat{\mathbf{b}}_{bw}^+, \quad \hat{\mathbf{u}}^+ = \bar{\mathbf{y}}^+ - \bar{\mathbf{x}}^+ \hat{\mathbf{b}}_{bw}^+.$$

Define

$$\eta_{iT} = \hat{\bar{u}}_i^* - \hat{\bar{u}}_i^+, \quad \mathbf{X}_{iT} = \bar{\mathbf{x}}_i^{*\prime} \bar{\mathbf{x}}_i^* - \bar{\mathbf{x}}_i^{+\prime} \bar{\mathbf{x}}_i^+.$$

Then the covariance matrix can be written as

$$\left(\sum_i^n \mathbf{X}_{iT} \right)^{-1} \left(\sum_i^n \hat{\eta}_{iT}^2 \mathbf{X}_{iT} \right)^{-1} \left(\sum_i^n \mathbf{X}_{iT} \right)^{-1}.$$

When there is no heteroskedasticity, the covariance matrix further becomes

$$\frac{1}{n}\sum_i^n \hat{\eta}_{iT}^2 \left(\sum_i^n \mathbf{x}_{iT}\right)^{-1},$$

and it converges in probability to the true covariance matrix.

6.4.3 Appendix C: econometric application

Many empirical panel regressions have the following form

$$y_{it} = \alpha + \mathbf{z}_i \mathbf{b}_1 + \mathbf{x}_{it}\mathbf{b}_2 + u_{it}, \quad u_{it} = a_i - \alpha + e_{it}, \tag{6.42}$$

where parameters of interest are both $\mathbf{b}_1$ and $\mathbf{b}_2$. Usually, $\mathbf{z}_i$ variables are time invariant individual characteristics, such as gender, education attainment, and race. Because of the time invariant variables in $\mathbf{z}_i$, the within group transformation for the fixed effects regression completely eliminates the $\mathbf{z}_i$ variables. Hence the within group transformation is not an option.

Let

$$\mu_{yi} = \alpha + \mathbf{z}_i \beta_1 + \boldsymbol{\mu}_{xi}\beta_2 + v_i,$$

and

$$y_{it}^o = a_i + \mathbf{x}_{it}^o \gamma + \varepsilon_{it},$$

where we assume that $E(\mathbf{z}_i \cdot v_j) = E(\boldsymbol{\mu}_{xi} \cdot v_j) = 0$, but $E(\mathbf{z}_i \cdot \boldsymbol{\mu}_{xi}) = \sigma_{z\mu} \neq 0$ and $\beta_2 \neq \gamma$, where '$\cdot$' stands for the Hadamard product. Then the pooled estimators of β become inconsistent. To see this, we expand y_{it} as

$$y_{it} = \mu_{yi} + y_{it}^o = \alpha + \mathbf{z}_i \beta_1 + \left(\boldsymbol{\mu}_{xi} + \mathbf{x}_{it}^o\right)\gamma + v_i + a_i + \boldsymbol{\mu}_{xi}(\gamma - \beta_2) + \varepsilon_{it}. \tag{6.43}$$

Hence, u_{it} in (6.42) becomes

$$u_{it} = v_i + a_i + \boldsymbol{\mu}_{xi}(\gamma - \beta_2) + \varepsilon_{it}, \tag{6.44}$$

and

$$E(\mathbf{z}_i \cdot u_{it}) = E[\mathbf{z}_i \cdot \boldsymbol{\mu}_{xi}(\gamma - \beta_2)] = \sigma_{z\mu} \cdot (\gamma - \beta_2) \neq 0, \tag{6.45}$$

$$E(x_{it} \cdot u_{it}) = E[\boldsymbol{\mu}_{xi} \cdot \boldsymbol{\mu}_{xi}(\gamma - \beta_2)] \neq 0. \tag{6.46}$$

Hence both estimators for $\mathbf{b}_1$ and $\mathbf{b}_2$ become inconsistent.

Hausman and Taylor (1981) considered exactly this case. Their critical assumption is that some variables in $\mathbf{z}_i$ and $\mathbf{x}_{it}$ are not correlated with the regression errors. To find such variables, Hausman and Taylor suggested three tests, which are basically to identify whether some of γ is equal to β_2. If there is no such a variable, then there is no appropriate instrumental variable.

However, we can easily overcome this issue by running the following two regressions. The first regression is the fixed effects regression with only time-varying variables – that is x_{it}.

$$y_{it} = \alpha_i + x_{it}b_2 + \text{ error.}$$

These within group estimators are consistently estimating the dynamic relationship γ. That is, $\hat{b}_{2wg} \to^p \gamma$.

The second regression is the modified between group regression. For time invariant variables, regressors do not need to be modified. But for time-varying variables, the regressors should be modified to reduce the small T bias. For example, the modified between group estimators are given by

$$\begin{bmatrix} \hat{b}_{1,bw} \\ \hat{b}_{2,bw}^+ \end{bmatrix} = \begin{bmatrix} \tilde{z}'\tilde{z} & \tilde{z}'\bar{x}^* \\ \tilde{z}'\bar{x}^* & \bar{x}^{*\prime}\bar{x}^* - \bar{x}^{+\prime}\bar{x}^+ \end{bmatrix}^{-1} \begin{bmatrix} \tilde{z}'\bar{y}^* \\ \bar{x}^{*\prime}\bar{y}^* - \bar{x}^{+\prime}\bar{y}^+ \end{bmatrix}. \tag{6.47}$$

Then it is straightforward to show that

$$E\begin{bmatrix} \hat{b}_{1,bw} - \beta \\ \hat{b}_{2,bw}^+ - \beta_2 \end{bmatrix} = \begin{bmatrix} 0 \\ O(T^{-2}) \end{bmatrix}.$$

The covariance matrix is given by

$$\frac{1}{n}\sum_{i=1}^{n}\hat{\eta}_{iT}^2 \begin{bmatrix} \tilde{z}'\tilde{z} & \tilde{z}'\bar{x}^* \\ \tilde{z}'\bar{x}^* & \bar{x}^{*\prime}\bar{x}^* - \bar{x}^{+\prime}\bar{x}^+ \end{bmatrix}^{-1}.$$

In this section, we discussed the economic meaning of the static relationship and how to estimate it consistently and efficiently. All these discussions, however, are valid only when the panel data are free from cross-sectional dependence. It is well known that the cross-sectional regressions are not well defined when the data are cross-sectionally dependent (Andrews, 2005). In practice, many empirical studies have used simple, common, time-fixed effects to handle cross-sectional dependence. That is, the inclusion of the time-fixed effects in (6.42) becomes

$$y_{it} = \alpha + z_i b_1 + x_{it}b_2 + \theta_t + u_{it}. \tag{6.48}$$

The next chapter discusses under what conditions the simple time-fixed effects in (6.48) can effectively handle cross-sectional dependence.

Notes

1   The number of observations is just ten. College Board considers ten different income groups: The lowest income group is between \$0 and \$20,000. The highest income group is more than \$200,000. For each income group, College Board reports the average of SAT scores.
2   Let the true means of λ_{yi} and λ_{xi} be λ_y and λ_x. Since the common dynamic relationship can be identified only with the cross-sectional averages, this relationship can be written as $h_t^y = \phi h_t^x + e_t$ where $h_t^y = \lambda_y' F_{yt}$ and $h_t^x = \lambda_x' F_{xt}$.
3   See Levitt (2004) for the excellent survey on this topic.
4   The data are obtained from uniform crime report.
5   It is important to address that the firm-level data should be considered the aggregate data as long as a firm consists of many individuals.
6   Of course, a mass hysteria death toll by a disease – for example, a pest outbreak in Europe in the 14th century – can influence the common factor directly. We exclude such a case here.

7

CONVERGENCE

In this chapter, we study the notion of the convergence or divergence and review how to test convergence. The convergence has been a prominent element in social science. Karl Marx is the first economist who predicted the income divergence. In fact, he predicted the divergence of individual incomes and such divergence would lead to an economic crisis. Later, Maynard Keynes refined Marx's business cycle theory and suggested a state intervention to moderate a cyclical movement. Even though the notions of divergence and convergence are well understood by social scientists, it was not easy to define statistically. In this chapter, we will study how the statistical notion of the convergence has been developed recently.

Researchers have used three different concepts of the convergence, depending on how to test the convergence: β-convergence, relative convergence, and σ-convergence. The β-convergence is the most popularly used concept in economic growth. In the early 1990s, Robert Barro and Xavier Sala-i-Martin suggested this concept to test the growth convergence. They further developed the β-convergence concept to the conditional and absolute β-convergence. A typical verbal interpretation for the β-convergence goes like this: "*Initially poor countries grow faster than initially rich countries.*" As Milton Friedman pointed out in his short communication in 1992 under the title of "Do Old Fallacies Ever Die?," this interpretation was originally suggested by Horace Secrist in his book *The Triumph of Mediocrity in Business* in 1933. In this book, Secrist showed that initially, most successful firms tended to do worse over time; meanwhile, initially less successful firms tended to improve later. Harold Hotelling, however, gave the critical review in 1933 that the Secrist's finding was just a statistical illusion and suggested that the true notion of the convergence should be related to the variance of the distribution. Later, Milton Friedman cited Hotelling's critics in his communication in 1992: *The real test of a tendency to convergence would be in showing a consistent diminution of variance.* This concept is called 'σ-convergence.' In fact, during the 1990s, many applied econometricians, including Evans (1996) and Quah (1996), attempted to test for σ-convergence under very restrictive conditions.

Later, a more flexible test and precise econometric modeling for the convergence is proposed by Phillips and Sul (2007). However, what they proposed is not exactly σ-convergence but is called the relative convergence, which holds if the relative ratio of any pair of variables is converging unity in the long run. The notion of the relative convergence is particularly useful when the panel data show distinct trending behaviors.

A formal test for σ-convergence appears recently. Kong, Phillips, and Sul (2018) propose the notion of 'weak' σ-convergence and provide a simple trend regression approach to test the weak σ-convergence.

7.1 β-Convergence: pitfalls of cross-country regressions

The β-convergence was born from the Solow growth model, where all countries share the same but exogenous technology. If other parameters in the model, such as population growth rates and discount rates, are homogeneous across countries, the steady-state growth rate becomes identical. The transition path is the key for the β-convergence.

Write the production function in the neoclassical theory of growth with labor augmented technological progress as $Y = F(K, LHA)$ and define

$$\tilde{Y} = f(\tilde{k}), \quad \tilde{Y} = Y/LHA, \quad \tilde{K} = K/LHA, \quad Y = \tilde{Y}HA = \tilde{Y}A,$$

where Y is total output, L is the quantity of labor input, H is the stock of human capital (here normalized to unity), A is the state of technology, K is physical capital, and $\tilde{Y}$ is output per effective labor unit. Using a Cobb-Douglas technology, the log-linearized approximation to the Solow model – which is the transitional path – is given by

$$y_{it} = \tilde{y}^* + [\tilde{y}_{i0} - \tilde{y}^*] \exp(-\delta t) + a_t \tag{7.1}$$

where y_{it} is log per capita real income, $\tilde{y}^*$ is the corresponding log steady-state level, a_t is the log technology progress, which is homogenous for all countries. The transition path in (7.1) implies that if there exists any deviation from the equilibrium path, then the deviation converges the steady-state level $\tilde{y}^*$ over time. The pitfalls of cross-country regressions start from the next interpretation.

Barro and Sala-i-Martin (1992) rewrote the log per capita real income in (7.1) as

$$y_{it} = \tilde{y}^*(1 - \exp(-\delta t)) + \tilde{y}_{i0} \exp(-\delta t) + a_t \tag{7.2}$$

and then under homogeneous technology, they claimed that[1]

$$\Delta y_{it} < \Delta y_{jt} \Leftrightarrow \tilde{y}_{i0} > \tilde{y}_{j0}. \tag{7.3}$$

The condition in (7.3) is called the β-convergence.

The empirical regression or non-augmented Solow growth regression is given by

$$\frac{y_{iT} - y_{i0}}{T} = a + \beta y_{i0} + u_i, \tag{7.4}$$

where $\beta = T^{-1}(1 - \exp(-\delta T))$. The null hypothesis is $\beta = 0$ or no β-convergence. If $\hat{\beta}$ is negative and statistically significant, then this empirical evidence has been interpreted that Solow model is correct. If the steady-state in the long run is different across countries, then the non-augmented Solow regression in (7.4) becomes misspecified, which results in inconsistent estimation of $\hat{\beta}$. In this case, the variables that affect the long-run, steady-state level should be included in the regression.

Let z_{it} be a vector of variables that affect the long-run, steady-state level. Further, let z_i be the long-run average of z_{it}. Then the augmented Solow regression is given by

$$\frac{y_{iT} - y_{i0}}{T} = a + \beta y_{i0} + z_i'\gamma + e_i. \tag{7.5}$$

If the estimate of the slope coefficient on the initial income is negative and significantly different from zero, then evidence has been interpreted that y_{it} converges conditionally.

Simply, this concept was used to explain the conditions for poor countries to catch up with rich countries. This interpretation is exactly the same as Horace Secrist's concept. Both concepts examine the convergence pattern of initially poor and rich firms (or countries), but the β-convergence deals with individual units; meanwhile, Secrist's concept applies to the convergence pattern among the subgroups based on the initial observations. They sound similar to each other, but statistically these two concepts are different. To see this, consider the following example.

$$y_{it} = b_i t + e_{it}, \quad e_{it} = \rho e_{it-1} + v_{it}, \tag{7.6}$$

where $b_i \sim iidN(0, \sigma_b^2)$ and $v_{it} \sim iidN(0, 1)$. Under this setting, there is a positive relationship between the initial observation $- b_i + e_{i1} -$ and the growth rate of y_{it}, b_i. That is,

$$\mathbb{E}\frac{1}{n}\sum_{i=1}^n (b_i + e_{i1}) b_i = \sigma_b^2 > 0.$$

In other words, initially rich countries grow faster than initially poor countries. Hence the β-convergence should not hold at all.

However, due to the statistical illusion, the β-convergence may hold. To see this, consider the followings: Sort y_{it} by the first observation and form three subgroups – initially low, median, high – and then take the cross-sectional means. Figure 7.1 shows the cross-sectional means of these three subgroups based on the initial observation ordering. Evidently, the initially rich group seems to grow slowly compared with the initially poor group. The underlying reason is simple. The subgroups are made based on the initial observations. Consider the low subgroup. Those who have smaller b_i may be included in this group, but more likely those who have smaller e_{i1} are assigned to this group since the values of b_i are bounded between zero and 0.1. Meanwhile, the values of e_{i1} are not bounded, but distributed as a normal. Since e_{it} follows an AR(1) process, e_{it} converges zero over time. Hence as t increases, the cross-sectional mean in the low subgroup will increase faster than that in the high subgroup.

It seems to be innocent to derive (7.3) from (7.1). However, the transitional path in (7.1) is simply a stability condition that y_{it} is converging $\tilde{y}^*$ over time. And the condition in (7.3) is just a necessary condition for the convergence. In fact, if the condition in (7.3) holds for every t, then it implies the divergence rather than the convergence. To see this, consider the two following data-generating processes.

Model A: $y_{it} = a_i + b_i t + y_{it}^o,$

Model B: $y_{it} = a_i + (b_i + c_i t^{-\alpha})t + y_{it}^o$ for $\alpha > 0,$

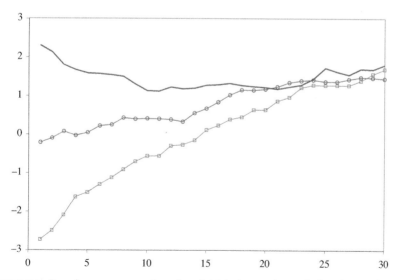

FIGURE 7.1   Pseudo convergence based on initial observation ordering (true DGP: no β-convergence, wrong initial subgrouping leads to statistical illusion of the β-convergence)

where $t = 0, 1, ..., T$. When $t = 0$, the initial incomes in both models become a_i under the assumption of $y_{i0}^o = 0$. For a time being, let's ignore the random part, y_{it}^o. The β-convergence has been tested in the following way.

$$\beta\text{-convergence} : Cov\left(y_{i0}, \frac{y_{iT} - y_{i0}}{T}\right) < 0.$$

Note that $(y_{iT} - y_{i0})/T$ is called 'long-run average,' which estimates the long-run growth rate of y_{it}. In fact, the limit of the long-run average becomes the growth rate in the steady-state in both Model A and B. When we ignore the random part, y_{it}^o, the negative covariance between the initial income and the long-run growth rate exists if

Model A: $Cov(a_i, b_i) < 0,$

Model B: $Cov(a_i, b_i) < 0$ or $Cov(a_i, c_i) < 0.$

In both Model A and B, the negative covariance between a_i and b_i implies a permanent divergence of y_{it} as $t \to \infty$. Note that in Model A, b_i represents heterogeneous technology. Hence the negative correlation between the initial income and the technology growth rate leads to temporal convergence initially but permanent divergence in the long run. In Model B, the growth rate of technology progress is time varying: $b_i + c_i t^{-\alpha}$. Even when there is no correlation between a_i and b_i, the temporal convergence holds as long as $Cov(a_i, c_i) < 0$. However, as long as $b_i \neq b_j$, the difference between y_{it} and y_{jt} gets larger in the long run. Only when $b_i = b$ for all i, but $Cov(a_i, c_i) < 0$, do initially poor countries grow faster than initially rich countries, but the growth rate of poor countries decreases over time as t increases and eventually reach at the steady-state level b. If initially rich countries have $c_i = 0$, then their growth rates would be around the steady-state level. Of course, Model B is just an example of what the growth economists actually want to capture in the rapid initial catching up and then slowing down the growth rate after a certain point. Therefore, the β-convergence condition is just a necessary condition but not a sufficient condition for the convergence. In other words, the evidence for the β-convergence does not support the Solow growth model at all, but the Solow growth model can lead to the β-convergence condition.

7.2 Relative convergence

Phillips and Sul (2007) propose the notion of the relative convergence to examine whether the actual data supports the Solow growth model. If the technology progress is homogeneous, then the growth rate of the log per capita real income must converge the steady-state level. In other words, in the long run, the slope coefficients on the time trend must be identical.

7.2.1 Notion of relative convergence

Phillips and Sul (2007) allow temporal time-varying slope coefficients on the trend term. In fact, they go beyond this and write up y_{it} as

$$y_{it} = b_{it}\theta_t, \tag{7.7}$$

where θ_t is a dominant (non)stochastic trend component, and b_{it} is just a leftover term. For example, Model A and B can be rewritten as

Model A: $\quad y_{it} = \left(b_i + a_i/t + y_{it}^o/t\right)t,$

Model B: $\quad y_{it} = \left(b_i + a_i/t + c_i t^{-\alpha} + y_{it}^o/t\right)t.$

In the long run (as $t \to \infty$), b_{it} in both models converges b_i. The convergence condition for y_{it}, hence, requires that the long-run slope coefficients, $b_i = b$. The relative convergence holds if and only if

$$\lim_{t \to \infty} \frac{y_{it}}{y_{jt}} = 1 \text{ for } i \neq j. \tag{7.8}$$

The condition in (7.7) can be interpreted as a model with time-varying factor loadings. If y_{it} converges θ_t, then this implies that y_{it} is perfectly correlated with y_{jt} in the long run. Rewrite (7.7) as

$$y_{it} = (b_i + \varepsilon_{it})\theta_t$$

where ε_{it} is cross-sectionally independent with a zero mean. Then the condition in (7.8) is equivalent to state as

$$b_i = b, \text{ and } V(\varepsilon_{it}) \to 0 \text{ as } t \to \infty. \tag{7.9}$$

If either $b_i \neq b$ for some i or $V(\varepsilon_{it})$ is fluctuating over time, then y_{it} diverges. Also the relative convergence implies the decrease in the cross-sectional dispersion among y_{it} over time.

7.2.2 How to test: log t regression

If $\theta_t \neq 0$ for all t, then the relative value of the time-varying factor loadings, b_{it}, can be retrieved by using the ratio formula. For example, the relative value of b_{it} to the cross-sectional average can be obtained by

$$h_{it} = \frac{y_{it}}{n^{-1}\sum_{i=1}^{n} y_{it}} = \frac{b_{it}}{n^{-1}\sum_{i=1}^{n} b_{it}}, \tag{7.10}$$

where h_{it} is called 'relative transition curve.' Depending on the denominator, the economic meaning of h_{it} changes.[2] The convergence condition in (7.9) implies that the variance of h_{it} converges zero. Define H_t as

$$H_t = \frac{1}{n}\sum_{i=1}^{n} (h_{it} - 1)^2.$$

Then the inverse variance ratio, H_1/H_t, will increase over time if the cross-sectional dispersion of h_{it} or b_{it} decreases over time. If $b_i \neq b$ for some i but $V(\varepsilon_{it}) \to 0$, the inverse variance ratio must be increasing initially but should be fluctuating over time in the long run. To compensate for the initial and temporal increase in H_1/H_t under the divergence, Phillips and Sul (2007) introduced a penalty function $L(t)$. The penalty function is a class of slowly varying function over time. For example, $\log t$ is a slowly varying time function in the sense that $\log t/t^a \to 0$ with any $a > 0$. Under the convergence, the increasing speed of H_1/H_t is much faster than the rate of divergence of $L(t)$. But under the divergence, the increasing speed of H_1/H_t is slower than that of $L(t)$. The following simple $\log t$ regression can distinguish the convergence case from the divergence case.

$$\log\left(\frac{H_1}{H_t}\right) - 2\log L(t) = a + b \log t + u_t.$$

Since the $\log t$ function is rapidly increasing initially, Phillips and Sul (2007) suggested to eliminate the first third of the sample. Also u_t is serially correlated, the long-run variance or HAC (heteroskedasticity autocorrelation consistent) estimator should be used. Under the null of the convergence, the t-ratio of $\hat{b}$ converges positive infinity. Meanwhile, under the alternative of the divergence, the t-ratio of $\hat{b}$ converges negative infinity. Define the t-ratio as

$$t_{\hat{b}} = \frac{\hat{b}}{\sqrt{\hat{\Omega}_u^2 / \sum_{t=r}^{T}\left(\log t - (T-r)^{-1}\sum_{t=r}^{T}\log t\right)^2}},$$

where $r = \text{int}(T/3)$ and $\hat{\Omega}_u^2$ is the long run variance of $\hat{u}_t$. Then the null of the convergence cannot be rejected if $t_{\hat{b}} \geq 1.65$ at the 5% level (one side test).

When a panel data of interest is, for example, a panel of price indexes, the convergence occurs at the point of the base year since all price indexes become identical at the base year. In this case, the long differenced data can be used to eliminate the base year effect. Let y_{it}^* be the true latent variable, but the observed data y_{it} is indexed by the based year. That is,

$$y_{it} = y_{it}^* - y_{i\tau}^*,$$

where τ is the base year. Then the long differenced series eliminates the base year term.

$$y_{it} - y_{i1} = y_{it}^* - y_{i1}^*$$

However, instead of $y_{i\tau}^*$, the long-differenced series includes the initial observations. To eliminate the impact of the initial observation, some initial observations should be discarded further.

7.2.3   Clustering algorithm

The log t regression has been popularly used partly because the automatic clustering algorithm has been available. Also Du (2017) provides STATA codes for the clustering algorithm.[3] When the null of the convergence is rejected, still some individual units form a sub-convergent group. The following automatic clustering algorithm selects the club members.

Step 1 (Last income ordering):

Order individuals in the panel according to the last observation in the panel. In cases where there is substantial time series volatility in y_{it}, the ordering may be done according to the time series average, $(T - [Ta])^{-1} \sum_{t=[Ta]+1}^{T} y_{it}$, over the last fraction $(f = 1 - a)$ of the sample (for example, $f = 1/3$ or $1/2$).

Step 2 (Core group formation):

Selecting the first k highest individuals in the panel to form the subgroup G_k for some $n > k \geq 2$, run the log t regression and calculate the convergence test statistic $t_k = t(G_k)$ for this subgroup. Choose the core group size k^* by maximizing t_k over k according to the criterion:

$$k^* = \arg \max_k \{t_k\} \quad \text{subject to} \quad \min \{t_k\} > -1.65. \tag{7.11}$$

The condition $\min \{t_k\} > -1.65$ plays a key role in ensuring that the null hypothesis of convergence is supported for each k. If the condition $\min \{t_k\} > -1.65$ does not hold for $k = 2$, then the highest individual in G_k can be dropped from each subgroup and new subgroups $G_{2j} = \{2,..., j\}$ formed for $2 \leq j \leq n$. The step can be repeated with test statistics $t_j = t(G_{2j})$. If the condition minimum $\{t_j\} > -1.65$ is not satisfied for the first $j = 2$, the step may be repeated again, dropping the highest individuals in G_j and proceeding as before.

Step 3 (Sieve individuals for club membership):

Let $G_{k^*}^c$ be the complementary set to the core group G_{k^*}. Adding one individual in $G_{k^*}^c$ at a time to the k^* core members of G_{k^*}, run the log t test. Denote the $t-$ statistic from this regression as $\hat{t}$. Include the individual in the convergence club if $\hat{t} > c$, where c is some chosen critical value. Run the log t test with this first sub-convergence group and make sure $t_{\hat{b}} > -1.65$ for the whole group. If not, raise the critical value, c, to increase the discriminatory power of the log t test and repeat this step until $t_{\hat{b}} > -1.65$ with the first sub-convergence group. Note that Phillips and Sul (2007) used $c = 0$.

Step 4 (Stopping rule):

Form a subgroup of the individuals for which $\hat{t} < c$ in Step 3. Run the log t test for this subgroup to see if $t_{\hat{b}} > -1.65$ and this cluster converges. If not, repeat Step 1 through Step 3 on this subgroup to determine whether there is a smaller subgroup of convergent members of the panel. If there is no k in Step 2 for which $t_k > -1.65$, then the remaining individuals diverge.

It is important to note that the clustering results may be influenced by the choice of the core members. If all core members are in the same convergent club, then asymptotically – when T is very large – the clustering results must be robust. To select convergent members conservatively, one can increase the threshold value c. As the value c increases, the number of sub-convergent clubs increases as well. Once all sub-convergent clubs are collected, it is important to check whether a union of two or three sub-convergent clubs is converging.

7.2.4 Pitfalls of the log t regression and alternative solutions

The log t regression has the following two problems. Both problems happen usually when some of individuals or cross-sectional units do not have distinct (stochastic) trending behaviors. Let's look at the issues in detail.

Issue 1 (Strong restriction: all $y_{it} \geq 0$ for all i and t) First, the relative transition is not well defined if some of y_{it} are negative. In an extreme case, if the sample cross-sectional mean for a particular t becomes zero, then the relative transition curve cannot be defined. Even when the true cross-sectional averages of y_{it} are all positive, the sample cross-sectional mean can be close to zero if some of y_{it} are negative. In this case, the relative transition curve increases suddenly so that the variance of h_{it} increases as well, which hampers the testing result seriously.

Solution 1 (Add cross-sectional mean) Let $\bar{y}_{nt}$ be the sample cross-sectional average. Check if $\bar{y}_{nt} > 0$ for all t. As long as the sample cross-sectional averages are positive, the following modification works well. Let's define y_{it}^+ as

$$y_{it}^+ = y_{it} + c\frac{1}{n}\sum_{i=1}^{n} y_{it} > 0 \text{ for all } t. \tag{7.12}$$

Then from the direct calculation, the modified sample variance of h_{it}^+ becomes

$$H_t^+ = \frac{\frac{1}{n}\sum_{i=1}^{n}\left(y_{it}^+ - \frac{1}{n}\sum_{i=1}^{n} y_{it}^+\right)^2}{\left(\frac{1}{n}\sum_{i=1}^{n} y_{it}^+\right)^2} = \frac{\frac{1}{n}\sum_{i=1}^{n}\left(b_{it} - \frac{1}{n}\sum_{i=1}^{n} b_{it}\right)^2}{c^2\left(\frac{1}{n}\sum_{i=1}^{n} b_{it}\right)^2}.$$

Taking the logarithm yields

$$\log \frac{H_1^*}{H_t^*} = \log \frac{H_1}{H_t},$$

since c is just a constant. As long as the sign of the cross-sectional mean of y_{it} does not change for all t, the simple transformation with an arbitrary large c in (7.12) always provides the true log H_1/H_t ratio.

Issue 2 (Unit of measurement issue) Let $Y_{it} = Y_{it}^* \times k$, where k is the unit of measure. For an example, \$1,000 ($k = 1$) can be written as 1K ($k = 1,000$). Further let

$$y_{it}^* = \log Y_{it}^* = b_{it}\theta_t,$$

then

$$y_{it} = \log Y_{it} = b_{it}\theta_t + \log k.$$

The relative transition curve with y_{it} is defined as

$$h_{it} = \frac{b_{it}\theta_t + \log k}{\frac{1}{N}\sum_{i=1}^{N} b_{it}\theta_t + \log k},$$

and its cross-sectional variance is given by

$$H_t = \frac{\frac{1}{N}\sum_{i=1}^{N}\left(b_{it} - \frac{1}{N}\sum_{i=1}^{N} b_{it}\right)^2 \theta_t^2}{\left(\frac{1}{N}\sum_{i=1}^{N} b_{it}\right)^2 \theta_t^2 + (\log k)^2 + 2\log k\left(\frac{1}{N}\sum_{i=1}^{N} b_{it}\theta_t\right)}$$

$$\neq \frac{\frac{1}{N}\sum_{i=1}^{N}\left(b_{it} - \frac{1}{N}\sum_{i=1}^{N} b_{it}\right)^2}{\left(\frac{1}{N}\sum_{i=1}^{N} b_{it}\right)^2} = H_t^*.$$

By using the direct calculation, the difference between H_t and H_t^* can be written as

$$\log H_t = \log H_t^* - \log\left[1 + \log k \frac{\log k + 2\bar{y}_{n,t}^*}{\left(\bar{y}_{n,t}^*\right)^2}\right] = \log H_t - f(k),$$

where $f(k)$ is an increasing function of t if the cross-sectional average of y_{it}^* increases over time. Hence the role of $f(k)$ becomes more or less a penalty function. In other words, as the observed samples are expressed as a smaller unit (alternatively as k increases), the penalty function increases so that the evidence for the convergence becomes weakened.

Solution 2: Using long difference or minimum value The unit problem can be easily avoided if the long difference is used. Let $y_{it} = b_{it}\theta_t + \log k$. Then

$$\Delta_L y_{it} := y_{it} - y_{i1} = b_{it}\theta_t - b_{i1}\theta_1 = y_{it}^* - y_{i1}^*.$$

This method is actually suggested by Phillips and Sul (2007) to avoid the base year problem. But this long differenced method makes $\Delta_L y_{i1} = 0$ for all i. In other words, the first modified observations become identical across i. To avoid the initial effects, one needs to discard some initial observations. However, taking a long difference can produce negative observations if $y_{i1} > y_{it}$ for some t. In this case, one can utilize Solution 1 shown earlier. However, when the length of time series observations is not enough, this method leads to the decrease of the power of the test (hard to reject the null of convergence even when the alternative is true). The alternative method is rather ad hoc, but useful in practice. Define $y_m^* = \min_{1 \le i \le n, 1 \le t \le T}\{y_{it}^*\}$. Similarly, define $y_m = \min_{1 \le i \le n,\ 1 \le t \le T}\{y_{it}\}$. Then it is straightforward to show that

$$y_{it} - y_m = y_{it}^* - y_m^* = y_{it}^\dagger. \tag{7.13}$$

When $t = 1$,

$$y_{i1}^\dagger = y_{i1}^* - y_m^* \ne y_{j1}^* - y_m^* \text{ if } i \ne j. \tag{7.14}$$

Hence the initial observations are different across i so that this method does not require to eliminate some initial observations.

In sum, when y_{it} does not have a distinct (stochastic) trend, the notion of the relative convergence does not hold. We will examine several empirical examples in detail later. Nonetheless, in this case, the notion of weak σ-convergence works better, which we will study next.

7.3 σ-Convergence

Testing the relative convergence becomes impossible when y_{it} changes signs over time, or the common factor θ_t does not contain any (non)stochastic trend. In such cases, a more appropriate notion is σ-convergence, a concept that is defined in terms of declining cross-sectional dispersion over time. This concept was originally suggested by Hotelling (1933) and is formally defined later by Kong, Phillips, and Sul (2018, KPS hereafter). Note that the relative convergence focuses only on the σ-convergence in the relative transition curves (or time-varying factor loading coefficients). Only when y_{it} shares the same long-run average ($a_i = a$ for all i), the cross-sectional variance of y_{it}, K_t, is possibly converging zero. Otherwise, the cross-sectional variance of y_{it} converges a non-zero constant as n, $T \to \infty$. KPS call this type of the σ-convergence "weak σ-convergence" and define it statistically as

$$Cov(K_t, t) \leq 0. \tag{7.15}$$

The weak σ-convergence is more restrictive than the relative convergence when the common factor has a distinct trend behavior. The difference between the σ-convergence and the relative convergence can be shown by using the following example.

$$y_{it} = a_i + (b + \varepsilon_i t^{-1/2})t + \epsilon_{it}t^{-\beta}, \text{ with } \beta > 0, \tag{7.16}$$

where $\epsilon_{it} \sim iid(0, \sigma_\epsilon^2)$ over (i, t), $\varepsilon_i \sim iid(0, \sigma_\varepsilon^2)$, and the components $(a_i, \varepsilon_i, \epsilon_{it})$ are all independent. Instead of the linear trend term in (7.16), a stochastic common factor can be placed. It is easy to see that relative convergence holds but not weak σ-convergence. In particular, taking a pair (y_{it}, y_{jt}) we have

$$\text{plim}_{t\to\infty} \frac{y_{it}}{y_{jt}} = \text{plim}_{t\to\infty} \frac{b + \varepsilon_i t^{-1/2}}{b + \varepsilon_j t^{-1/2}} = 1, \tag{7.17}$$

but when considering cross section variances, such as $K_{nt}^y = n^{-1}\sum_{i=1}^n (y_{it} - n^{-1}\sum_{i=1}^n y_{it})^2$, we have

$$K_t^y = \text{plim}_{n\to\infty} K_{nt}^y = \sigma_a^2 + \sigma_\varepsilon^2 t + \sigma_\epsilon^2 t^{-2\beta} \text{ with } \beta > 0, \tag{7.18}$$

where σ_a^2 is the variance of a_i. As long as $\sigma_\varepsilon^2 > 0$, the cross-sectional dispersion of y_{it} increases over time. Thus, the condition of $\varepsilon_i \neq \varepsilon_j$ for some $i \neq j$ is sufficient to prevent σ-convergence.

Meanwhile, when the common factor contains a weak trend component, the relative convergence does not hold, but the weak σ-convergence holds. Consider the next example.

$$y_{it} = a_i + \varepsilon_i t^{-1/2} + \epsilon_{it}t^{-\beta} \text{ with } \beta > 0 \tag{7.19}$$

In this case, the relative convergence does not hold because

$$\text{plim}_{t\to\infty} \frac{y_{it}}{y_{jt}} = \text{plim}_{t\to\infty} \frac{a_i + \varepsilon_i t^{-1/2} + \epsilon_{it}t^{-\beta}}{a_j + \varepsilon_j t^{-1/2} + \epsilon_{jt}t^{-\beta}} = \frac{a_i}{a_j} \neq 1. \tag{7.20}$$

But the weak σ-convergence holds since

$$K_t^y = \sigma_a^2 + \sigma_\varepsilon^2 t^{-1} + \sigma_\epsilon^2 t^{-2\beta} \to \sigma_a^2. \tag{7.21}$$

Therefore, the notion of the σ-convergence is more generally applicable, but also more restrictive than the relative convergence when the common factors have distinct stochastic trends.

KPS propose the following the weak σ-convergence test. Let K_{nt}^y be the sample cross-sectional variance of y_{it}. Next, construct the t-statistic of the OLS estimate $\hat{\phi}$ based on the Newey-West HAC estimator with $L = \text{int}(T^{1/3})$ from the following simple trend regression.

$$K_{nt}^y = a + \phi t + u_t,$$ (7.22)

$$t_{\hat{\phi}} = \frac{\hat{\phi}}{\sqrt{\hat{\Omega}_u^2 / \sum_{t=1}^T \left(t - T^{-1} \sum_{t=1}^T t\right)^2}},$$ (7.23)

where $\hat{u}_t = K_{nt}^y - \hat{a} - \hat{\phi}t$,

$$\hat{\Omega}_u^2 = \frac{1}{T}\sum_{t=1}^T \hat{u}_t^2 + 2\frac{1}{T}\sum_{\ell=1}^L \vartheta_{\ell L} \sum_{t=1}^{T-\ell} \hat{u}_t \hat{u}_{t+\ell},$$ (7.24)

and $\vartheta_{\ell L}$ is the Bartlett lag kernel weight. Then the t-ratio has the following bounds.

$$\begin{array}{ll} t_{\hat{\phi}} < -\sqrt{3} \text{ or } t_{\hat{\phi}} \to -\infty & \text{if } y_{it} \text{ is weakly } \sigma\text{-converging,} \\ t_{\hat{\phi}} > \sqrt{3} \text{ or } t_{\hat{\phi}} \to +\infty & \text{if } y_{it} \text{ is diverging,} \\ t_{\hat{\phi}} \to^d \mathcal{N}(0,1) & \text{if } y_{it} \text{ is fluctuating.} \end{array}$$ (7.25)

Note that $\sqrt{3} \simeq 1.73$ so that usual 5% critical value (one side test, 1.65) can be used for testing the weak σ-convergence. That is, depending on the t-ratio, one can check whether or not y_{it} is weakly σ-converging, fluctuating, or diverging.

$t_{\hat{\phi}} < -1.65$	$-1.65 < t_{\hat{\phi}} < 1.65$	$1.65 < t_{\hat{\phi}}$
weak σ-convergence	fluctuating	σ-divergence

The trend regression in (7.22) is misspecified unless y_{it} is fluctuating over time (in this case, $\phi = 0$). Also, as $n, T \to \infty$, the OLS estimate of ϕ converges zero, but its t-ratio is either diverging $\pm\infty$ if y_{it} is diverging (or weakly σ-converging). In other words, even when the $t_{\hat{\phi}} < -1.73$, it does not mean that K_{nt}^y will diverge negative infinity in the long run.

When y_{it} includes a (non)stochastic trend (or includes common factors with heterogeneous factor loadings), the time-varying pattern of the cross-sectional variance of y_{it} is mainly dependent on the time-varying patterns of the square of the stochastic trend. To see this, assume that y_{it} follows a static factor structure with a single factor.

$$y_{it} = a_i + \lambda_i F_t + u_{it}$$

Then K_t^y becomes

$$K_t^y = \text{plim}_{n\to\infty} K_{nt}^y = \sigma_a^2 + \sigma_\lambda^2 F_t^2 + \sigma_u^2.$$

Hence, regardless of whether u_{it} is weakly σ-converging, K_{nt}^y fluctuates over time.

However, after eliminating the common components, one can re-run the weak σ-convergence test. To be specific, let $\hat{F}_t$ be an estimator of the common factors. Then run the following regression with the estimates of $\hat{F}_t$ for each i.

$$y_{it} = a_i + \lambda_i' \hat{F}_t + u_{it},$$

where the number of the common factors is more than single. If the factor number is single, then the sample cross-sectional average can be used instead of $\hat{F}_t$. Note that for the PC estimation of F_t, the standardization is necessary. However, for the estimation of y_{it}^o, one should not standardize y_{it}.

Next, construct the following measure. It is important to include fixed effects in z_{it}.

$$z_{it} = y_{it} - \hat{\lambda}_i' \hat{F}_t = a_i + y_{it}^o + (\lambda_i' F_t - \hat{\lambda}_i' \hat{F}_t)$$

Finally, run the trend regression with z_{it}.

7.4   Empirical example I: household expenditure data from KLIPS

The following trend regression was run to estimate the initial log expenditure and the expenditure growth rate for each household.

$$\frac{\log C_{iT} - \log C_{i1}}{T - 1} = a + \beta \log C_{i1} + u_i,$$

where C_{it} is the nominal expenditure for the ith household at time t. Figure 7.2 plots the log initial expenditure and the long-run growth rates. Evidently, there is a negative correlation between the two, hence the β-convergence holds. To check whether the negative correlation is due to some outliers, two subgroups are formed based on the Mahalanobis depth (MD) function.[4] The MD values for the first subgroup are greater than 0.2, and those for the second subgroup are greater than 0.4. Evidently, regardless of the MD values, there is negative correlation between the two.

Table 7.1 reports the formal regression results. Evidently, the estimated slope coefficients are all negative and significantly different from zero. Hence there is a strong evidence for the β-convergence. However, as we discussed early, one should not rely on the result of the β-convergence due to its statistical pitfalls.

Next, we ran the log t regressions with various measurement units. The unit of the original data is 10,000 Korean won (more or less around 10 USD). As we

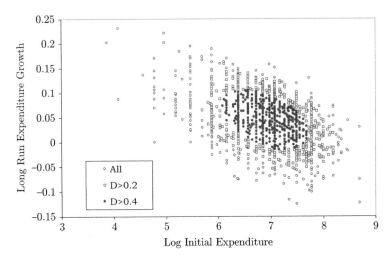

FIGURE 7.2 The negative correlation between log initial expenditure and expenditure growth

TABLE 7.1 Various convergence tests

β-Convergence	Case	$\hat{\beta}$	$t_{\hat{\beta}}$	Convergence
	All	−0.033	−21.84	Yes
	$D_i > 0.2$	−0.034	−18.79	Yes
	$D_i > 0.4$	−0.034	−14.97	Yes
Rel. Convergence	Units	$\hat{b}$	$t_{\hat{b}}$	
	10K. Won	−1.010	−42.92	No
	100K. Won	−0.985	−43.33	No
	1K. Won	−1.101	−40.59	No
	100 Won	−1.156	−39.00	No
	10 Won	−1.166	−38.74	No
	Minimum	−0.831	−39.84	No
Weak σ-Convergence		$\hat{\phi}$	$t_{\hat{\phi}}$	
	n.a.	0.013	9.949	No

discussed earlier, the results of the log t regression are dependent on the choice of measurement units, but the conclusion of the test is not dependent on the choice of the measurement units in this case: All samples are relatively diverging over time. The underlying reason is that the common stochastic trend, θ_t, is dominant in the household expenditure panel. To see this, the sample cross-sectional average is plotted in Figure 7.3. Evidently, the common stochastic trend (which

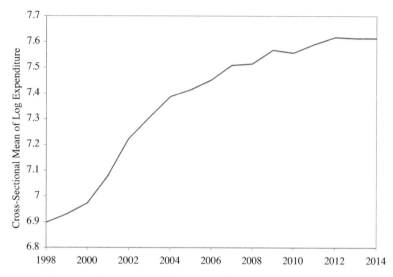

FIGURE 7.3 Cross-sectional mean of log expenditure

can be approximated by the sample cross-sectional average) is distinctly increasing over time.

The weak σ-convergence test is free from any restriction. The t-ratio is greater than 1.65 so that the panel of household expenditure clearly diverges over time.

7.5 Practice: convergence tests

In this section, we study how to use log t and weak σ convergence tests to examine the convergence behavior of the crime rates across 50 US states from 1965 to 2014. Note that from previous practices, we already knew that all crime rates have a single common factor with homogeneous factor loadings. We will utilize this information to examine the convergence behavior of the crime rates. It always useful to test the weak σ-convergence first. If the panel data of interest has a distinct (non)stochastic trend – all time series have either significantly positive or negative coefficients on the linear trend term – then the weak σ-convergence usually imply the relative convergence statistically. The opposite is not true, theoretically, but in almost of all cases, if the relative convergence is rejected, then the weak σ-convergence is also rejected usually. Meanwhile, the disagreement between the relative and weak σ-convergences can be easily seen when the panel data of interest does not have any distinct (non)stochastic trend. In this case, the notion of the relative convergence is not well defined. Hence, in this case, testing the weak σ-convergence is more meaningful.

If the weak σ-convergence is rejected, then the relative convergence may be performed. Furthermore, if the relative convergence is rejected as well, then the clustering algorithm can be performed. Of course, the panel data of interest should share a distinct (non)stochastic trend. Otherwise, the relative convergence test does not work well so that the clustering results are not reliable anymore. In this case, the notion of co-divergence is useful, but we will not study this concept in this monograph.

We will study MATLAB codes first and then show the corresponding GAUSS and STATA codes.

7.5.1 Practice with MATLAB I: weak σ-convergence test

Download `weakc.m` and `nwest.m` in the same directory where the panel data of interest is. Also copy `pc.m` as well. As shown in Table 5.1, crime rates have a single factor with homogenous factor loadings. Here the following two variances are constructed. The first one, $\hat{K}_{nt}^y$, is the sample cross-sectional variance of the log-level crime rates. Since crime rates have a single factor with homogenous factor loadings, this measure will reflect the cross-sectional dispersion of the idiosyncratic terms. The second one, $\hat{K}_{nt}^z$, is the sample cross-sectional variance of the PC-estimated idiosyncratic term.

$$\hat{K}_{nt}^y = \frac{1}{n}\sum_{i=1}^{n}\left(y_{it} - \frac{1}{n}\sum_{i=1}^{n}y_{it}\right)^2, \quad \hat{K}_{nt}^z = \frac{1}{n}\sum_{i=1}^{n}\left(z_{it} - \frac{1}{n}\sum_{i=1}^{n}z_{it}\right)^2, \tag{7.26}$$

where

$$z_{it} = y_{it} - \hat{\lambda}_i\hat{F}_t = a_i + y_{it}^o + (\lambda_i F_t - \hat{\lambda}_i\hat{F}_t). \tag{7.27}$$

Note that as we emphasized in Section 7.3, z_{it} should include the fixed effects.

'weakc.m' is the function for the weak σ-convergence test. The usage of the function goes like this.

```
[bhat, tb-ratio] =weakc(x,p).
```

bhat is a (2×1) vector of the LS estimates from the regression of $\hat{K}_{nt}^y = a + \phi t + u_t$. tb-ratio is the (2×1) vector of the associated t-ratios. 'p' is the lag length for Newey and West lag. The default value must be int($T^{1/3}$).

MATLAB EX 7-1

```
clear;
load property_mat.csv; x1 = property_mat;
[T,n]  = size(x1);
x = log(x1(:,2:n));
[b1,tr1]  = weakc(x,3);
[b2,tr2]  = weakc(x,4);
```

Note that we have $T = 50$ so that the nearest integer of $50^{1/3}$ is either 3 or 4. Hence the two *t*-ratios with three and four lags are reported together. Alternatively, you can use the 'round' command to pin down the choice of the lag length. That is, you can use the following command.

```
x = log(x1(:,2:n));
k1 = round(T^(1/3)); % will give k1 = 4
[b1,tr1] = weakc(x,k1);
```

Since we have nine different crime rates, you can load them altogether and run the weak σ-convergence test. Here is an example (a case of two data files).

```
clear;
load violent_mat.csv; x1 = violent_mat;
load murder_mat.csv; x2 = murder_mat;
[T,n] = size(x1);
x1 = log(x1(:,2:n));
x2 = log(x2(:,2:n));
for i = 1:2;
  if i == 1; x = x1; end
  if i == 2; x = x2; end
  [b11,tr11] = weakc(x,3); [b12,tr12] = weakc(x,7);
  [b11*100 tr11 tr12]
end
```

The first three columns in Table 7.2 show the results with all nine crime rates. All crime rates are weakly σ-converging their national crime rates over time. The results with four lags weaken slightly, but all of *t*-ratios are less than the critical value of -1.65. Since the *t*-ratios are smaller than -1.65, the following null

TABLE 7.2 Weak σ-convergence tests with various crime rates

		With $\hat{K}^y_{nt}$			With $\hat{K}^z_{nt}$		
		$\hat{\phi} \times 100$	$t_{\hat{\phi}}(3)$	$t_{\hat{\phi}}(4)$	$\hat{\phi} \times 100$	$t_{\hat{\phi}}(3)$	$t_{\hat{\phi}}(4)$
Violent		−1.491	−4.504	−4.120	−0.780	−1.910	−1.744
	Murder	−0.447	−5.402	−5.238	−0.282	−2.440	−2.287
	Robbery	−0.518	−2.204	−2.026	−0.488	−2.309	−2.126
	Rape	−0.382	−9.667	−8.900	−0.163	−2.490	−2.280
	Assault	−0.277	−2.344	−2.153	−0.222	−2.065	−1.892
Property		−0.192	−5.749	−5.276	−0.190	−5.855	−5.670
	Burglary	−0.490	−4.668	−4.264	−0.401	−3.592	−3.280
	Larceny	−0.240	−6.321	−5.794	−0.176	−10.70	−10.15
	Motor Theft	−0.189	−2.097	−1.968	−0.242	−2.630	−2.449

hypothesis can be constructed and rejected. You are not supposed to accept the null, but the alternative. Hence you can construct the following null and alternative hypotheses: $\mathcal{H}_0 : t_{\hat{\phi}} \geq -1.65$ v.s. $\mathcal{H}_A : t_{\hat{\phi}} < -1.65$. Since the t-ratios are less than -1.65, you can accept the alternative hypothesis of the weak σ-convergence.

Next, we will study how to test the weak σ-convergence with z_{it} in (7.27). See the following MATLAB codes.

```
[f1,l1,v1,e1] = pc(x,1);
xx = [ones(T,1) f1];
be = inv(xx' * xx)*xx' *x;
z = x - f1*be(2,:);
[b11,tr11] = weakc(z,3);
```

The first line estimates the PC common factor and then constructs z_{it} in the fourth line. Note that pc(x,k) standardizes x automatically. However, z_{it} should not be standardized for the test for the weak σ-convergence. The last three columns in Table 7.2 show the results with z_{it}. The evidence becomes weakened since z_{it} includes the additional term of $\lambda_i F_t - \hat{\lambda}_i \hat{F}_t$. However, all t-ratios are less than -1.65 so that overall the results are robust.

7.5.2 Practice with MATLAB II: relative convergence test

'logt.m' function is for the relative convergence or log t test. The usage of the function goes like this.

```
[chat, tc-ratio] =logt(x)
```

chat is a (2×1) vector of the LS estimates from the log t regression of log $(H_1/H_t) - 2 \log (\log t) = a + b \log t + u_t$. tc-ratio is the vector of the associated t-ratios. All other parameters are automatically assigned inside of 'logt' function. Before you use the log t regression, you need to check whether the panel data used in the regression satisfies the requirement of $y_{it} \geq 0$ for all i and t. Also, you need to check whether the panel data has all strong trend behaviors. The first requirement is easy to check by printing out the minimum value of y_{it}. The second one is rather ambiguous, but you can check by running the following simple trend regression.

$$y_{it} = \alpha_i + \beta_i t + v_{it}, \text{ for each } i.$$

If $\hat{\beta}_i$ is significantly positive or negative for all i, then we can say that the trending behavior is very strong. If most of $\hat{\beta}_i$ are significantly positive, but the rest of them are not significantly negative, then we can say that the trending behavior is relatively strong. If some of $\hat{\beta}_i$ are significantly positive, some of them are significantly negative, and the rest of them are not significantly different from zero, then we can say that there is no strong trending behavior. In the first two cases, you can use the log t regression. Otherwise, do not run the log t regression. See the following.

MATLAB EX 7-2
```
for i = 1:1;
   if i == 1; x = x1; end
                :
                :
      outf = [] ;
        for i1 = 1:n-1;
          my = min(x(:,i1)); % Checking the requirement
              of y_it ≥ 0
          trd = 1:T;
          xx = [ones(T,1) trd'] ; % Checking trend coefficient
            be = inv(xx'*xx)*xx'*x(:,i1);
            re = x(:,i1) - xx*be;
          sig = nwest(re,3);
          sig = sig*diag(inv(xx'*xx));
            tr = be./sqrt(sig);
          outf =[outf; i1 my be(2,1) tr(2,1)] % Stacking up output
        end
      [outf]
   end
```

Output file looks like this.
```
1.0000 8.8416 0.0182 3.6999
2.0000 5.9322 0.0427 6.9257
3.0000 8.0366 0.0393 7.4844
              :
              :
```

Table 7.3 shows the results of these screening procedures and the results of the log t regression. The requirement for all $y_{it} > 0$ is binding for all cases except for murder and rape. However, only in the cases of burglary and violent, we can observe the strong trending behavior. For other crime series, at least one series has a significantly negative trend. Hence the relative convergence test should not be used for these seven crime rates. In fact, in the cases of murder and motor theft, almost half of the series have significantly different signs of trend coefficients. Naturally, the notion of the relative convergence does not hold in these cases. Hence the result of relative divergence ($t_{b} < -1.65$) should not be taken seriously.

When you reject both the weak σ-convergence and the relative convergence, you can think of the clustering option in Section 7.2.3. Automatic clustering programs are available in GAUSS and STATA.

TABLE 7.3 Relative convergence tests with crime rates

		Frequency		logt Regression	
		$t_b \leq -1.65$	$y_{it} < 0$	$\hat{b}$	$t_{\hat{b}}$
Violent		0/50	0/250	0.234	1.726
	Murder	33/50	5/250	−0.508	−3.825
	Robbery	6/50	0/250	−0.185	−1.502
	Rape	1/50	1/250	0.810	7.243
	Assault	1/50	0/250	0.020	0.161
Property		9/50	0/250	0.320	2.913
	Burglary	0/50	0/250	0.234	1.726
	Larceny	4/50	0/250	0.623	5.769
	Motor Theft	20/50	0/250	−0.354	−3.194

7.5.3 Practice with GAUSS

Download EX7_1.pgm, which contains a number of procedures, including 'pc' 'weakc' and 'logt'. In the following, GAUSS version codes for MATLAB EX 7-1 and MATLAB EX 7-2 are presented.

GAUSS EX 7-1

```
new; cls;
t = 50; n = 50;
load x1[t,n+1] = violent.csv;
load x2[t,n+1] = murder.csv;
        ⋮
load x9[t,n+1] = motorv.csv;
x1= ln(x1[.,2:n+1]);
        ⋮
x9= ln(x9[.,2:n+1]);
i = 1; do while i <= 9;
  if i == 1; x = x1; endif;
        ⋮
  if i == 9; x = x9; endif;
  k = int(t^(1/3)); p = int(t/3);
  {b1,t1} = weakc(x,k);
  {f1,l1,v1,e1} = pc(x,1);
  xx = ones(rows(x),1)~f1;
  be = invpd(xx' xx)*xx' x;
  z = x - f1.*be[2,.];
  {b2,t2} = weakc(z,k);
  i~b1~b2~t1~t2;
i = i + 1; endo;
```

GAUSS EX 7-2

```
new; cls;
t = 50; n = 50;
  :
i = 1; do while i <= 9;
  if i == 1; x = x1; endif;
    :
  if i == 9; x = x9; endif;
    k = int(t^(1/3));
    p = int(t/3);
  outf = {};
    i1 = 1; do while i1 <= n-1;
    my = minc(x[.,i1]);
    xx = ones(rows(x),1)~seqa(1,1,t);
    be = invpd(xx' xx)*xx' x[.,i1];
    re = x[.,i1] - xx*be;
    sig = nwest(re,k);
    sig = sig*invpd(xx' xx);
    tr = be./sqrt(diag(sig));
    outf = outf|i1~my~be[2,1]~tr[2,1];
    i1 = i1 + 1; endo;
  outf;
i = i + 1; endo;
```

Clustering algorithm

'exm.pgm' includes the procedure called 'sorthat,' which automatically finds out the subconvergent clusters.

7.5.4   Practice with STATA

In the following, the STATA versions of MATLAB EX 7-1 and EX 7-2 are presented. For automatic clustering code, see Du (2017), or visit https://sites.google.com/site/kerrydu2016/home/stata-files. For the weak σ-convergence test, one needs to download pcweaks.ado and weaks.ado as well. The 'weaks.ado' provides the trend regression results of $\hat{K}_{nt}^y = a + \phi t + u_t$. To get z_{it} in (7.27), one has to use pcweaks.ado first and call the variable z.

STATA EX 7-1

```
xtset id year
keep lmur id year
reshape wide lmur, i(id) j(year)
order _all, alphabetic
```

```
weaks lmur1965-lmur2014, lag(3)
weaks lmur1965-lmur2014, lag(4)
pcweaks lmur1965-lmur2014, k(1)
matrix z = r(z)
svmat z
weaks z1-z50, lag(3)
```

'lag(3)' indicates that the lag length for Newey and West's (1987) HAC estimator is set by three. The usual selection rule is int($T^{1/3}$). Here we have $T = 50$, $50^{1/3} \simeq 3.7$, so we choose lag(3) and lag(4). You will get the following outputs.

```
. order _all, alphabetic
. weaks lmur1965-lmur2014, lag(3)
-----------------------------------------------------
    bhat: -.00446665
    t-ratio: -5.4016011
-----------------------------------------------------
. weaks lmur1965-lmur2014, lag(4)
-----------------------------------------------------
    bhat: -.00446665
    t-ratio: -5.2374812
-----------------------------------------------------
. pcweaks lmur1965-lmur2014, k(1)
. matrix z = r(z)
. svmat z
. weaks z1-z50, lag(3)
-----------------------------------------------------
    bhat: -.00281888
    t-ratio: -2.4400676
-----------------------------------------------------
```

Note that the 'bhat' is the least-squares estimate of ϕ from the regression of $K_{nt} = a + \phi t + u_t$. The values of 'bhat' are not dependent on the choice of the lag length. Hence with lag(3) or with lag(4), the values of 'bhat' remain the same. Meanwhile, the t-ratio is dependent on the choice of lag. Since both t-ratios are less than the critical value of -1.65, y_{it} is weakly σ-converging. Next, 'pc lmur1965-lmur2014, k(1)' is providing z_{it} in (7.27). 'svmat z' generates a $(n \times T)$ matrix of z.

To check the significance level for the trend coefficient, one can do the following.

STATA EX 7-2

```
xtset id year
keep lmur id year
reshape wide lmur, i(year) j(id)
forvalue i=1/50{
  reg lmur'i' year
}
```

Note that here you reshape the data by $T \times n$ rather than $n \times T$.

Notes

1 Let $\log A_t$ grows at x rate per year. Then $\Delta \log A_t = \Delta a_t = x$. Under this assumption, $\Delta y_{it} = \left(-\tilde{y}^* + \tilde{y}_{i0}\right)\left(e^{-\beta t} - e^{-\beta(t-1)}\right) + x$. Naturally, $\Delta y_{it} - \Delta y_{jt} = \left(\tilde{y}_{i0} - \tilde{y}_{j0}\right)\left(e^{-\beta t} - e^{-\beta(t-1)}\right)$. Since $e^{-\beta t} - e^{-\beta(t-1)} = e^{-\beta t}(1 - e^{\beta}) < 0$, the condition in (7.3) holds.

2 Suppose that y_{it} is the log per capita real income. To compare the relative transition of the ith non-OECD countries to the OECD average, one can use the following relative transition: $h_{it} = y_{it}/n^{-1}\sum_{j \in \text{OECD}} y_{jt}$, where n is the total number of the OECD countries.

3 For GAUSS code, visit at http://www.utdallas.edu/-d.sul/papers/RecentWorking%20Papers1.htm. For STATA code, visit at https://sites.google.com/site/kerrydu2016/home/stata-files.

4 Let X_i be a $(k \times 1)$ vector of random variables with a finite mean μ_X and covariance of Σ_X. Then the empirical version of the MD is given by $\left[1 + (X_i - \hat{\mu}_X)' \hat{\Sigma}_X^{-1} (X_i - \hat{\mu}_X)\right]^{-1}$, where $\hat{\mu}_X$ is the sample mean and $\hat{\Sigma}_X$ is the sample covariance matrix.

8

APPENDIX

Basic panel regressions

8.1 Standard two-way fixed effects estimation

Before we introduce the two-way fixed effects model, we briefly review other pooled estimators first. Consider the following two panel regressions.

$$\text{Pooled OLS:} \qquad y_{it} = \alpha + \beta x_{it} + e_{it}, \tag{8.1}$$

$$\text{Fixed Effect:} \qquad y_{it} = \alpha_i + \beta x_{it} + \varepsilon_{it}. \tag{8.2}$$

The first regression in (8.1) is called 'pooled ordinary least squares' (POLS) regression, where all slope coefficients are restricted to be homogeneous. The second regression in (8.2) allows heterogeneous constants for each individual.

8.1.1 POLS estimation

The POLS estimator, believe it or not, had been popularly used in the '70s and even '80s. Surprisingly, many old, empirical stylized facts were established based on the pooled OLS estimation. The underlying logic of the POLS regression goes like this. Consider a cross-sectional regression for a particular year (for example $t = 1$) given by

$$y_{i1} = \alpha + \beta x_{i1} + e_{i1}. \tag{8.3}$$

If the data are available for another year (let's say $t = 2$), then we have

$$y_{i2} = \alpha + \beta x_{i2} + e_{i2}. \tag{8.4}$$

If the relationship between y and x is not time varying, then more efficient estimation can be done by pooling (8.3) and (8.4). Why more efficient? Because the pooled regression in (8.4) use more observations so that the least-squares estimator must be more efficient if all slope coefficients are homogeneous. Researchers realized, however, that running the POLS regression becomes problematic if the fixed effect α_i is correlated with the individual mean of x_{it}. See chapters 1 and 6 for a more detailed discussion of why the POLS regression becomes problematic in practice.

8.1.2 One-way fixed effect estimation

The individual fixed effect model in (8.2) was developed in the early '60s but in practice, this model was not popularly used until the '70s. In the treatment literature, the fixed effect model was useful in eliminating unobserved variables. Rewrite (8.3) and (8.4) as

$$y_{i1} = \alpha + \beta x_{i1} + z_i'\delta + \epsilon_{i1}, \ t = 1 \text{ or before treatment,}$$

$$y_{i2} = \alpha + \beta x_{i2} + z_i'\delta + \epsilon_{i2}, \ t = 2 \text{ or after treatment,}$$

where z_i is a vector of other time invariant but unobserved regressors, which may be correlated with the treatment dummy variable x_{it}. Then it is easy to see that the fixed effect in (8.2) includes $z_i'\delta$, which is unobserved heterogeneity.

To estimate β, consider the following overall and time series means. If $\alpha_i = \alpha$, then we consider the overall mean. That is,

$$\frac{1}{nT}\sum_{i=1}^{n}\sum_{t=1}^{T}y_{it} = \alpha + \beta\frac{1}{nT}\sum_{i=1}^{n}\sum_{t=1}^{T}x_{it} + \frac{1}{nT}\sum_{i=1}^{n}\sum_{t=1}^{T}e_{it}. \tag{8.5}$$

Subtracting (8.5) from (8.1) yields

$$y_{it} - \frac{1}{nT}\sum_{i=1}^{n}\sum_{t=1}^{T}y_{it} = \beta\left(x_{it} - \frac{1}{nT}\sum_{i=1}^{n}\sum_{t=1}^{T}x_{it}\right) + e_{it} - \frac{1}{nT}\sum_{i=1}^{n}\sum_{t=1}^{T}e_{it}. \tag{8.6}$$

Hence the estimator of β in (8.1) is exactly identical to the estimator of β in (8.6). If $\alpha_i \neq \alpha$, then we consider the time series mean.

$$\frac{1}{T}\sum_{t=1}^{T}y_{it} = \alpha_i + \beta\frac{1}{T}\sum_{t=1}^{T}x_{it} + \frac{1}{T}\sum_{t=1}^{T}\varepsilon_{it}. \tag{8.7}$$

Subtracting (8.7) from (8.2) yields

$$y_{it} - \frac{1}{T}\sum_{t=1}^{T}y_{it} = \beta\left(x_{it} - \frac{1}{T}\sum_{t=1}^{T}x_{it}\right) + \varepsilon_{it} - \frac{1}{T}\sum_{t=1}^{T}\varepsilon_{it}. \tag{8.8}$$

This transformation is called 'within group' transformation. Hence the estimator of β in (8.8) is called the 'within group (WG)' estimator as well.

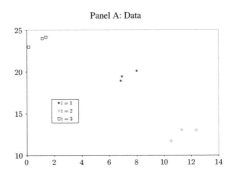

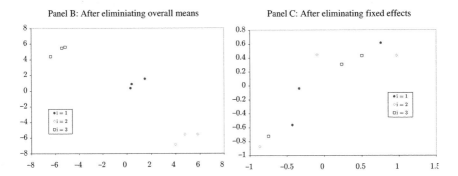

FIGURE 8.1   Importance of fixed effects on the estimation

Figure 8.1 shows three panels of panel data sets: Raw data set (Panel A), after eliminating overall mean (Panel B), and after eliminating the time series mean (Panel C). In Panel A, three individuals and three time series observations are plotted. Panel B looks exactly the same as Panel A, except for changing the center point. Eliminating the overall mean simply moves the center point of the graph of Panel A. Running the pooled OLS is equivalent to plotting a straight line in Panel B, which minimizes the sum of the distance between the line and each point. Similarly, the within group estimator is the slope of the straight line in Panel C, which gives the minimum mean squares errors. Obviously, the fixed effect estimate is positive (Panel C); meanwhile, the POLS estimate is negative (Panel B).

8.1.3   Two-way fixed effect estimation

The importance of the two-way fixed effect estimator had been addressed somewhat differently depending on the literature. In the treatment effect literature, the two-way fixed effects lead to estimate consistently (or correctly) the marginal effect of an idiosyncratic change (or treatment) on an outcome. In macro or finance studies, the year dummy or common time effects are included to avoid cross-sectional dependence in the error terms. We will study the first case here.

Consider two individuals, A and B, before and after a treatment. Individual A received a treatment ($x_{A1} = 0$ but $x_{A2} = 1$) at the second period; meanwhile, B has not received any treatment. Outcomes of A and B are reported in the following table.

	Before	After	Difference
A	α_A	$\alpha_A + \gamma + \delta$	$\gamma + \delta$
B	α_B	$\alpha_B + \gamma$	γ
Difference	$\alpha_A - \alpha_B$	$\alpha_A + \delta - \alpha_B$	δ

Denote y_{it} and x_{it} as the outcome and treatment, respectively. Then α_i can be interpreted as individual fixed effects, γ as the overall year effect, and δ as the treatment effect. In the earlier case, the treatment effect is exactly identified. However, if the number of individuals increases and treatment years are different, then it is convenient to run the following two-way fixed effect regression.

$$y_{it} = a_i + \theta_t + \beta x_{it} + u_{it}, \tag{8.9}$$

where θ_t is called 'year fixed effect' or 'common time effect.' To see how the two-way effect regression in (8.9) identifies the parameters in the earlier table, we consider the following expectations.

$$\mathbb{E}(y_{A0}|x_{A0} = 0) = a_A + \theta_0 = \alpha_A,$$
$$\mathbb{E}(y_{A1}|x_{A1} = 1) = a_A + \theta_1 + \beta = \alpha_A + \gamma + \delta,$$
$$\mathbb{E}(y_{B0}|x_{B0} = 0) = a_B + \theta_0 = \alpha_B,$$
$$\mathbb{E}(y_{B1}|x_{B1} = 0) = a_B + \theta_1 = \alpha_B + \gamma.$$

Hence the treatment effect, δ, can be estimated by taking the difference-in-difference.

$$[\mathbb{E}(y_{A1}|x_{A1} = 1) - \mathbb{E}(y_{A0}|x_{A0} = 0)] - [\mathbb{E}(y_{B1}|x_{B1} = 0) - \mathbb{E}(y_{B0}|x_{B0} = 0)] = \delta \tag{8.10}$$

The common time effect, θ_t, is correlated with the common factor with the treatment x_{it} as long as the treatment is given in a different year or time. Naturally, if θ_t is not included, then the one-way fixed effect estimator in (8.2) becomes inconsistent due to the so-called omitted variable bias. Note that the common factor θ_t can influence on y_{it} differently. In this case, the so-called factor-augmented regression needs to run to estimate the idiosyncratic relationship between outcomes and treatments. See Chapter 6 for more detailed discussions.

Next, we study how the year fixed effect can reduce the cross-sectional dependence. Assume that $\mathbb{E}\theta_t = 0$ and θ_t is strongly exogenous, or $\mathbb{E}\theta_t x_{is} = 0$ for all t and s. Under these conditions, the one-way fixed effect estimator in (8.2) becomes consistent, even though there is no year fixed effect in the regression, since the year fixed effect, which is included in the regression error, is not correlated with the regressor. However, it is very difficult to get any consistent estimator for variance and covariance matrices of the fixed effect estimator. We will study this issue in the next subsection.

8.2 Valid test statistics

Before we study how to estimate the variance and covariance matrices for the two-way fixed effect estimator, we consider much simpler cases.

8.2.1 Basic inference theory

First, we consider the following simple cross-sectional regression for the estimation of a sample mean.

$$y_i = \beta x_i + \varepsilon_i = \beta + \varepsilon_i \text{ with } x_i = 1 \text{ for all } i, \tag{8.11}$$

where y_i is a 'time invariant' variable. Then it is easy to show that

$$\hat{\beta} = \frac{\sum_{i=1}^n x_i y_i}{\sum_{i=1}^n x_i^2} = \frac{1}{n}\sum_{i=1}^n y_i = \beta + \frac{1}{n}\sum_{i=1}^n \varepsilon_i. \tag{8.12}$$

Next, we need to evaluate whether the estimate of $\hat{\beta}$ is statistically significant. We need to rely on its asymptotic property. First, we need to calculate the variance of the sample mean. By definition, we have

$$
\begin{aligned}
\sigma_{\hat{\beta}_n}^2 &= \mathbb{E}(\hat{\beta} - \beta)^2 = \mathbb{E}\left[\frac{1}{n}\sum_{i=1}^n \varepsilon_i\right]^2 \\
&= \frac{1}{n^2}\mathbb{E}[\varepsilon_1^2 + \varepsilon_2^2 + \cdots + \varepsilon_n^2] + \frac{2}{n^2}\mathbb{E}[\varepsilon_1\varepsilon_2 + \varepsilon_1\varepsilon_3 + \cdots + \varepsilon_{n-1}\varepsilon_n] \\
&= \frac{1}{n}\sigma_\varepsilon^2 + \frac{1}{na^2} \times [\text{sum of the cross sectional covariances}],
\end{aligned}
\tag{8.13}
$$

where the last equation is obtained under the assumption of $\mathbb{E}\varepsilon_1^2 = \mathbb{E}\varepsilon_2^2 = \cdots = \mathbb{E}\varepsilon_n^2 = \sigma^2$.

Suppose that there is no cross-sectional correlation. Then

$$\sigma_{\hat{\beta}_n}^2 = \frac{1}{n}\sigma_\varepsilon^2 \to 0 \text{ as } n \to \infty. \tag{8.14}$$

The condition in (8.14) implies that as the number of observations increases, the variance of the estimator – or uncertainty of the estimator – becomes smaller and eventually goes to zero. In other words, the estimator becomes consistent. Since $\sigma_{\hat\beta}^2$ or σ_ε^2 is a true parameter, it must be estimated. The sample variance of ε_i can be a consistent estimator for σ_ε^2. Then from a standard central limit theorem (Lindeberg and Levy CLT), the t-ratio of the sample mean under the null hypothesis of $\beta = 0$ becomes

$$t_{\hat\beta} = \frac{\hat\beta}{\sqrt{\hat\sigma_{\hat\beta}^2}} = \frac{\sqrt{n}\left(\hat\beta - 0\right)}{\sqrt{\frac{1}{n-1}\sum_{i=1}^n \varepsilon_i^2}} \to^d \mathcal{N}(0,1), \tag{8.15}$$

where $\hat\sigma_{\hat\beta}^2 = \hat\sigma_\varepsilon^2/n$, $\hat\sigma_\varepsilon^2 = (n-1)^{-1}\sum_{i=1}^n \hat\varepsilon_i^2$, and $\hat\varepsilon_i = y_i - \hat\beta$. In other words, the t-ratio of $\hat\beta$ converges a standard normal distribution with a large n (usually $n > 15$).

8.2.2 Cross-sectional dependence

What if there is cross-sectional dependence? Unlike time series data, it is unknown how to calculate or estimate the cross-sectional correlations unless a particular assumption – for example, spatial dependence – is made. Typically, empirical researchers had assumed no cross-sectional correlations simply because they did not know how to estimate them. Suppose that $\mathbb{E}\varepsilon_i\varepsilon_j = \sigma_\theta^2$ for $i \neq j$. In other words, there is identical dependence across individuals. Then for a large n, we have

$$\sigma_{\hat\beta_n}^2 = \frac{1}{n}\sigma_\varepsilon^2 + \frac{2\sigma_\theta^2}{n^2}[n-1+n-2+\cdots+1] \simeq \frac{1}{n}\sigma_\varepsilon^2 + \sigma_\theta^2. \tag{8.16}$$

In this case, the uncertainty does not go away, even with a large n, so that we can say $\hat\beta$ becomes inconsistent since $\hat\beta$ is always random, even when $n \to \infty$.

Next, we assume that $\mathbb{E}\varepsilon_i\varepsilon_j = \sigma_\theta^2/n$ for $i \neq j$. Under this assumption, we have

$$\sigma_{\hat\beta_n}^2 = \frac{1}{n}\sigma_\varepsilon^2 + \frac{2\sigma_\theta^2}{n^2}\left[\frac{n-1}{n} + \frac{n-2}{n} + \cdots + \frac{1}{n}\right] \simeq \frac{\sigma_\varepsilon^2 + \sigma_\theta^2}{n}. \tag{8.17}$$

The correct t-ratio, $t_{\hat\beta}^*$, becomes

$$\left|t_{\hat\beta}^*\right| = \left|\frac{\sqrt{n}\hat\beta}{\sqrt{\hat\sigma_\varepsilon^2 + \hat\sigma_\theta^2}}\right| < \left|\frac{\sqrt{n}\hat\beta}{\sqrt{\hat\sigma_\varepsilon^2}}\right| = \left|t_{\hat\beta}\right|. \tag{8.18}$$

Hence the conventional t-ratio, $t_{\hat\beta}$ (after ignoring the cross-sectional dependence), is always higher than the true t-ratio in absolute value. More importantly, the difference between $|t_{\hat\beta}|$ and $|t_{\hat\beta}^*|$ becomes larger as n increases. As n increases, the rejection rate of the null hypothesis based on the conventional test increases, even when the null is not true.

8.2.3 Solution: use two-way fixed effect

This simple example can be extended to a general panel regression.

$$y_{it} = a_i + \beta x_{it} + \varepsilon_{it}, \quad \text{with } \varepsilon_{it} = \theta_t + \epsilon_{it}, \tag{8.19}$$

where we assume that $\varepsilon_{it} \sim iid(0, \sigma_i^2)$ and θ_t are stationary random variables with zero mean and finite variance. Then the standard t-ratio of $\hat{\beta}$ with one-way fixed effect can be written as

$$|t_{\hat{\beta}}| = \left| \frac{\sqrt{nT}\hat{\beta}}{\sqrt{\hat{\sigma}_\varepsilon^2/\hat{\sigma}_x^2}} \right|, \tag{8.20}$$

where $\hat{\sigma}_x^2 = [n(T-1)]^{-1} \sum_{i=1}^n \sum_{t=1}^T \tilde{x}_{it}^2$ with $\tilde{x}_{it} = x_{it} - T^{-1}\sum_{t=1}^T x_{it}$, and

$$\hat{\sigma}_\varepsilon^2 = \frac{1}{n(T-1)} \sum_{i=1}^n \sum_{t=1}^T \hat{\varepsilon}_{it}^2. \tag{8.21}$$

Obviously, the t-ratio in (8.20) and the sample variance of ε_{it} in (8.21) ignore the cross-sectional correlation among ε_{it}. Hence the null hypothesis must be rejected more often, even when the null is true. To reduce the false rejection rate, the correct t-ratio should be used. To construct the correct t-ratio, simply include the two-way fixed effect in the regression.

Table 8.1 shows the rejection rates of the one-way and two-way fixed effect regressions. Artificial data are generated from (8.19), where $x_{it} \sim iid\mathcal{N}(0,1)$,

TABLE 8.1 Rejection rate of the null when the null is true (Nominal Rate: 5%)

		One-Way FE			Two-Way FE		
n	T	$\hat{\beta}$	$t_{\hat{\beta}}$	$t_{\hat{\beta},\text{rob}}$	$\hat{\beta}$	$t_{\hat{\beta}}$	$t_{\hat{\beta},\text{rob}}$
25	5	0.997	0.447	0.508	0.999	0.055	0.075
50	5	0.999	0.568	0.607	1.000	0.057	0.069
100	5	1.001	0.672	0.703	1.000	0.050	0.057
200	5	0.993	0.781	0.801	1.000	0.050	0.055
500	5	0.994	0.849	0.864	1.000	0.050	0.048
25	200	0.999	0.451	0.528	1.000	0.053	0.070
50	200	0.999	0.604	0.658	1.000	0.048	0.059
100	200	0.999	0.687	0.726	1.000	0.050	0.053
200	200	1.000	0.786	0.813	1.000	0.052	0.056
500	200	1.001	0.855	0.873	1.000	0.054	0.055

$\theta_t \sim iidN(0,1)$, and $\varepsilon_{it} \sim iidN(0,1)$. Since there is no correlation between x_{it} and θ_t (they are generated from separated and independent distributions), both one-way and two-way fixed effect estimators do not suffer from any bias. However, the t-ratio based on the one-way fixed effect is always higher (in absolute value) than that based on the two-way fixed effect. As we studied, the size of T is not important, but the size of n matters. As n increases, the rejection rate increases with the one-way fixed effect regression. Note that $t_{\hat{\beta},\text{rob}}$ stands for the t-ratio based on the robust covariance estimation, which we will study soon. Nonetheless, the result does not change whether we are using a robust covariance estimation.

Before we study the role of the panel robust covariance, we provide a mid-summary here. To avoid a false rejection and to get a consistent estimator, one should run a two-way fixed effect regression. However, there is another serious issue to use a two-way fixed effect regression. Study Chapter 6 for more detailed issues and solutions.

8.2.4 Serial dependent panel: use panel robust covariance

In order to understand the role of panel robust covariance, we need to study the following simple time series case. Assume that a time series data, z_t, is serially correlated. For, particularly, we assume that z_t follows an AR(1) process given by

$$z_t = a + e_t, \quad e_t = \rho e_{t-1} + \epsilon_t. \tag{8.22}$$

We want to estimate the mean of z_t. The sample mean is a consistent estimator if there is no outlier. Let

$$\hat{a} = \frac{1}{T}\sum_{t=1}^{T} z_t = a + \frac{1}{T}\sum_{t=1}^{T} e_t. \tag{8.23}$$

Next, we need to calculate the variance of $\hat{a}$.

$$
\begin{aligned}
V(\hat{a}) \quad &= \quad \Omega_e^2 = \mathbb{E}(\hat{a}-a)^2 = \mathbb{E}\left[\frac{1}{T}\sum_{t=1}^{T} e_t\right]^2 = \frac{1}{T^2}\mathbb{E}(e_1 + \cdots + e_T)^2 \\
&= \quad \frac{1}{T^2}\mathbb{E}\left(e_1^2 + \cdots + e_T^2\right) + \frac{2}{T^2}\mathbb{E}(e_1 e_2 + e_1 e_3 + \cdots + e_{T-1}e_T) \tag{8.24}
\end{aligned}
$$

The first term can be estimated accurately, even when $\mathbb{E}e_t^2 = \sigma_{e,t}^2 \neq \sigma_e^2$ always. The second term – which is the sum of cross-product terms – is not easy to estimate. With time series data, the variance of $\hat{a}$ is always approximated by the heteroskedasticity autocorrelation consistent (HAC) estimator. For example, Newey and West's (1987) estimator is a good example.

However, with panel data, the second term in (8.24) can be more accurately estimated. Let

$$z_{it} = a + e_{it}, \quad e_{it} = \rho e_{it-1} + \epsilon_{it}. \tag{8.25}$$

If there is no cross-sectional dependence, then we can approximate the entire term in (8.24) by

$$\mathbb{E}\left[\frac{1}{T}\sum_{t=1}^{T}e_{it}\right]^2 \simeq \frac{1}{n}\sum_{i=1}^{n}\left[\frac{1}{T}\sum_{t=1}^{T}e_{it}\right]^2 = \Omega_e^2 \text{ as } n \to \infty. \tag{8.26}$$

Next, we apply this method to a panel regression. Consider a simple two-way fixed effect regression.

$$y_{it} = a_i + \theta_t + \beta x_{it} + \varepsilon_{it}. \tag{8.27}$$

To eliminate a_i and θ_t, we transform y_{it} and x_{it} as follows: First, we take the time series average in (8.27).

$$\frac{1}{T}\sum_{t=1}^{T}y_{it} = a_i + \frac{1}{T}\sum_{t=1}^{T}\theta_t + \beta\frac{1}{T}\sum_{t=1}^{T}x_{it} + \frac{1}{T}\sum_{t=1}^{T}\varepsilon_{it}. \tag{8.28}$$

Second, subtracting (8.28) from (8.27) yields

$$y_{it} - \frac{1}{T}\sum_{t=1}^{T}y_{it} = \theta_t - \frac{1}{T}\sum_{t=1}^{T}\theta_t + \beta\left(x_{it} - \frac{1}{T}\sum_{t=1}^{T}x_{it}\right) + \varepsilon_{it} - \frac{1}{T}\sum_{t=1}^{T}\varepsilon_{it}. \tag{8.29}$$

Now, the individual fixed effect is gone in (8.29). To eliminate the common time effect or year effect, we take the cross-sectional average in (8.29).

$$\frac{1}{n}\sum_{i=1}^{n}\left(y_{it} - \frac{1}{T}\sum_{t=1}^{T}y_{it}\right) = \theta_t - \frac{1}{T}\sum_{t=1}^{T}\theta_t + \beta\frac{1}{n}\sum_{i=1}^{n}\left(x_{it} - \frac{1}{T}\sum_{t=1}^{T}x_{it}\right)$$
$$+ \frac{1}{n}\sum_{i=1}^{n}\left(\varepsilon_{it} - \frac{1}{T}\sum_{t=1}^{T}\varepsilon_{it}\right). \tag{8.30}$$

Lastly, subtracting (8.30) from (8.29) leads to

$$y_{it}^+ = \beta x_{it}^+ + \varepsilon_{it}^+, \tag{8.31}$$

where

$$y_{it}^+ = y_{it} - \frac{1}{T}\sum_{t=1}^{T} y_{it} - \frac{1}{n}\sum_{i=1}^{n}\left(y_{it} - \frac{1}{T}\sum_{t=1}^{T} y_{it}\right)$$

$$= y_{it} - \frac{1}{T}\sum_{t=1}^{T} y_{it} - \frac{1}{n}\sum_{i=1}^{n} y_{it} - \frac{1}{nT}\sum_{i=1}^{n}\sum_{t=1}^{T} y_{it}.$$

x_{it}^+ and ε_{it}^+ are defined similarly.

Next, the least-squares estimator $\hat{\beta}$ in (8.31), which is the two-way fixed effect estimator, is given as

$$\hat{\beta} = \frac{\sum_{i=1}^{n}\sum_{t=1}^{T} x_{it}^+ y_{it}^+}{\sum_{i=1}^{n}\sum_{t=1}^{T}\left(x_{it}^+\right)^2} = \beta + \frac{\sum_{i=1}^{n}\sum_{t=1}^{T} x_{it}^+ \varepsilon_{it}^+}{\sum_{i=1}^{n}\sum_{t=1}^{T}\left(x_{it}^+\right)^2}. \qquad (8.32)$$

Let $\Delta_{nT} = (nT)^{-1}\sum_{i=1}^{n}\sum_{t=1}^{T}\left(x_{it}^+\right)^2$. Then

$$\hat{\beta} - \beta = \left(\Delta_{nT}^{-1}\right)\frac{1}{nT}\sum_{i=1}^{n}\sum_{t=1}^{T} x_{it}^+ \varepsilon_{it}^+. \qquad (8.33)$$

The variance of $\hat{\beta}$ can be calculated as

$$V(\hat{\beta}) = \mathbb{E}(\hat{\beta} - \beta)^2 = \mathbb{E}\left(\Delta_{nT}^{-1}\right)^2 \mathbb{E}\left[\frac{1}{nT}\sum_{i=1}^{n}\sum_{t=1}^{T} x_{it}^+ \varepsilon_{it}^+\right]^2. \qquad (8.34)$$

Let $z_{it} = x_{it}^+ \varepsilon_{it}^+$. We know (by assumption) that z_{it} is not correlated with z_{jt} since there is no cross-sectional dependence. Hence,

$$\mathbb{E}\left[\frac{1}{nT}\sum_{i=1}^{n}\sum_{t=1}^{T} x_{it}^+ \varepsilon_{it}^+\right]^2 = \frac{1}{n^2}\sum_{i=1}^{n}\mathbb{E}\left[\frac{1}{T}\sum_{t=1}^{T} z_{it}\right]^2. \qquad (8.35)$$

To estimate it, we use the regression residuals, $\hat{\varepsilon}_{it}^+$, instead of ε_{it}^+. Then the panel robust covariance matrix is written as

$$V(\hat{\beta}) = \left(\sum_{i=1}^{n}\sum_{t=1}^{T}\left(x_{it}^+\right)^2\right)^{-1}\sum_{i=1}^{n}\left(\sum_{t=1}^{T} x_{it}^+ \varepsilon_{it}^+\right)^2\left(\sum_{i=1}^{n}\sum_{t=1}^{T}\left(x_{it}^+\right)^2\right)^{-1}. \qquad (8.36)$$

Then the t-ratio based on the panel robust covariance estimator becomes

$$t_{\hat{\beta},\mathrm{rob}} = \frac{\hat{\beta}}{\sqrt{V(\hat{\beta})}}, \qquad (8.37)$$

where $V(\hat{\beta})$ is given in (8.36). Originally, a general formula was derived by White (1984), and later a more explicit formular was derived by Arellano (1987). Interestingly, empirical researchers had ignored this estimator and used the wrong t-ratio until Bertrand, Duflo, and Mullainathan (2004) mentioned the statistical inference issue in the *Quarterly Journal of Economics*.

REFERENCES

Ahn, S. C., & Horenstein, A. R. (2013). Eigenvalue ratio test for the number of factors. *Econometrica, 81,* 1203–1227.

Almond, D., Chay, K. Y., & Lee, D. S. (2005). The costs of low birth weight. *The Quarterly Journal of Economics, 120*(3), 1031–1083.

Anderson, J. E., & Van Wincoop, E. (2003). Gravity with gravitas: A solution to the border puzzle. *American Economic Review, 93*(1), 170–192.

Andrews, D. W. K. (2005). Cross-section regression with common shocks. *Econometrica, 73*(5), 1551–1585.

Bai, J. (2003). Inferential theory for factor models of large dimensions. *Econometrica, 71,* 135–171.

Bai, J. (2004). Estimating cross-section common stochastic trends in nonstationary panel data. *Journal of Econometrics, 122*(1), 137–183.

Bai, J. (2009). Panel data models with interactive fixed effects. *Econometrica, 77*(4), 1229–1279.

Bai, J., & Ng, S. (2002). Determining the number of factors in approximate factor models. *Econometrica, 70,* 181–221.

Bai, J., & Ng, S. (2006). Evaluating latent and observed factors in macroeconomics and finance. *Journal of Econometrics, 131*(1–2), 507–537.

Bai, J., & Ng, S. (2013). Principal components estimation and identification of static factors. *Journal of Econometrics, 176*(1), 18–29.

Barro, R. J., & Sala-i-Martin, X. (1992). Convergence. *Journal of Political Economy, 100,* 223–251.

Behrman, J. R., & Rosenzweig, M. R. (2002). Does increasing women's schooling raise the schooling of the next generation? *American Economic Review,* 323–334.

Bertrand, M., Mullainathan, S., & Shafir, E. (2004). A behavioral-economics view of poverty. *American Economic Review, 94*(2), 419–423.

Black, S. E., Devereux, P. J., & Salvanes, K. G. (2007). From the cradle to the labor market? The effect of birth weight on adult outcomes. *The Quarterly Journal of Economics, 122*(1), 409–439.

Breitung, J., & Choi, I. (2013). 11 Factor models. In N. Hashimzade & M. A. Thornton (Eds.), *Handbook of research methods and applications in empirical macroeconomics* (pp. 249–265). Cheltenham: Edward Elgar Publishing.

Choi, I., & Jeong, H. (2018). Model selection for factor analysis: Some new criteria and performance comparisons. *Econometric Reviews.* https://doi.org/10.1080/07474938. 2017.1382763.

Chudik, A., & Pesaran, M. H. (2013). Large panel data models with cross-sectional dependence: A survey. In B. Baltagi (Ed.), *The Oxford handbook on panel data.* Oxford: Oxford University Press.

Du, K. (2017). Econometric convergence test and club clustering using Stata. *Stata Journal, 17*(4), 882–900.

Engel, C., Mark, N. C., & West, K. D. (2007). Exchange rate models aren't as bad as you think. *NBER Macroeconomics Annual, 22,* 381–441.

Engel, C., Mark, N. C., & West, K. D. (2015). Factor model forecasts of exchange rates. *Econometric Review, 34,* 32–55.

Evans, P. (1996). Using cross-country variances to evaluate growth theories. *Journal of Economic Dynamics and Control, 20,* 1027–1049.

Evans, P., & Karras, G. (1996). Convergence revisited. *Journal of Monetary Economics, 37*(2), 249–265.

Friedman, M. (1992). Do old fallacies ever die? *Journal of Economic Literature, 30,* 2129–2132.

Gaibulloev K., Sandler, T., & Sul, D. (2013). Common drivers of transnational terrorism: Principal component analysis. *Economic Inquiry, 51*(1), 707–721.

Greenaway-McGrevy, R., Han, C., & Sul, D. (2012a). Asymptotic distribution of factor augmented estimators for panel regression. *Journal of Econometrics, 169*(1), 48–53.

Greenaway-McGrevy, R., Han, C., & Sul, D. (2012b). Estimating the number of common factors in serially dependent approximate factor models. *Economics Letters, 116,* 531–534.

Greenaway-McGrevy, R., Mark, N., Sul, D., & Wu, J. (2017). Exchange rates as exchange rate common factors. *International Economic Review,* forthcoming.

Hallin, M., & Liska, R. (2007). The generalized dynamic factor model determining the number of factors. *Journal of the American Statistical Association,* 603–617.

Hausman, J. A., & Taylor, W. E. (1981). Panel data and unobservable individual effects. *Econometrica, 49*(6), 1377–1398.

Hotelling, H. (1933). Review of the triumph of mediocrity in business by Horace Secrist. *Journal of the American Statistical Association, 28,* 463–465.

Kong, J., Phillips, P. C. B., & Sul, D. (2018). The weak σ-convergence: Theory and Applications. *Journal of Econometrics,* forthcoming.

Kuznets, S. (1946). *National product since 1869* (assisted by L. Epstein & E. Zenks). New York, NY: National Bureau of Economic Research.

Levitt, S. D. (2004). Understanding why crime fell in the 1990s: Four factors that explain the decline and six that do not. *Journal of Economic Perspectives, 18*(1), 163–190.

Mark, N. C., & Sul, D. (2001). Nominal exchange rates and monetary fundamentals: Evidence from a small post-Bretton Woods panel. *Journal of International Economics, 53,* 29–52.

Moon, H. R., & Weidner, M. (2015). Linear regression for panel with unknown number of factors as interactive fixed effects. *Econometrica, 83*(4), 1543–1579.

Newey, W.K. and K.D. West (1987). A simple positive semi-definite, heteroskedasticity and autocorrelation consistent covariance matrix. *Econometrica, 55*(3). 703–708.

O'Connell, P. G. J. (1988). The overvaluation of purchasing power parity. *Journal of International Economics, 44,* 1–19.

Onatski, A. (2009). Testing hypotheses about the number of factors in large factor models. *Econometrica, 77,* 1447–1479.

Onatski, A. (2010). Determining the number of factors from empirical distribution of eigenvalues. *Review of Economics and Statistics, 92*(4), 1004–1016.

Parker, J., & Sul, D. (2016). Identification of unknown common factors: Leaders and followers. *Journal of Business & Economic Statistics, 34*(2), 227–239.

Pesaran, M. H. (2006). Estimation and inference in large heterogeneous panels with a multifactor error structure. *Econometrica, 74*(4), 967–1012.

Phillips, P. C. B., & Sul, D. (2007). Transition modeling and econometric convergence tests. *Econometrica, 75*(6), 1771–1855.

Phillips, P. C. B., & Sul, D. (2009). Economic transition and growth. *Journal of Applied Econometrics, 24*(7), 1153–1185.

Quah, D. (1996). Empirics for economic growth and convergence. *European Economic Review, 40,* 1353–1375.

Royer, H. (2009). Separated at girth: US twin estimates of the effects of birth weight. *American Economic Journal: Applied Economics, 1*(1), 49–85.

Verdelhan, A. (2015). The share of systematic variation in bilateral exchange rates. *Journal of Finance,* forthcoming.

INDEX